NATIONAL LAMPOON® PRESS

Also on sale from NATIONAL LAMPOON® PRESS

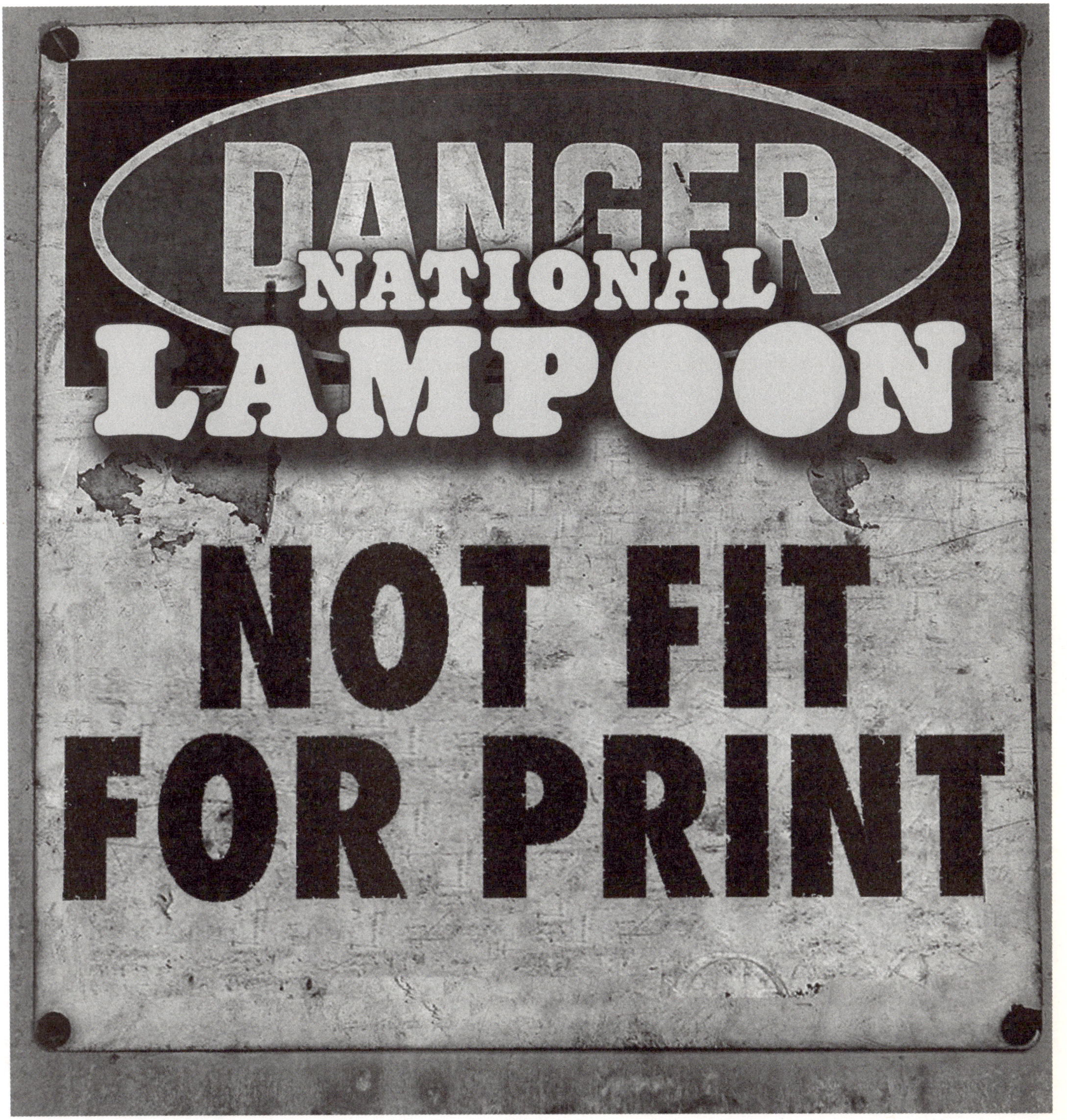
DANGER
NATIONAL
LAMPOON
NOT FIT
FOR PRINT

NATIONAL LAMPOON® PRESS

Published by National Lampoon Press

National Lampoon, Inc. • 8228 Sunset Boulevard • Los Angeles • California • 90046 • USA • AMEX:NLN

Not fit for print / edited by Phil Haney and Taii K. Austin
-- 1st ed.
p. cm.

ISBN 0-977871-835
978-0977871-834

$17.95 US / $21.95 Canada

Book Design and Production by
JKN

PRINTED IN THE UNITED STATES OF AMERICA

1 3 5 7 9 10 8 6 4 2

NOVEMBER 2006

WWW.NATIONALLAMPOON.COM

Firstly, I'd like you to put aside your preconceived notions of what constitutes "funny"...

Chapter 1: The Man & The System
(politics, race & religion)

Chapter 2: A Compendium Of Poop
Putting the Scat Back in Scatological

Chapter 3: Death Is Funny When It Happens To Someone Else

Chapter 4: The Finer Intricacies of The Hot Lunch vs The Cleveland Steamer

Chapter 5: School Shootings, Religious Cults, Serial Killers, Alien Abductions ...these are a few of my favorite things

HANS DICK
#27 "HEAVEN"
by: Marc M.
Up on a cloud somewhere in heaven, Rocky sneered down at Amanda. Still bitter about the whole stabbing him in his sleep thing.

Chapter 1
The Man & The System
(politics, race & religion)

Slave Training Manual

by Duncan Trussel

SLAVE TRAINING MANUAL
FRANKLIN PLANTATIONS
Caught on Cotton for 50 years
You have officially been purchased by Jeb Franklin,Proprietor of Franklin's Plantation.
You are now part of the last surviving slave-driven cotton plantation in the USA, a plantation where all "employees"—paid or non-paid—take pride in their work and are glad to be members of the FP family.
This guide-book will answer any questions you might have during the exciting beginning of your life as a slave. Pay close attention as you read the following pages—and be sure to say hello to your new friends King Cotton and Jester Gin. They are here to help you learn!
DUNCE
KING COTTON
JESTER GIN

Jeb Franklin
Owner

Honorary Sheriff, 33rd degree Mason, and loving father of 22 sons and daughters both living on the plantation and off, Jeb Franklin has turned the business of slave ownership into a subtle art form. Jeb's revolutionary approach to slave management has won him the Franklin Plantation "Merciful Master" award for 50 years running. If you happen to see him sipping mint julips on the porch of Springwell Manor or enjoying a ride through the fields on his Stallion Burnbone, never ever ever look him in the eye. And of course only speak when spoken to.

Alexander Legree
Human Resources

Mr. Legree got his doctorate in behavioral science at the University of North Carolina. After working in the nicotine enhancement division of the Phillip Morris Tobacco Company for over 15 years, Legree opted to turn his knowledge of enslavement to nicotine into a life-time career centered around the enslavement of others. See Mr. Legree if you have any questions or complaints regarding life on the plantation.

MISSION STATEMENT

As the last surviving slave owning entity in the United States, it is our mission to produce the highest quality cotton at the lowest cost. That's where you come in! Our goal is to bring Franklin Plantations to the forefront of the non-compensated labor industry, and have fun doing it! In the words of our President and CEO Jeb Franklin, "The only thing better than hymns to Jesus is the sweet blessed singing of the slaves toiling in the fields."

FREQUENTLY ASKED QUESTIONS

WILL I EVER SEE MY FAMILY AGAIN?
The answer to this question is yes—if you mean your new family at Franklin Plantations. You will see them every morning at 6AM sharp and all through the day!

WHAT'S THE UNDERGROUND RAILROAD?
The Underground Railroad is what Santa Claus uses to send elves home on vacation.

HOW MUCH FOOD IS TOO MUCH FOOD?
More than 2 meals a day is enough to make you guilty of the "whippin" offense of gluttony. (see punishments)

At least you can't get fired!
KING COTTON

BENEFITS

We consider the natural joy of being a part of the last slave-run Cotton Plantation in the USA to be the primary benefit of working at **FP**, but we do offer some special perks to all of our slaves both young and old alike.

1 **All the water you can drink!** The river running through Franklin Plantations produces an endless supply of nature's finest beverage.

2 **Sunshine.** It's something most folks take for granted, but ask any of our slaves who have been deprived of it in the Thinking Box™ (see punishments 5a) and they will tell you that it's the "Bees Knees."

3 **Room and Board.** You heard right! From now on, you won't have to worry about that pesky rent check or going to the grocery store. And just wait until you sink your teeth into some Salted Possum or suck down a spoonfull of "Plantation Mash™." You're gonna wish you had two mouths™.

4 **Free Burial.** At the end of your employment term, you will be given one free burial and your own engraved wooden headstone.

PUNISHMENTS

Jesus tells us that a slave's true occupation is to be punished. But Jeb Franklin allows slaves to take a vacation from this punishment for exactly as long as they keep picking cotton with an FP smile.

HERE ARE A FEW THINGS A BAD SLAVE CAN LOOK FORWARD TO!

THINKIN BOX

THE RELAXER

MARRIAGE

CAREER ADVANCEMENT

Picking cotton's just the beginning! There are many other opportunities that await a slave who works hard and develops a marketable skill set. Here are just a few of the positions you could move into:

BLACKSMITH Imagine the sense of pride you will feel when you see a shiny pair of your carefully crafted manacles on the leg of one of your best friends. "Taint nuttin like it."

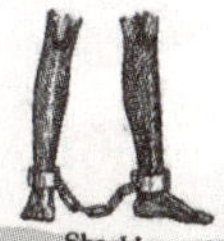

Shackles

MOTHER The only feeling greater than bringing a baby into the world is knowing that the child has job security for the rest of his living years. And you get an entire day of maternity leave!

ORGAN DONOR Jeb Franklin prides himself on his charitable contribution to the Birmingham community. The job of Organ Donor takes a big heart—especially when the recipient is an adult male.

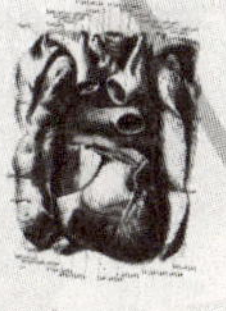

DRESS CODE
Franklin Plantations prides itself on being the foremost trend setter in Alabama slave fashion.
You will be provided with one custom-fit slave uniform supplied by Jay Krul.
Alterations to your uniform will result in immediate disciplinary action.
REVOLTS
That's Revolting!
DUNCE
It may be hard to believe, but some slaves just can't get into the slave life-style! They use "Devil-Talk" to convince other weak-minded "bugaboos" to actually raise arms against the master.
Even in the old days, revolts almost always failed. But now with the invention of the Machine Gun, we can turn any angry mob into hamburger meat in less than 30 seconds...You do the math!

PERSONALITY TEST

At Franklin Plantations we like to know our slaves. The following is a personality test designed to help us get to know you better. Please answer the following 2 questions as honestly as possible. You will not be "punished" for your response.

SECTION A

Please Finish The Following Sentences. Please circle your answers.

1.) A good slave:

A. Knows that it is his duty in life to render service to his gracious and forgiving master. He knows that he is lucky to be a slave in this life, because if he does a good job, he will be a king in heaven.

B. Thinks on his own accord. He comes up with newfangled ideas and gets all puffed up thinking that he is smarter than everyone else. He uses his brains to get away with breaking rules.

C. There is no such thing as a good slave. Slavery—whether it is wage slavery or old fashioned bondage—is founded on outdated hierarchical value systems that presume certain people are entitled to more while others suffer. This premise is innately flawed because blah blah blah blah.

2.) If given the opportunity to escape I would:

A. Make sure my supervisor knew that I was given that opportunity, and who gave it to me. I would then graciously accept my punishment knowing that, even though I didn't do anything wrong, I still need to teach my body a lesson.

B. Leave, but come back after having some fun. Chances are no one will notice that I am gone, and if they do, I will have a clever excuse to explain why my breath reeks of gin and vaginal secretion. Sure my slave outfit is now covered with my filthy sinful spunk, but I think that I am so smart I can outwit Master and his henchmen. I am really smart.

C. Find my way home and do what I can to outlaw slavery in all of its horrible forms.

If you choose anything other than A) then you're going to get a big reward for your honesty! Please bring this test to the " Honesty Cabin" and turn it in to recieve a prize for being so smart and special. You deserve it.

WELCOME ABOARD!

You now know everything it takes not just to be a slave, but to be the best slave you can be!

That great feeling you are experiencing in your heart is not your imagination—it's the joy and pride that comes from being a happy slave. Its the joy of pure submission to a force you couldn't resist even if you wanted to. So get your slave-ass moving and start picking cotton, you miserable wretch.

You Have No Choice!™

Jesus Christ: Substandard Employee

by Brendan K. O'Grady

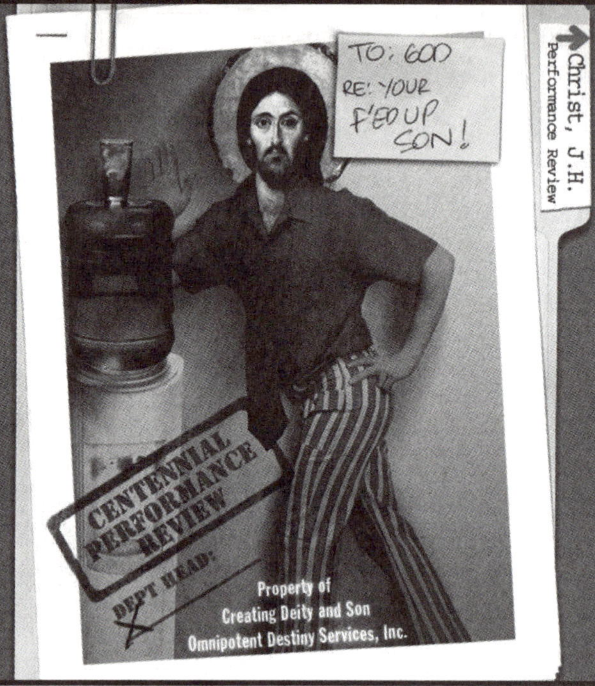

Creating Deity and Son Omnipotent Destiny Services, Inc. 111 Heaven Road Heaven, HV 1.800.555.HEAVEN

Intra-office Memorandum
To: Brian Harper, Assistant Director of Human Resources
From: Tom Atkinson, Personnel Manager
CC: God, Executive Director/Company Founder
Re: Christ, Jesus H. Centennial Performance Review

Brian,

As per your request, I have compiled all on-the-job citation notices for Jesus Christ, employee #012351, in preparation for his centennial performance review.

On a personal note, I feel compelled to say that despite having a lot of obvious natural talent for the job, Jesus is pretty clearly working to only a fraction of his potential. On more than one occasion, I have strolled past his cubicle only to see him, head down on his desk, fast asleep and drooling on the latest *Hustler*. Worse still, he is frequently not even present at all, having either arrived late, left early, or gone on yet another cigarette break. And while his easygoing demeanor once made him a well-liked employee, many of his coworkers have begun complaining about his irresponsibility affecting their workloads.

I hope these documents will be sufficient to begin your performance evaluation, and if there is anything else I, or my office, can do please do not hesitate to ask.

Sincerely,
Tom Atkinson
Personnel Manager
Heaven

Infraction Record
Jesus H. Christ

Event: Assassination of Archduke Franz Ferdinand
Date: 06/28/1914
Number of Humans Affected: Approx. 211 Million
Company Liability: Sparked the start of World War One; millions dead in war; civil conflict/ethnic cleansing resulting from ensuing power vacuum; post-war European economy devastated; a Lost Generation.
Employee Negligence/Malpractice: Jesus effectively ignored the prayers of 17 million peoples of the Balkans and Eastern Europe when he allowed this powder keg to ignite. While it is difficult to understand the nuance and momentum of preventing conflict escalation, I am hesitant to write this off as "early-century jitters." Given that he has been at this job for over a millennia, it's plain to see that his attempts at halting mankind's decline into chaos were half-hearted at best. He planned to project his angered visage onto the full moon, prompting all to become humble and throw down their arms in the wonderment of His divine glory. He instead appeared slightly obscured by guacamole in a flour tortilla in Oaxaca, Mexico. The tortilla was then eaten. Despite Jesus wishes, I am unwilling to "help a brother out" on this report.

Event: The Dust Bowl
Date: Fall 1933-Spring 1938
Number of Humans Affected: Approx. 430,000
Company Liability: A prolonged period of harsh weather in the United States' most fertile farmland; thousands of farmers in the central US forced to immigrate to an overcrowded West; massive levels of poverty, starvation, malnourishment; crippled American economy in conjunction with stock market crash.
Employee Negligence/Malpractice: Jesus maintains that the Dust Bowl was a calculated effort and completely conscious. I reprimanded his shortsightedness and explained that answering John Steinbeck's prayers for inspiration was not sufficient enough cause for turning the greatest industrial power on Earth into a barren wasteland. He should have just recommended Steinbeck start a heroin habit or something a bit more conventional. Jesus then explained that his intention was to usher in a "Get-People-the-Fuck-Out-of-Oklahoma" movement, which, while admirable in theory, is hardly in his job description. Jesus' own progress reports on ending the drought claimed that the American Midwest is in an aberrant climate zone and required several years of repair, though I secretly suspect that he simply disappeared for around 3 years in the middle. If this is to signify the beginning of a pattern in his work ethic, I think Jesus may be sorely in need of a formal performance evaluation.

Event: The Holocaust
Date: 1933-1945
Number of Humans Affected: Estimates between 5.5 and 10.5 million
Company Liability: Torture/murder camps designed to carry out systematic genocide; millions of marginalized minorities slaughtered; enforced Hitler's regime in Germany; main factor behind second world war.
Employee Negligence/Malpractice: In his defense, Jesus raises a fair point: Hitler was a struggling artisan who came from an impoverished background. He claimed to perform God's will as spoken to him from On High, and rose amongst his peers as a leader among men and a true believer in a time of great sorrow and despair. He was even clean cut, a snappy dresser and a vegetarian to boot. Quite simply put, Jesus thought we were endorsing him. As odd as it may sound, I have, personally, mixed opinions regarding this story. On the one hand, this is all stuff that legitimately could have come out of the Old Testament. On the other, Jesus may still be sore at the Jews for, well, killing him. Discretion being the better part of management, I think we have to let this one slide.

Event: Altamont

Date: 12/06/69

Number of Humans Affected: 200,000 concert goers

Company Liability: Several hundred accounts of sexual assault; violent stabbing of a young black man by motorcycle gang; the death of peace and the 1960s; several hundred "bad-trips."

Employee Negligence/Malpractice: With regards to the very public and brutal death of idealism and altruism in the modern age, Jesus claims that this happening was under Buddha's responsibility, though no shift-change form was ever signed by a supervising manager. It was soon revealed that Jesus was, himself, present at the site of the atrocities. Apparently, he regularly visits the Grateful Dead when they "smoke up," and was in the company of a Mr. Jerry Garcia for the better part of six hours backstage. Others present at the event claimed Jesus was "under the influence." although he points out that what employees do on time off is confidential, and company drug testing policy unfortunately agrees with him. I have my own theories though, mostly based on the contact high I received while filing this report. Lastly, Christ would like me to officially state that he did not write off his ticket on the company expense account.

Event: The Super Bowl Shuffle

Date: 2/26/85

Number of Humans Affected: Millions of Americans tormented by their radio.

Company Liability: A gold-selling single for the Bears Shuffling Crew; paved the way for solo joints by Shaquille O'Neil and "Neon" Deion Sanders; thousands of subsequent suicides.

Employee Negligence/Malpractice: Allowing a group of professional football players to make a pop musical record is one of Christ's most egregious lapses in judgment to date. The 1985 Chicago Bears are clearly becoming prime contenders in the "false idols" category. And, frankly, I don't see how justifying William "The Refrigerator" Perry's messiah complex is excusable in any sense, even if the royalties did pay for Mike "Samurai" Singletary's back child-support.

Event: Terrorist Attacks of 9/11

Date: 9/11/01

Number of Humans Affected: Approximately 3,000 dead or missing.

Company Liability: Billions cast into shock as the world recoils in horror beneath the shadow of an uncertain tomorrow; subsequent "War on Terror" throws the globe into political turmoil; serious windfall for competing companies [esp. Allah's Mighty Creation Co.]

Employee Negligence/Malpractice: An event of this magnitude defines generations of humans on Earth and changes the face of humanity for all times to come. This cannot be dismissed with a simple "Ooh, damn...my bad," as Jesus apparently wishes it could. This is exactly the sort of shortsighted, inappropriate, downright incompetent behavior that has been synonymous with his work since the day he started. Furthermore, "Well c'mon...who the fuck saw the second plane coming?" is no excuse.

Event: *Sex and the City* goes off the air

Date: Final episode February 22, 2004

Number of Humans Affected: Weekly viewership average topping 7 million; culture at large.

Company Liability: Inexplicable riots in the streets of Manhattan; water coolers silent across America.

Employee Negligence/Malpractice: I don't care if Jesus didn't like the show; he's simply crossed out of line. When the credits rolled, the tremendous disappointment and subsequent violence was both predictable and preventable. Mobs of single 30-something women, obvious homosexuals, and high-end designers crazed on neon-colored novelty cocktails and psychotropic mood stabilizers wreaking havoc across the upper west side? Prada looted? Tiffany and Co. firebombed into nothingness? Vera Wang and Narcisco Rodriguez missing and presumed dead! Such willful dereliction of duty to public safety has characterized his work for the last hundred years, and should be duly noted for consideration in his upcoming centennial performance evaluation.

Creating Deity and Son   Omnipotent Destiny Services, Inc.   111 Heaven Road Heaven, HV   1.800.555.HEAVEN

Intra-office Memorandum

To: Tom Atkinson, Personnel Manager

From: Brian Harper, Assistant Director of Human Resources

Re: re: Christ, Jesus H. Centennial Performance Review

Tom,

Thanks for the expeditious delivery of those citations on #012351 [Christ, Jesus H.]. We'll start the processing work on his performance review immediately.

Between you and I, Christ has been skating by on his name for entirely too long. I'm not going to be one calling nepotism or anything, but if this were my kid we were talking about, we'd have fucking canned him after the whole "Black Death" thing in the 14th century.

Anyway, thanks again for keeping on point in office C, and I'll see you for 18 on Saturday.

Sincerely,
Brian Harper,
Assistant Director of Human Resources
Heaven

Brian,   GOD

I appreciate your concern about the quality of Jesus' work here at CD&S, and the time and effort that undoubtedly are being put into his performance review. I've had several personal talks with him over the last thousand years or so, and I think he's really ready to buckle down and start taking his position seriously. Thank you again for you continued patience, and don't worry: I think he'll find his groove soon.

-G

Ten Things I Don't Understand About Black People

by Justin Rebello

But first, a disclaimer...

Listen, I'm not racist. So if you're looking at the title and thinking, "Oh boy, here he goes, get out your ACLU handbooks and humorless views on life," save it. Yes, I make my fair share of jokes about African-American Human Beings, but the way I see it, how am I any different from those Original Kings of Comedy-types whose entire schtick consists of variations of "white people walk like this...black people walk like this..." jokes? I'm not. Furthermore, if I'm allowed to say this shit unfettered, it provides yet another aspect of our culture that the two races have in common. Personally, I think of myself as a fucking pioneer. I like black people. I have black friends. I enjoyed *Baby Boy*. I've watched porn involving black people (either that or the lighting was bad). So in conclusion, if you read this column and still think I'm a racist, please go fuck yourself.

1. The N-word.

Let's talk about it. I know it's a horrible word, something akin to dropping the C-bomb around a chick. I guess what baffles me is it's cool for blacks to say it to each other.

To continue my parallel, isn't this something like one girl saying to the other: "Oh, is that Sarah? Is that my cunt Sarah? Cunt, get over here! Damn, cunt, how you been? It's been ages." They don't. Now fine, you consider it a sign of solidarity and that's cool. (By the way, I loved being able to write "cunt" that many times and it's not even all that offensive given the context.) I guess my question is: I know whites shouldn't say it to blacks, but is it okay if we say it to other whites? Like if I met my white friend Timmy and was like, "Hey nigga, want to go to the Gap? No don't invite Steve. I hate that nigga. Oh nigga please." Can I say that without black guys giving me the old stink-eye? I think that should be okay. But I figured I'd get the "it's all good" from you first.

2. Why are black girls so damned loud?

The reason I ask is I'm afraid the affirmative action people are going to get involved with espionage, and then we got Monique and Shaniqua sneaking into Kim Jong Il's palace in the middle of the night and suddenly being all, "OH SHIT. MOTHERFUCKER I BROKE A MOTHERFUCKING NAIL! SHANIQUA CHECK THIS MOTHERFUCKING SHIT OUT!" I'm just concerned for the welfare of this country.

3. Black guys, do you really like white girls or do you do that just to piss white guys off?

Because when a cute white chick gets with some crazy ghetto black dude it pisses me off. Not that I'm against interracial dating, that's fine. I just wonder, because black girls don't really like white guys. You have to realize, too, white girls are kind of insane. Seriously, they spend ridiculous amounts of money on *The OC* DVDs; I don't think they truly understand the plight of the black man.

4. Are you guys really still mad about slavery?

I mean, geez it was over a hundred years ago. And it's not like you personally were held slaves. Yeah, slavery sucked but Jews still don't piss and moan about the Holocaust. Shouldn't there be a statute of limitations on bitching about something that happened over a century ago and not even directly to you?

5. Do you guys really like pigs' feet?

Because it looks disgusting. If you like the taste that's fine, it just baffles me is all. How about cow uterus? Is that any good? Dog pelvis?

And what the fuck is a "chitling?"

6. Do you guys actually think D.L. Hughley is funny?

Because I've watched a few of his comedy specials, and honestly he's about as funny as a documentary on child abuse. But I see black guys in the audience just whooping it up.

And that leads me to my second question: What is wrong with black audiences at black comedy specials? Nobody just laughs, it's like a full body dry heave, like they're trying to hack up a Toyota Land Cruiser. I get scared, that's all.

7. Is everything really racist?

I hear this all time. "I asked for no tomatoes. There's tomatoes on this. That guy's a racist!" Do you really mean this or is it just an easy way to call somebody out? You know who I think is a racist? George W. Bush. Seriously, I realize nobody's said this yet, but his reaction post-Katrina leads me to only one inexorable conclusion: George Bush doesn't care about black people. Seriously, I know I'm the first person to say this.

8. What rapper is it okay to like?

And which rappers are too watered down for lame-ass white folk? Oooh, can I guess? Ok. I think you're cool with DMX. And I guess Jay-Z, even though honestly all his songs essentially sound like "Uh, Rockafella uh-uh..." and so on and so forth. Is Eminem okay? Well, let me rephrase. If he wasn't white, would he be okay? I think 50 Cent blows. I'm not scared of you, 50 Cent. Bitch-ass ho. How about Vanilla Ice? Just kidding. Let me know. By the way, black guys, how come rap music sucks now? Huh? Seriously, the two pioneers of early-90s gangsta rap have been relegated to Coors Light commercials and coming up with incomprehensible lingo for Eugene Levy to spout in the next Queen Latifah catastrophe. Fashizzle my dizzle? C'mon Snoop, in 1993 that talk could get you killed in the LBC. It's depressing, that's all. I'm just kind of disappointed, black guys, that you let this happen on your watch.

WTF?

9. How come you all look alike?

Just kidding. But seriously, do you think all white people look alike? Because, no offense, I think all blacks look alike. Same with Asians. Even Jews. People from Connecticut? They ALL look alike. Same with gays. And pretty much any minority group I may have forgotten. You know who looks a lot alike? Portuguese people who write shitty college humor columns. See, can't get mad now, because I self-deprecated. Self-deprecation. It's like a life jacket.

10. Did you really spend $200 on shoes?

And what does Avirex mean? Those seem like awfully big pants, is that really necessary? Do you spend more on laundry? How come you guys don't have to fold the bill on your baseball hats? And why is the tag still on there? Sorry, I'm trying to get as many questions in as possible. Please don't hate me. I love black people. Fresh Prince! ■

I Am So Sorry We Led Your Son To Christ

by Peter Lynn

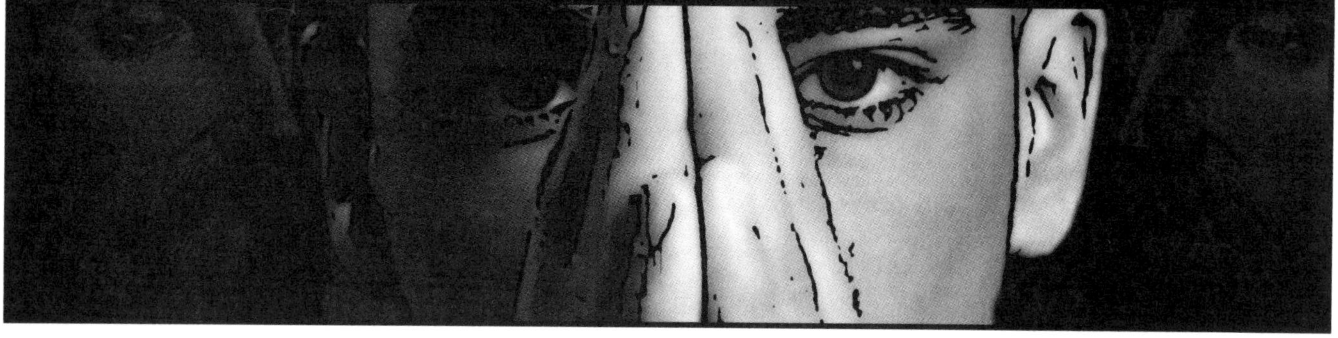

Dear Mrs. McMillan,

I am so very sorry that we tricked your son Jody into surrendering himself unto the bosom of Jesus Christ. Who knew he'd actually fall for it? I mean really.

Believe me, it all started as an innocent prank. The last thing we wanted to do was actually lead our high school buddy to the eternal salvation of the King of Kings. I'm sure you can imagine our surprise when our practical joke backfired—big time—and Jody's sins were washed away by the blood of the True Creator. Foot: meet mouth.

It happened when we were all at the video store, and I found one of those free Christian tract pamphlets tucked behind a copy of *Harry Potter and the Prisoner of Azkaban.* The tract was about some Christian rock band that signs a contract with this guy named "Lew Siffer." It turns out rock music is a powerful demonic force controlled by Satan, and the whole band is cast into everlasting torment—except the guitarist Paul, who at the last second receives Jesus as the way, the truth, and the light.

I know how much Jody loves Mötley Crüe, so I figured he'd laugh his ass off. I handed it to him and said, in this really serious voice, "Here man, I think you need to read this." I was totally expecting him to bust a gut. But instead, he read it through for a long time, then looked up with this serious face and asked me, "Is this true?"

I didn't know what to say for a minute. But then Craig told Jody very solemnly that it was indeed God's truth and that Jody needed to give himself fully to our Lord and Savior, Jesus Christ. I don't even know where he pulled that one from—it was inspired.

To be honest, I can't remember half the silly things we told him. After that—and I'm not proud of this—we begged Jody to kneel down with us and give his heart to the Lord. Up until then, I'd sort of half-figured he'd just been playing along—but then, his eyes wet with tears, Jody said "Dear God, I am a sinner and need forgiveness. I believe that Jesus Christ shed his precious blood and died for my sins. I am willing to turn from sin. I now invite Christ to come into my heart and life as my personal Savior." It was so weird.

Mrs. McMillan, you have to admit your son Jody is pretty gullible. I'm pretty sure he still thinks Spider-Man is a real guy. I want you to know that we tried our best after that to explain to Jody that bringing him to God's embrace had just been a big joke that'd gotten waaaay out of hand. But he just kept thanking us for leading him down the Roman road to walk in the light with the Savior, so we ended up going for tacos without him.

I just wanted you to understand that *actually* leading Jody to Christ was the last thing we meant to do. I know it's got to be hard for you to live with a good and faithful servant of the Lord, always talking about how you're going to Hell because your soul is stained with the sin of Satan's deceit. Still, at least when he goes to church; it gets him out of the house for a while, am I right? Glass half full.

I hope this apology note will suffice, since I don't think you'll be seeing us come over to visit Jody anytime soon. I guess he'll always have a friend in Jesus, though.

Again, ***really*** *sorry.*
Peter ■

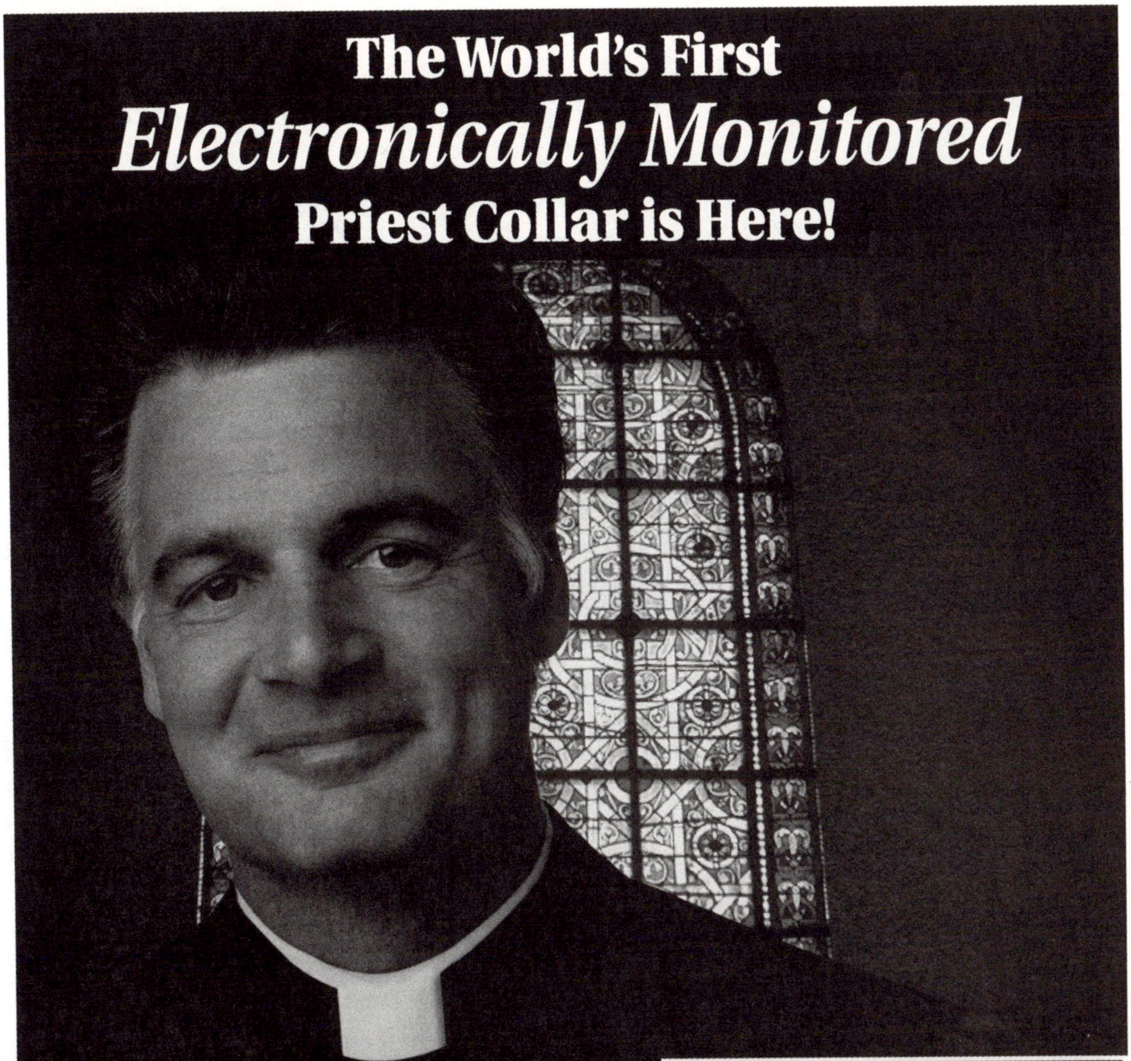

Cleric Tracker
9800 Series

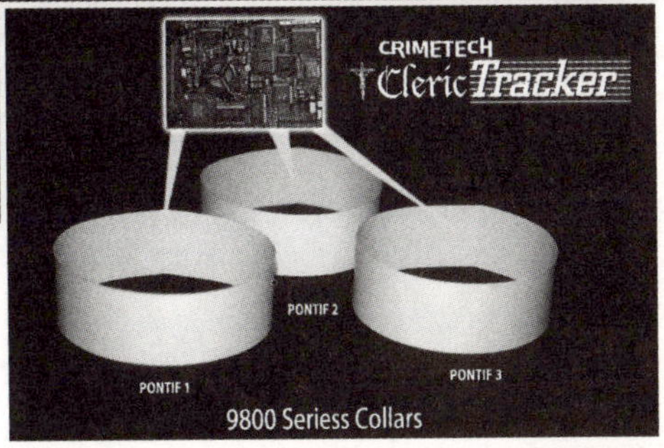

Have faith again in your faith. Thanks to advancements in modern penalogical science, the same technology used in court-ordered home detention ankle bracelets is now available to churches! No more do parishioners have to worry about the whereabouts of their Priests!

The Clerictracker 9800 series integrates the latest in GPS (Global Positioning Satellite) technologies and home detention electronic monitoring systems with a traditional Priest's collar!

Remarkably, the Crimetech 9800 computer processor and radio signal circuit board have been seamlessly concealed within the inner layers of white linen found in a traditional Catholic Priest's collar.

CRIMETECH

The Immigration Situation

by Scott Rubin

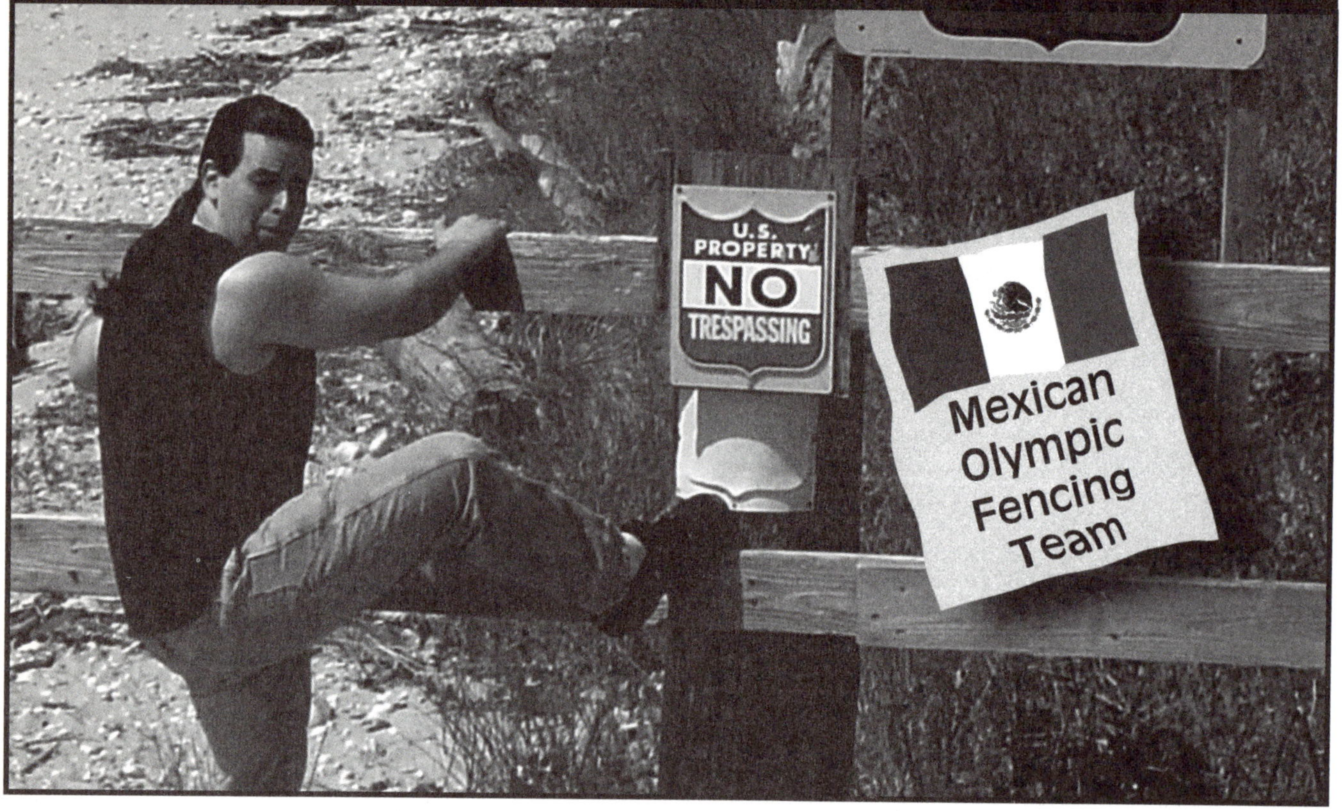

We can't live without Mexicans! Who's going to do those jobs? No American wants to do those jobs anyway!

Bullshit! My 12-year-old kid wants them. He can't cut a lawn, deliver the newspaper, baby-sit or even wash dishes in the restaurant across the street. Why? Because those **pesky Mexican Illegals** have taken all the kids' jobs. He can't even cut our own lawn because I've got like eighteen Mexicans doing it. I'm hooked: I got three cleaning the house, two washing my car, and one typing this article. This is fucking up our children.

Yes, the children! *Think of the children, America!* They're all playing **video games** or shooting those **air-soft guns** instead of working their asses off for a paycheck. Right now, I hear some Mexican in a truck pulling up in our driveway tossing the newspaper. My son wants that job! How is he supposed to earn his allowance? No wonder that Justin Berry kid sold himself online. What else was he supposed to do? Internet child porn is the new paper route. Get a webcam and a PayPal account and you're in business. I don't advocate such despicable part-time work, but it beats knocking off the corner liquor store. Well maybe not, but it's an honest day's living.

Kids should be **revolting.** A *million kids* should march down the streets of L.A. demanding their jobs back and making signs: "*You Can't Make a Living Killing Zombies in Resident Evil.*" "*Grounded for Six Weeks After Selling My Parents' Furniture on eBay.*" "*Don't Make Me Do Internet Porn!*"

And where does this all leave parents? I can *not* teach my kid the value of a buck because there's nothing for him to do to earn it. Good ol' American values down the drain. I propose if the government is going to continue letting Mexican Illegals cross the border, it's the government's responsibility to put our kids back to work. Mexicans have all the kid jobs, so *let's put the kids on the border* to keep them out. We can pay them $1.50 an hour. They can put in a few hours after school and on weekends. The government won't have to bus these kids to Arizona or Texas—we can install video cameras along the border and have the kids monitor them on their PS2 screens. Make it a video game called *Border From Hell.* Point and shoot. Who could possibly be **more qualified** for such a job? Our children. ■

NORTH AMERICAN SUPER HERO
"Uh oh, watch it! Invisible Woman is on th' rag!"

A "Fabulous" Slave Narrative

by Bashir Salahuddin & Diallo Riddle

William "Jupiter" Crabtree was known for his love of well-seasoned rhubarb and mutton pie, a good smoke of hickory root in his pipe, and butt sex.

While most people believe our country's first gay marriage took place between San Franciscans Del Martin and Phyllis Lyon in 2004, documents recently unearthed suggest the existence of same-sex matrimony far earlier.

Scholars in the Department of Afro-American, African, Indian, East Indian & Eskimo Affairs at Newark College have discovered a 19th century slave memoir penned by Augustus Merriweather, a field worker who found homosexual love on a Sorghum plantation in Tupelo, Mississippi.

JUNE 11, 1861:

... we was in the field pullin' up dat Sauhgum, when ol' Jupiter come over to my plot and says he need hepn' wit his own work seein' as he wasn't gon finish in time and I owed him for the teeth he let me borry to chew lass night's dirt pone. I walked over wit him and we worked side by side.

Time an' 'gin my arms rubbed up'n against his as we worked. I never took no notice befo' 'bout how his arms was strong like that ol' mule Massa kept for kickin' slaves in the head when they got outta line.

Yet, when he wasn't workin' them same arms' was soft like that patch of grass under the hickory tree where massa took the slaves so the mule could kick 'em.

Strong yet soft.

Jupe said, that since'n we worked so well together, we should become a team. I ain't have no prollem wit that. The last slave I work'd with was old GetGoat who was hung for lookin' at Massa's Wife when she would come down to da stables and "reverse ride da horse." I told Jupe I'd be at his side.

Jupe also asked if he could rub up on my chest a mite, before the sun went down.

I said yes.

AUGUST 8, 1862:

...Sunday was upon us like a mule on a hardheaded slave.

Ol' Jupe said that since'n we had worked together so well'n for the past few months, this Sunday, instead of usin' the two hours massa gave us to be with our lill'uns, we should head down to that ol' crick by Tunney Road and see if we can't scare up'n some red tail snappers, catfish and dead slave heads.

I said "shol," since wattin' nuttn' to do on Sunday anyway but wait for Massa to get done rapin' Annie Mae so I could have my dinner.

As we walked to the river' ol' Jupe kept lookin' in my face like he want to say sumn' but can't get the words to workin' like they should. I figured the deer n' leaf pone we'd been eatin' was givin him the skeeters.

Then he just stopped walkin, looked at me, farted up a mite, like he's layin' down his burdens and, in the haze of a wilted elm, he reached over and tookn' me in arms.

He kissed me hard like momma used to fore' daddy strangled her with my overalls for birthin' another girl.

Jupe said that we didn't have time now, but that next Sunday he would take me into the tall grasses down by the water, and show me a new way to lov'n.

I assume he mean to have his way with me like we did with that ole' mule when it was younger to the point where all it wants to do is kick slaves all day and night.

...I can't wait.

AUGUST 15, 1862:

...sweet agony...

AUGUST 16, 1862:

...spent most of the day in that outhouse.

My food just goin' right through me like my butt ain't got no way to stay closed. Can't get yestuday offn' my mind is all. I want some more.

I wondered, as I sat there blasting out the mo'nin grits pone, am I a sinner? Does this new thang that had a hold of me and made me wanna bend over and grab my ankles whenever Jupe was around, like Massa's Wife whenever she smelled paint dryin', mean sumn' is wrong?

How could sumn' so feel so painful? Yet so good?

FEBRURY 11, 1863:

...man come runnin' up say ol' Presdent' Lincun gon set us free soon.

Freedom.

Don't even know what dat dere word mean. Even if I leavin' this place I ain't gon be "Free" like'n I want to. Free to go where I please or do as I will or have Jupe get behin' me and "Drive that ox train through the mountains" for three or for hours.

Ol' Jupe felt the same way. He says'n that he wish they was some way for us to keep our love true and good. Like if we was'n to get marrid.

At first I thought he was crazy as a raped mule. But then I got to thinkin' maybe he right? I snuck out past massa's wife who was fondlin' one of my Youngins while she straddled the brazier, and headed over to Jupe's cabin.

We made our way down to the barn dat nite. Den, wit just the scent of honeysuckle and the wails of lynched relatives as witness, me and Jupe had a lil' ceremony like the one me and Annie Mae had after she bore our fifth mulatto chile.

I became Missus Apple Sauce Jupiter Crabtree. In the eyes of each other, our Lawd, and that ol' mule that woked up and kicked us both in the back as soon as the ceremony was over.

Crabtree's life partner on a Sorghum plantation, Augustus "Apple Sauce" Merriweather ("Bottom"). Pictured decades after the death of Jupiter in the small Ohio town where spent his final days cobbling shoes and jumping off low hanging trees into cornfields. ■

Clerics Order Danishes Renamed "Freedom Doughnuts"

by Mark Arenz

KABUL, AFGHANISTAN - Days have passed since the Danish cartoon row began, and still the rage in the Muslim community over the allegedly blasphemous drawings continues to grow. According to the throngs of incensed Muslims lining the streets of major capitols all over the world, the anger is no longer just about the offensive artwork itself. Adding fuel to the fire, they say, is the West's apparent lack of sympathy. Some Western leaders have seemed dismissive, even downright callous, about the scope of damage done to Islam.

"Just because a few thousand people get murdered by hijacked planes slammed into landmarks, Americans suddenly think they understand cultural victimization," scoffed Mullah Ibrahim Al Unatic. "Big deal. Somebody drew cartoons about us. That's right, cartoons. Try to live with *that,* infidels."

As the protesters grow bored with simple rioting and effigy burning, the battle over the offensive pictures has turned personal. In the past few days, there have even been calls for the cartoonists themselves to face justice in a Muslim court where experts say they may face traditional punishments such as finger amputation or even death by stoning. The newspaper's editor, however, says the unnamed illustrators are unafraid of such a fate.

"Come on, these people are from Denmark," said Carsten Juste. "I'm sure they get stoned all the time."

Eager victim or not, the international community has traditionally taken a dim view of such violent behavior on the part of Arab theocracies. So, to express this misunderstood outrage in a more acceptable manner, coffee shops and restaurants throughout the Muslim world have decided to alter their menus, crossing out the sticky-sweet breakfast item known as the Danish and giving it a far more palatable name, the "Freedom Donut."

"That will show them," said Al Unatic. "Mess with the foundation of our faith and we'll mess with your national pastry. Those murderous incest-crazed Danes will think twice the next time they want to stereotype an entire culture, I assure you."

Down at Uncle Salam's Potted Meat Emporium in downtown Kabul, the rechristened treats were selling like, well, hotcakes. Clerks had to restock the items several times over the course of the day as the shelf under the "God is great—and so are these delicious pastries" sign emptied out again and again. For the happy customers, Freedom Doughnuts are more than just a tasty way to start the day; they represent the power of the Muslim people to transform something bad into something good through clever repackaging.

"Usually I am not allowed to eat such things because my doctor says I am supposed to watch my intake of fat and sugar," said one heavy-set man as he stuffed half a dozen icing-covered morsels into the pockets of his chapan. "But now I can have as many Freedom Doughnuts as I want—all for the greater glory of Allah. Also, I'm pretty sure that if I die of a heart attack while striking out at the Western Satan in this way, my death will technically count as martyrdom, seventy-two virgins included."

Even though many American politicians, including President George W. Bush, have condemned the controversial cartoons as hurtful and counterproductive, there does not appear to be a move afoot to make the same name changes here in the States. At the Capitol Hill cafeteria, apple and cheese Danishes are still on the menu right next to old favorites like cheeseburgers and freedom fries.

Oddly enough, the idea has critics right in the heart of the Muslim world.

A boycott of products that actually come from Denmark is one thing, but this is just stupid," said Egyptian journalist Kareem Mahjeens. "I mean, a Danish is nothing like a donut at all."

A few hours later Mahjeens dictated a statement to the press recanting his earlier criticism of the Allah-approved name change. He apologized for the large number of typos in the press release, explaining that his typing skills are not what they used to be after having mysteriously lost a few fingers earlier in the day. ■

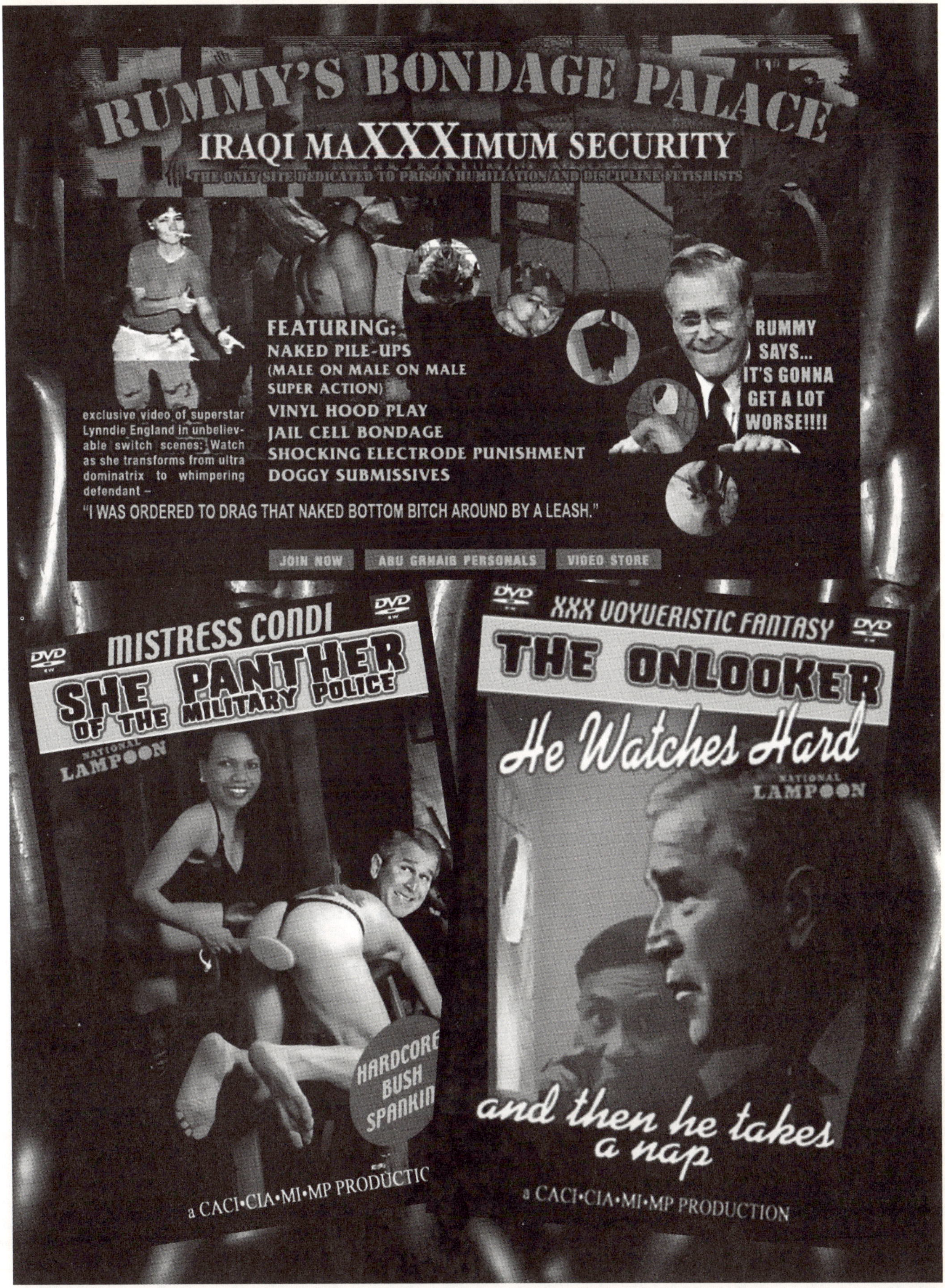
RUMMY'S BONDAGE PALACE
IRAQI MAXXXIMUM SECURITY
THE ONLY SITE DEDICATED TO PRISON HUMILIATION AND DISCIPLINE FETISHISTS
FEATURING:
NAKED PILE-UPS
(MALE ON MALE ON MALE
SUPER ACTION)
VINYL HOOD PLAY
JAIL CELL BONDAGE
SHOCKING ELECTRODE PUNISHMENT
DOGGY SUBMISSIVES
exclusive video of superstar Lynndie England in unbelievable switch scenes: Watch as she transforms from ultra dominatrix to whimpering defendant –
"I WAS ORDERED TO DRAG THAT NAKED BOTTOM BITCH AROUND BY A LEASH."
RUMMY SAYS... IT'S GONNA GET A LOT WORSE!!!!
JOIN NOW
ABU GRNAIB PERSONALS
VIDEO STORE
DVD
MISTRESS CONDI
SHE PANTHER OF THE MILITARY POLICE
NATIONAL LAMPOON
HARDCORE BUSH SPANKIN
a CACI•CIA•MI•MP PRODUCTIC
DVD
XXX VOYUERISTIC FANTASY
THE ONLOOKER
He Watches Hard
NATIONAL LAMPOON
and then he takes a nap
a CACI•CIA•MI•MP PRODUCTION

5 Steps To Dating A Black Chick

by Taii K. Austin

Dear Whiteboys,

In the heyday of American black-white relationships the courting process was fairly straightforward. After dusk, you'd wait for the missus to fall asleep–a heady cocktail of bourbon and complicity having claimed her 'til the morn. You would then take a stroll out to the Nigra patch, pluck you a purty wench, and drop your pantaloons. It really was that simple. Sure, sometimes her uppity husband or brambly-headed children would fuss, but that could be nipped in the bud with a well-timed boot to the jaw and the threat of revoking the family's Sunday night salt pork privileges. You know how Nigras love they salt pork.

But in 2006, interracial dating has evolved and therefore, my friend, so must you. Bear in mind, today black women have options and income. In many cases, *they* wear the pantaloons. The old techniques are thereby rendered obsolete and you must now appeal to her sensibilities in a subtler manner. The mind of the black-woman-who-dates-white-men is a complex minefield of physical preferences and emotional traps designed to confuse the fuck out of you at all times.

But don't worry, I'm here to help. What follows are five easy steps to bedding the black girl of your choice.

STEP 1: BE WHITE

This seems obvious, but you'd be surprised just how many guys make a wrong turn here. Fair-skinned Hispanics and Eminem types do not qualify. She's already got the black thing down, so your knowledge of underground hip-hop and fresh set of cornrows will get you nowhere.

STEP 2: HAVE MONEY

Seriously. If she wanted to pay for dinner, she'd date a black man.

STEP 3: AVOID ILLEGITIMATE KIDS, A CRIMINAL RECORD, POOR GRAMMAR

See also Step 2.

STEP 4: PURCHASE *THE COLOR PURPLE*: BOOK AND MOVIE, BOTH

Black women not only LOVE *The Color Purple*, but it is also the only oppression narrative where black men and white *women* are the villains. Think you're getting head after nine hours of foot-chopping and whipping? Notsomuch, Bradford; take *Roots* off your Netflix queue.

STEP 5: FOR GOD'S SAKE, GET HER DRUNK

This one supersedes all boundaries of race. Get a girl drunk or, better yet, get a girl in a position to *pretend* she's drunk and she'll do just about anything. This is how all meaningful relationships begin. I have read stories about how some couples started out as platonic friends or co-workers or met online and then allowed a romance to evolve organically, but I don't believe them. They're myths that serve to make those of us who are doing it right feel bad. It would be irresponsible of me to suggest otherwise.

After that, it's smooth sailing; simply proceed as you normally would in a loving relationship. Oh, and make sure you buy her something expensive each time Grandma Agnes calls you a Pickininny Nigger-loving Race-Mixer at dinner. Nothing says white guilt like white diamonds. ■

IT'S TEN O'CLOCK. DO YOU KNOW WHERE YOUR CHILDREN ARE?

Foreigners Around The World
A Brief Survey of the Various Foreigners, Their Chief Characteristics, Customs, and Manners

by P.J. O'Rourke

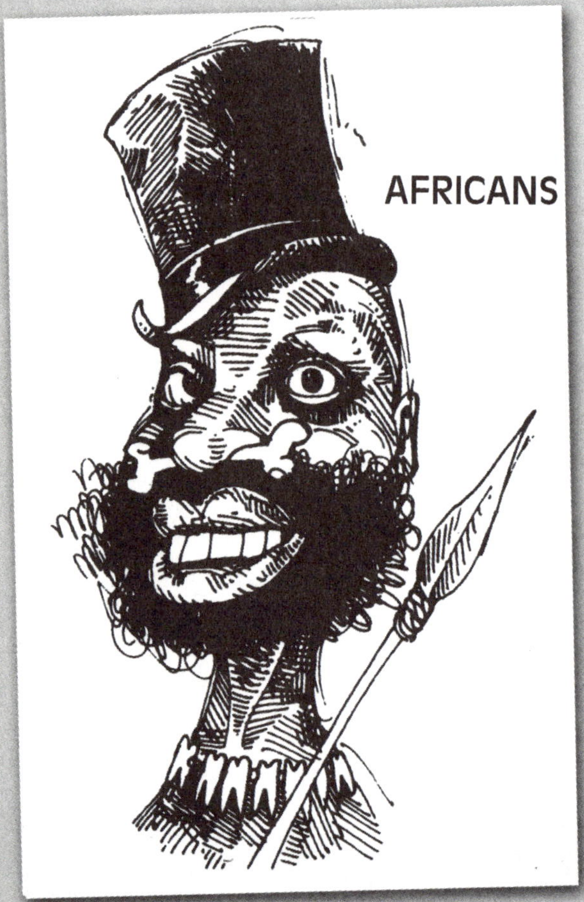

Racial Characteristics:

They eat each other and worship bundles of sticks and mud. You can never remember the names of their countries, which have a new Chief Na-Na-Click-And-Whistle every half hour and too many snakes and bugs anyway. They eat those, too. They put bones in their noses and wear plants for clothes. Best known for creating an American race known as "blacks" by selling their family members into bondage.

Good Points:

Don't feel pain the way we do.

Proper Forms of Address:

Fishmouth, shitskin, jungle jack.

Racial Characteristics:

Wear bed sheets and put bags over their women's heads. They burp and fart during meals and wash themselves in sand. They fuck little boys and practice some stupid, violent religion that they're trying to get all our blacks to believe in. They quite courageously murder each other and chop off people's hands for littering. They plant bombs everywhere they go and own all the Earth's oil. They hate Jews because Jews are the only people in the world with noses uglier than their own, and they're cornering the Cadillac market so that the Hebes will have to drive Buicks.

Good Points:

If they had any country clubs, they wouldn't let Jews in.

Proper Forms of Address:

Camel jockey, tent-head, desert Irish, gas-ass.

Racial Characteristics:

Violently loud alcoholic roughnecks whose idea of fun is to throw up on your car. The national sport is breaking furniture and the average daily consumption of beer in Sydney is ten and three-quarters gallons for children under the age of nine. All Australians are bilingual, speaking both English and Sheep. Possibly as a result of their country's being upside down, the local dialect has over 400 terms for vomit. These include "Technicolor yawn," "talking to the toilet," "round-trip meal ticket," and "singing lunch." It is illegal to employ the Aboriginal inhabitants as anything but toilets, and some of the peculiar forms of native wildlife have up to nine assholes.

Good Points:

Amusing zoos.

Proper Forms of Address:

Steady there, Cool off, For Christ's sake-not in the sink, Stay back, I've got a gun!

Racial Characteristics:

Hard to tell a Canadian from an extremely boring white person unless he's dressed to go outdoors. Very little is known of the Canadian country since it is rarely visited by anyone but the Queen and illiterate sport fishermen. It is thought to resemble a sort of arctic Nebraska. It's reported that Canadians keep pet French people. If true, this is their only interesting trait. At any rate, they are apparently able to train Frenchmen to play hockey, which is more than any European has ever been able to do.

Good Points:

Still have plenty of Indians to abuse.

Proper Forms of Address:

Bud, mac, mister, hey you.

Racial Characteristics:

Hordes of incomprehensible rat-eaters with a peculiar political philosophy and a dangerous penchant for narcotic drugs. No one can possibly know what dark and grotesque things pass through the minds of this hydra-headed racial anomaly which is, after all, more like a monstrous colony of flesh-crazed carpenter ants than a nation of rational men. Only a fool would deal with two-legged insects such as these. Our only hope is that the farsighted leaders of our own land will someday soon treat us to the welcome spectacle of a thermonuclear obliteration of this yellow menace.

Good Points:

They're almost as far away as it's possible to be.

Proper Forms of Address:

Zipper head, Chink, slant, ching-chong Chinaman, yellow peril.

Racial Characteristics:

Cold-blooded queers with nasty complexions and terrible teeth who once conquered half the world but still haven't figured out central heating. They warm their beers and chill their baths and boil all their food, including bread. An intensely snobbish group, but whom exactly they're snubbing is an international mystery. They all have large collections of something useless like lamp finials or toad eggs, and they would have lost both world wars if it were not for us. They like to be spanked with canes and that's just what they deserve.

Good Points:

It's relatively easy to make yourself understood with them.

Proper Forms of Address:

Limey, lime-eater, pom, poof, sister-boy.

Racial Characteristics:

Sawed-off sissies who eat snails and slugs and cheese that smells like people's feet. They take filthy pictures of each other with cheap cameras, wash nothing but their cunts, fight with their feet, and perform sex acts with their faces. Utter cowards who force their own children to drink wine, they gibber like baboons even when you try to speak to them in their own wimpy language.

Good Points:

Invented the blowjob.

Proper Forms of Address:

Froggy, froggy-wog, frog-eater, French-lips, Franco fuck-face, clit-lick.

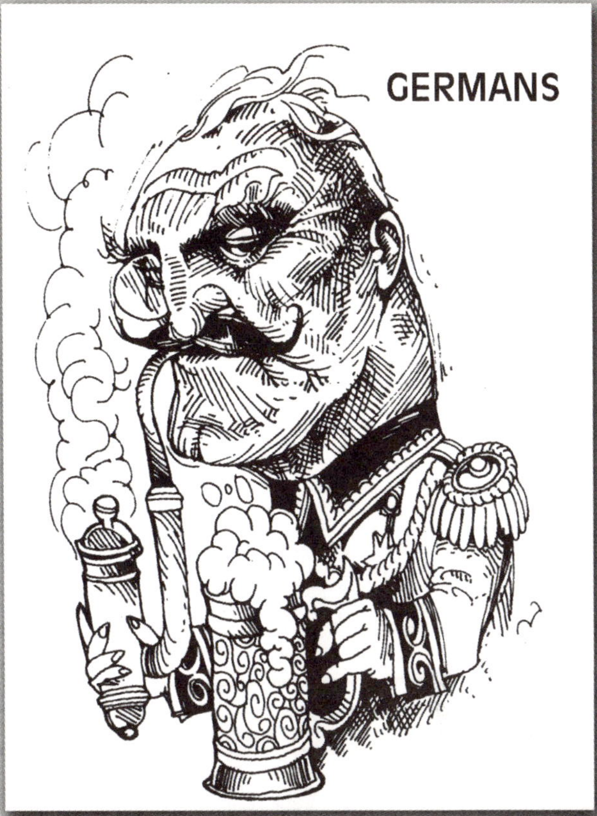

Racial Characteristics:

Piggish, sadomasochistic automatons whose only known forms of relaxation are swilling watery beer from vast tubs and singing the idiotically repetitive verses of their porcine folk tunes. Germans have never been successfully Christianized. Their language lacks any semblance of civilized speech. Their usual diet consists almost wholly of old cabbage and sections of animal intestines filled with blood and gore. Once every two or three decades, they set forth, lemming-like, on pointless military adventures during which great numbers of them are slaughtered—much to the improvement of the world in general. Their lardy women have long, tangled masses of sticky hair under their arms, and the men shave the sides of their heads.

Good Points:

Kill a lot of French.

Proper Form of Address:

Kraut, Hun, Heiny, spike-head, sausage-breath.

Racial Characteristics:

Degenerate, dirty, and impoverished descendants of a bunch of la-de-da fruit salads who invented democracy and then forgot how to use it while walking around dressed up like girls. Today they fuck sheep and are engaged in an international campaign to take over all the world's small, filthy grocery stores. They eat the insides of goats with their fingers. Their toilets are mere holes in the floor. And they cringe at the least threat from the imbecilic, taffy-yanking Turks next door.

Good Points:

Cute alphabet.

Proper Forms of Address:

Feta-face, sheep dip, dog fashion, GeekoEuropean, eek-a-Greek!

Racial Characteristics:

Dismal, obsequious curry-cunts whose gods have too many arms and legs. They wrap their heads in towels and wipe their asses with their hands. They are unable to feed themselves and what food they do have tastes as if it was mixed with the offal from muskrat dens. Their culture is moribund, their politics dictatory, their economy stagnant, their skins sebaceous, and their social order loathsome to the minds of decent men everywhere.

Good Points:

Dirty statues.

Proper Forms of Address:

Wog, towel head, human refuse.

Racial Characteristics:

Pie-faced, neckless, bandy-legged sots who almost never fuck. Ignorant and superstitious, they are in utter thrall to the vile, conniving priests of their dark and barbarous religion. Their women have their legs on upside down and no man in the country eats anything but potatoes. The principal delights of the Irish are in quarreling, fighting, and killing each other with bombs. They can be trained to do nothing useful that a dray horse can't accomplish in half the time, and they spew a continuous stream of mumbles and grunts which they fancy to be "poems." They sell their children for whiskey.

Good Points:

Many Irish are dead.

Proper Forms of Address:

Bogmouth, peat-face, Mr. Potato Head, nun-buns, dumb Mick.

Racial Characteristics:

Living proof that money can't buy love, these greedy, usurious, scheming Christ-killers (who won't eat pork because it reminds them of their parents) go around moving into other people's countries and buying up all the pawnshops and delicatessens. They were personally responsible for the fall of the Roman Empire, the 1929 stock market crash, and the loss of World War II by a prominent European country. Now they're ruining show business. Their fiendish heathen religious rituals include mutilating the penises of their own sons and drinking the blood of Christian babies during Lent. The world's nations have historically competed with each other to see who could get rid of them fastest. They control the legal, medical, psychiatric, and accountancy professions, and are the force behind international communism, sex education, the media, and freemasonry.

Good Points:

Lots of bullshit holidays

Proper Forms of Address:

Yid, kike, sheeny, Hebe, nickel-nose, knife-nose, gabardine stroking mockey, clip-tip.

Racial Characteristics:

This least appealing of the European peoples combines natural criminal propensities with an attitude of slavish idolatry toward that Whore of Rome, the Pope. When speaking, the Italians gesture frantically with their hands in an attempt to distract your gaze from their ugly faces—upon which are clearly etched the marks of their moral and intellectual degeneracy. They cannot stop stealing, and will sometimes go so far as to steal money that is rightfully theirs from the pockets of their own trousers even as they wear them. Worse yet, they rarely catch themselves doing so. (Not that it matters, since their currency is worth nothing.) Otherwise, they amuse themselves by kidnapping the neighbor's children, voting for Communists, and staying out on strike, where they've been since the 1940s. On the field of battle they are abject cowards, and in the kitchen they're enthralled with bruised tomatoes and the noodle only.

Good Points:

The women have big tits.

Proper Forms of Address:

Ginzo, guinea, dago, spaghetti-bender, wop.

Racial Characteristics:

Resembling the Chinese in many respects but mercifully less numerous. Their idea of a good time is to torture people, preferably by inserting a glass rod in the penis—and this is only for captured business competitors. During times of war, they resort to more drastic measures entirely. They have no new ideas of their own or any native creativity, but they are able to copy everything we do quite nicely, considering the color of their skin. Their diet consists principally of fish, which they do not cook or even, in many cases, kill. It's rumored that they know of sex acts peculiar unto themselves, and with any luck, so it will stay. The most frightening thing about the Japanese is that we've tried the atomic bomb on them twice and it doesn't seem to have much effect.

Good Points:

Frequently commit suicide.

Proper Forms of Address:

Nip, Jap, dink, gook, yellow rat.

Racial Characteristics:

Resembling the Spanish in all their more loathsome characteristics except lazier, dirtier, and more thieving. A large percentage of American Indian blood in the average Mexican deprives him of any natural human sympathies or moral sense and makes him a wholly unmanageable drunk. The principal industry of Mexico is the production of pornographic playing cards that depict their women corrupting the morals of donkeys. Completely untrustworthy, the Mexican will make food out of anything that will hold still. An attempt to conquer and hence eliminate this pesky breed of miscegenators was launched by our government during the last century, but wholesale nausea on the part of our troops after witnessing Mexican home life prevented our doing as thorough a job as we should have.

Good Points:

You can buy their twelve-year-old daughters.

Proper Forms of Address:

Wetback, beaner, chili-dipper, taco turd, flap hat.

Racial Characteristics:

A nation known as the Rudimental Reading Class of Europe. Its citizens are turkey-loaf look-alikes descended from a barbarian horde that took a wrong turn on its way to sack Rome. They spent the Middle Ages trying to fight Vikings on horseback and invented breech-loading artillery by pointing their cannons the wrong way around. They didn't know about sexual intercourse until the tenth century, having previously reproduced by raiding warthog litters. In 1947, the Poles became a Communist country under the impression that it was a rite of the Catholic church, and today their principal exports are snow tires manufactured from their own native deposits of snow.

Good Points:

Easy to beat at contract bridge.

Proper Forms of Address:

Polack, dumbo, lug wrench, kielbasa brain.

Racial Characteristics:

Brutish, dumpy, boorish lard-bags in cardboard double-breasted suits. Lickspittle slaveys to the maniacal schemes of their blood-lusting Red overlords. They make bicycles out of cement and can be sent to Siberia for listening to the wrong radio station. Their Communist party cuts the dicks off of high school boys to get women athletes, and shoots losing chess champions in the kneecaps. They shine their shoes with shit and spread Shinola on their wheat fields.

Good Points:

They aren't allowed to leave their country.

Proper Forms of Address:

Redski, Russki, Commie scum, stinking Red slime, puke-gutted Bolshevik assholesucker.

Racial Characteristics:

Sour, stingy, depressing beggars who parade around in schoolgirl skirts with nothing on underneath. Their fumbled attempt at speaking the English language has been a source of amusement for five centuries, and their idiot music has been dreaded by those not blessed with deafness for at least as long. The latter is produced on a device resembling five flutes that have grown a piss bladder. Formerly, the Scots painted themselves blue and ranged far and wide over the British Isles, but good fortune prevailed and they were conquered by their betters. What passes for an alcoholic beverage in the dreary province to which the Scots have been driven has enjoyed a short vogue among fairies and advertising types, but this appears to be giving way to cocaine.

Good Points:

Attractive plaids.

Proper Forms of Address:

Scotty, Jock, legs, plaid ass.

Racial Characteristics:

As hot of blood as they are dim of mind, a national situation dating back to the fifteenth century when they expelled the last of the Moors, and with them the only people south of the Pyrenees who could count above twenty. The deep-seated strain of masochistic homosexuality manifested in their love for watching ritualized forms of stooptag played with large male cows needs hardly be commented on, except to say that Ernest Hemingway's fondness for this country and its neolithic pastimes was enough to keep most educated people away through the better part of the present century. Spiritually, the Spanish are disfigured beyond help by a particularly greasy sort of religious fanaticism that manifests itself in morbid visions of the type in which our Savior is seen swallowing the menses of his Virgin Mother, and so on and so forth to an extent that it turns sensible people ill. The Spanish are largely notable for having set out some 500 years ago and found the only people on the face of the Earth primitive enough for them to conquer. (See Mexicans.)

Good Points:

Only one book that has to be read for Comparative Lit. courses.

Proper Forms of Address:

Spic, greaser, tight pants, hankie-crotch.

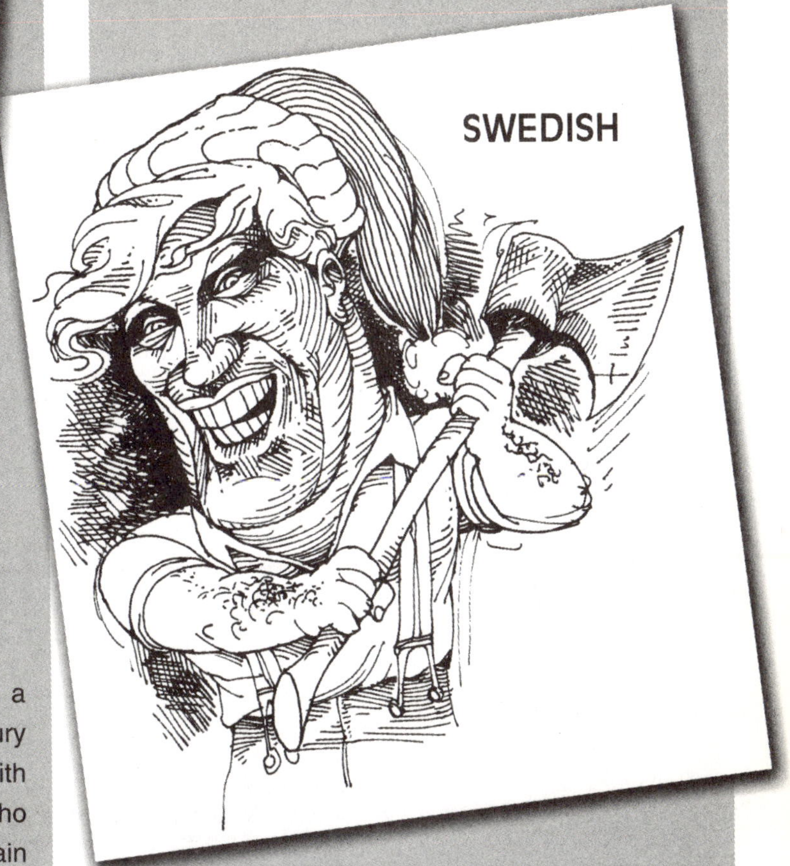

Racial Characteristics:

Tedious, clean-living Boy Scout types, strangers to graffiti and littering, but who are possessed of an odd suicidal mania. Speculation is that they're slowly boring themselves to death. This is certainly the case if their cars and movies are any indication. They eat a lot of fish, and perhaps this is more brain food than their modest cranial endowments can cope with. In other points they resemble Canadians, though better looking. Not that that's saying much. Maybe they're depressed because they have the silliest sounding language west of the Urals? No use asking them; what with their silly sounding language it's almost impossible for them to get anything across to anyone. Swedes fuck a lot, but only in the missionary position.

Good Points:

They're really, really white.

Proper Forms of Address:

Herring-choker, herring-knocker, squarehead, Swede.

Racial Characteristics:

Mountain Jews in whose icy clutches lay the fruits of grave misdeeds committed in every clime. Under cover of their sanctimonious Red Cross organization, they have penetrated all the governments on the planet and, concealed by a flutter of blood drives and nurses' caps, lie sucking like leeches at the marrow of the gold, chocolate, clock, and army knife industries of nations beyond number. Pathologically clean, they sterilize their children at birth, which accounts for their low rate of population growth and leaves them more room to hide heaps and piles of money in their tiny, Alp-ringed repository of snow-covered sin.

Good Points:

They rarely yodel in the home.

Proper Forms of Address:

Butter balls, cheese knees, big fat Swiss. ■

"SHOCK & AWE" YOUR FRIENDS WITH THE
100 PC.
NOW WITH ABUSE PHOTOS!
$1.25 DINARS
AL QAEDA TERRORIST PLAY SET
(MADE IN OVERSEAS SWEAT SHOPS)
COMES WITH THIS STURDY CARDBOARD ABU GHRAIB PRISON!
BLOW THE HELL OUT OF TERRORISM!
CRAMMED IN THIS FLIMSY CARDBOARD FOOT LOCKER TOY STORAGE BOX
ACTUAL SIZE
EACH FOOTLOCKER CONTAINS
4 CAMELS
4 HUMMERS
4 CRUISE MISSLES
4 DEPLETED URANIUM ROUNDS
8 DAISYCUTTERS
8 BUNKERBUSTERS
8 SAUDI "STUDENTS"
8 SLEEPERS
1 U.S. PRESIDENT IN FLIGHT SUIT
1 AYATOLLAH
1 SADDAM
1 BIN LADEN
1 COLIN
1 DICK
1 BUSH
RUSH THE CRAZY FANATICS TO ME!
Send ______ ☐ Cash ☐ Check ☐ Money Order
(No C.O.D.'s Please) Total amount enclosed $______
Name ....
Address ....
City.......... State.......... Zip ....
WRITTEN BY ROBERT S. RHINE ART BY JIM SMITH LAYOUT BY D.W. FRYDENDALL

There's No Poon At This Riot

by John Scheck

Yo, Salim. *Asalamu alaykum*, my man. I like your poster: *Death to America and all of the infidels who live there.* That's a good one, dog. What are we rioting about today, you ask? Fuck if I know, but I'm sure we have good reasons. Hey Hakim. What's happening, dude? Nice effigy of President Bush you're burning. Those four years you spent at art school in the U.S. really paid off. Let me just throw this Molotov cocktail at the embassy and then I can shake your hand.

Dude, why don't you ever bring your sister? There is never any hootchie at these anti-American mobs.

I wouldn't bring my sister, either. I'm just saying that we could use a little booty here. All I ever see at these things is the same group of swarthy dudes. I thought there was a woman at yesterday's riot, but it was just a hostage they had wrapped in a blanket. Imagine my embarrassment when I was trying to get her phone number and all I got was some French journalist's muffled plea for help. The sexual tension is so thick around here you could cut it with a strafing run from a Zionist F16.

I spit on the ground when I think of America, the Great Satan, but do you remember when we were going to school there? The street demonstrations had tons of hotties. That Freedom of Choice rally in Washington, DC was like *a Girls Gone Wild* video. Riding in the crowded Metro car on the way to the Mall was better than a lap dance. It's no wonder that our demonstrations here at home always turn violent.

At least here we get things accomplished. We've had four riots this month, and it's only the 10th. When we were studying in America we'd be sitting around planning a terrorist attack, and then someone would get the brilliant idea to hit Happy Hour. After that we'd waste the rest of the night trying to get laid. I know that it is the land of the Great Satan, but the wings at Hooters rock. And would it be such a terrible sin to have a couple of those waitresses at this riot?

Where is Ali? I haven't seen him at a demonstration since he got married. What? His wife has him at home painting their kitchen? Just leave it to women to screw it up for men when we want to go on a murderous rampage.

By the way, I can't make it tomorrow for the Death to Israel rally. I'm going to the mall. You guys should come. We can hook up with some girls. ■

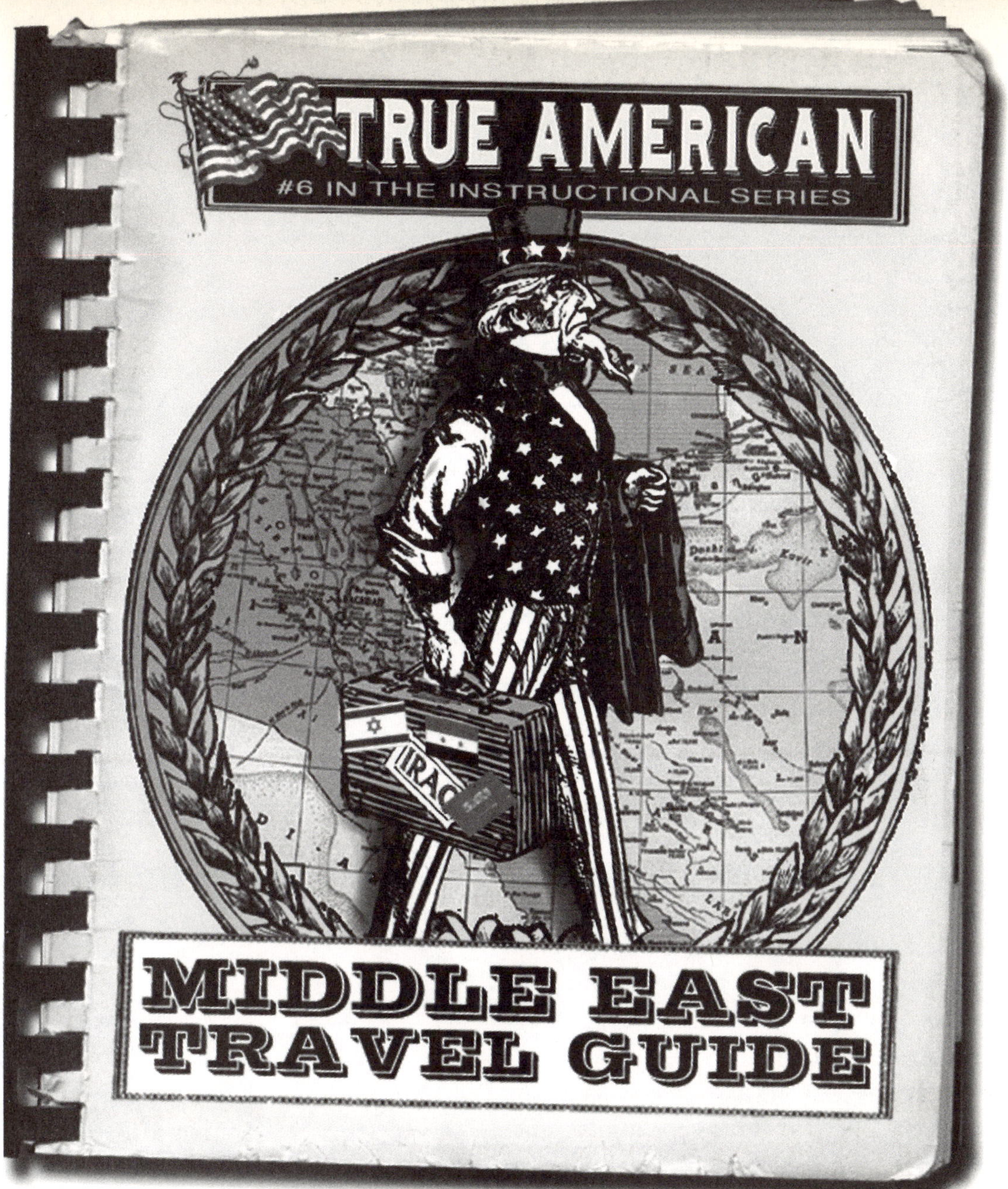

by David Wong

The Rest of the World and You

Traveling the True American Way

While leafing through the less important sections of your local newspaper, you may have noticed that the beautiful flower that is America is surrounded by a pot of damp, moldering dirt known as The Rest of the World.

No matter how well the True American may plan, you may at some point find yourself outside of America and among a group of what are known as **Exo-Americans**. These are people who are forced to live an alternative, non-American lifestyle, to the extent that they actually live outside of America and, in fact, may never have even been to America. There are over 6.2 billion of these poor souls on the planet.

Most of them are friendly and will carry your luggage in exchange for a crisp American dollar and a pat on the head. Some of them, however, are **Muslims**. There is a great deal of paranoid misinformation out there about this enigmatic group — that they refuse to eat even the juiciest ham; that the impoverished among them tend to spontaneously explode — but there is no need to fear. By using this guide, the True American traveler will be able to identify and judge Muslims with ease, making for a worry-free visit to the Middle Eastern regions of Exo-America.

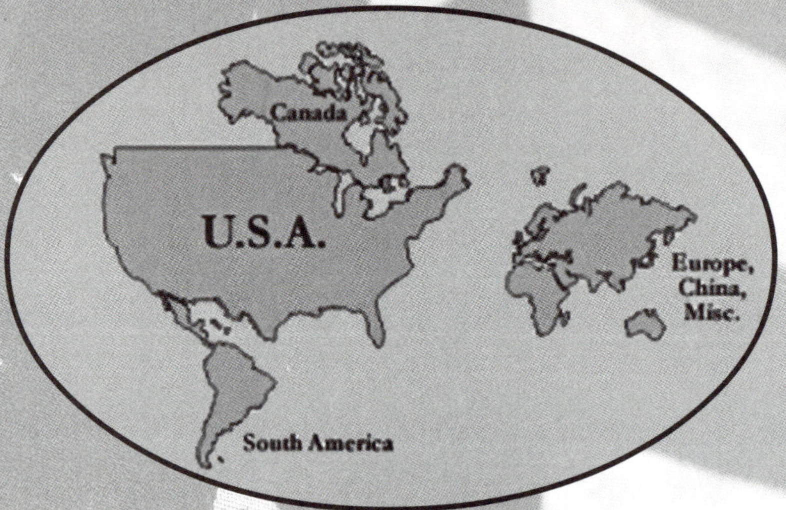

excerpts from Chapter 11
Dealing with the Modern Muslim

When first entering the Middle East, the True American traveler may at first be alarmed to see men who appear to be of **Muslim orientation**. Do not panic. In some cases, young Muslim men are not terrorists. Treat the man with respect and attempt to engage him in conversation. Explain to him **calmly** and **respectfully** that Allah is a false god, and that he should consider converting to a different, superior religion. Tell him the good news about Jesus Christ and let him know that there is no need to be jealous of Americans, as we are actively working to make his country just like the United States.

According to research, Muslims have 1,945 words for exploding suddenly, yet no concept of human love or joy.

The danger to you at this stage should be minimal. "Muslims rarely spontaneously explode on public thoroughfares," says researcher **Rey McDonald**, author of a study on human explosiveness as rated by nationality. "The Muslim's natural enemies are large bodies of public transportation."

Luckily, the spacious desert streets of the Middle East offer the True American traveler many opportunities for two-fisted American valor. If you find you have have insufficient arm room for valor, run in the opposite direction.

Battling the Muslim
Terrorist at a U.S. Embassy

The Middle East affords the True American tourist many pleasures, from exotic sand to hilarious local architecture and highly affordable prostitution. But no matter how enjoyable the sights and sounds, your heart will inevitably stray to your glorious homeland. Luckily, the weary True American traveler can enjoy the best a foreign country has to offer simply by visiting the nearest U.S. Embassy.

While there, however, be on guard for Muslim attack. "Statistically speaking, it is always logical to assume that any Muslim man within a hundred feet of a U.S. embassy will explode," explains travel expert **Jonathan Landeros**, author of *One Week to Retirement: A Guide to Law Enforcement With a Sassy Black Partner.* "But there's one embassy visitor they *haven't* counted on: one who doesn't play by the rules. Someone not content to lay down and die in the explosion. Someone who'd rather dive *away* from it, in slow motion."

That visitor? The True American. At the first sign of a Muslim, take immediately to the ventilation ducts and elevator shafts, where you will be better prepared to administer unstoppable martial arts-fuelled justice to terrorism. "Pin clever puns to any corpses you leave in your wake," advises John McCabe, author of *Hard to Kill: Using Air Vents To Your Advantage During Terrorist Attack.* "This will let Muslim terrorists know that you're clever and insightful as well as dangerous."

Also remember that in 97% of all terrorist hijackings of government buildings, cruise ships and aircraft carriers, Muslim terrorists will underestimate and even ridicule your attempt to kill dozens of armed terrorists by yourself. Use their ignroance of American street smarts and inexhaustible bravery to your advantage by being smart and brave at all times.

REMEMBER:
IF YOU ARE WEARING A WHITE UNDERSHIRT AND KHAKIS, FEEL FREE TO STRIP DOWN TO THEM NOW.

Spotting the Wily Muslim on a Tour Bus

STEP ONE:
REMAIN CALM

While aboard a Middle Eastern tour bus, the True American traveler should thus be on the alert **at all times** for a) exploding Muslims and b) the opportunity to dive away in slow motion from said exploding Muslims.

Any bus-riding Muslim men should be dealt with through the following two steps:

If you are unable to remain calm, proceed directly to two-fisted American valor. Whether calm or not, however, approach bus-riding Muslims carefully. **DO NOT CONFRONT THEM ALL AT ONCE**. Remember, you will most likely not have a firearm or explosive yet (unless you were planning to blow up the tour bus yourself, in which case use this opportunity to lay down suppressing fire).

If unarmed, attempt to isolate one of the (statistically likely) terrorist hijackers. Pick one who looks least likely to detonate suddenly. Speak to him calmly and away from his comrades.

"If you can get one terrorist away from the fatalistic mentality of the Muslim pack, you can begin a dialogue," says hostage expert and psychologist **Dr. Daniel Hoffstra**. "Remind him that you are both merely men. Perhaps demonstrate that by quickly and discreetly showing him your well-circumsized penis. Tell him you share the same interests. Mention that you have just converted to Islam. Then, speaking soothingly, place both hands gently on the sides of the his head and snap his neck with a quick twisting motion."

Hide the body and take any firearms you find on him. Take his shoes if you need them.

Speaking soothingly, place both hands gently on the sides of his head and snap his neck with a quick, twisting motion.

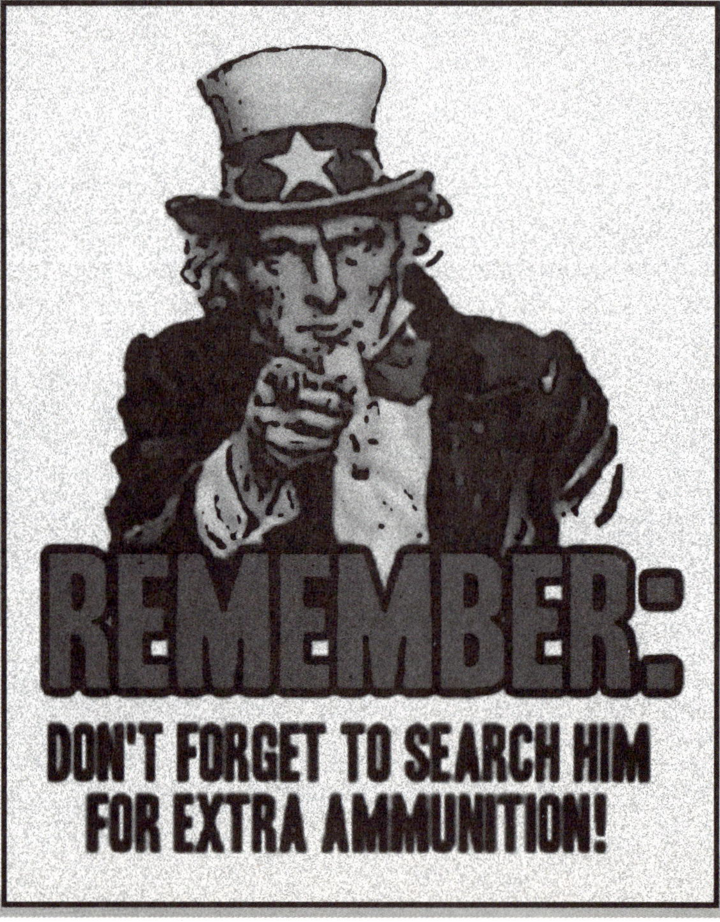

REMEMBER:
DON'T FORGET TO SEARCH HIM FOR EXTRA AMMUNITION!

Spotting the Wily Muslim on a Tour Bus

STEP TWO:
ASSESS THE SITUATION

The True American must ask himself: what are the hijackers' goals? Do they intend to blow up the tour bus, or ransom hostages?

If the terrorists' intention is to blow up the bus: You'll have no choice but to use your guile and martial arts skills to take out the Muslim men one by one. Save the most devious and devilishly charismatic assailants for last. If the Muslims have a bomb, strap it to one of the hijackers and toss him out of the side door while passing over a suspension bridge. As he falls to the water below, shout to him, "be sure to tell Allah that America is *da bomb!*"

Note that these rules apply to other modes of ground transportation as well, such as monorails and subway cars. Always be aware of your environment when choosing which deadly martial art to employ.

"Hand-to-hand combat on top of a subway car, for instance, is a different game altogether," says *Fifty Ways to Kill on Public Transportation* author **Kenneth Southerfield**. "Your first instinct will be to execute flawless backflips, helicopter punches and cartwheel kicks. But those require a great deal of headroom in the fighting arena, a luxury you do not have when speeding through a tunnel."

Limit your deadly repertoire to short punches and crotch-kneeings. Save the more elaborate moves for your plane trip home, when you find yourself on the wing dueling with the Muslim terrorist ringleader.

Muslim terrorists are unprepared for the tourst savvy enough to dive away from an explosion in slow motion.

If the terrorists' intention is to ransom the hostages: See above.

Fighting the Muslim Terrorist Ringleader on the Wing of an Airplane

Be aware of the wind factor. Remember, you'll have air rushing past you at 600 miles-per-hour. And stay away from those engines!

"The airline engine presents a dual problem," says Michael Zarzakov, author of Practical Wingfighting, 4th Edition. "The intakes are sucking air into the razor-sharp spinning turbofan engines, and the exhaust is hot enough to turn a ten-pound turkey into a charcoal briquette."

Zarzakov says a good tactic is to point past the Muslim's shoulder and say "look! Allah is flying behind the plane!" Then when he turns, shove him off the leading edge of the wing and into the engine. Timing and reaction are everything. You'll have only a split second to say "you're about to meet a big fan of Allah... a turbo fan!" before the blades shred him.

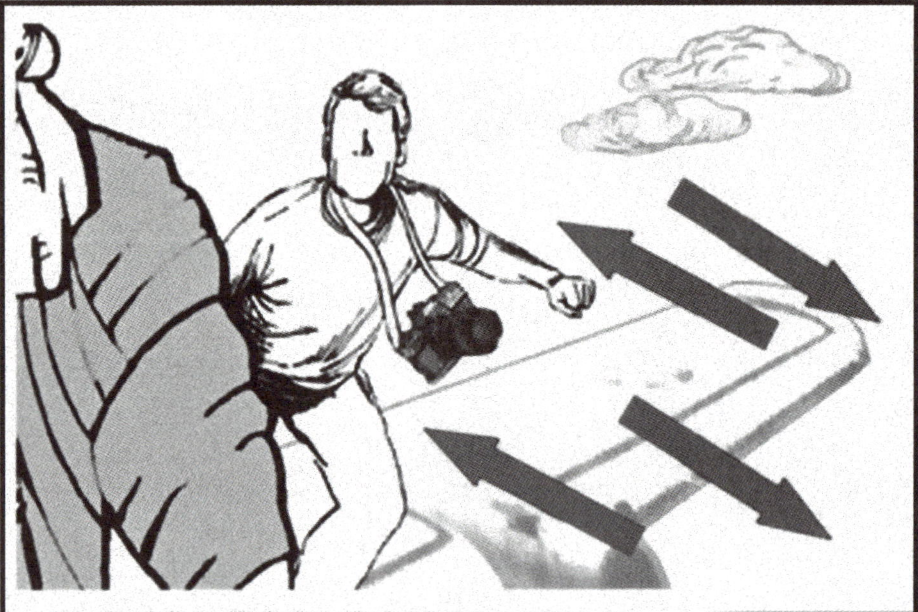

Be aware of the wind factor. Remember, you'll have air rushing past you at 600 miles per hour.

REMEMBER:
WHEN EMERGENCY LANDING THE PLANE,
ENLIST THE HELP OF A SPUNKY STEWARDESS

Other books in the True American Instructional Series

The True American Guide To Fighting Foreigners

If you can't beat them, try harder. This handy pocket-sized guide contains over 497 pages of fighting tactics from around the world. Learn which curses will offend most and what weaknesses can be exploited. Includes such useful chapters as *Fisticuffing With the Wrathful Mohammedan, Applying Salt to The Eyes of the Limber Nigerian* and *Getting a Taiwanese Vagrant in a Full Nelson.* An invaluable addition to the suitcase of any traveler unwilling to silence his beliefs in polite company, and makes a perfect gift for those yearning to fight someone with a different complexion.

ONLY $39.99 - BUY NOW!

The True American Guide To Diplomacy

Anything a foreigner can say tactfully, an True American can say **twice as tactfully!** The True American Guide ot Diplomacy contains over 234 pages of strategies in dealing with Exo-Americans diplomatically, with chapters such as *How To Compliment the Exo-American* ("I'm sure under favorable light conditions, your country would look much prettier") and *Avoiding Sex With a Foreign Diplomat's Wife* ("Everything you have heard about our legendary prowess as lovers is true; however, in the interests of diplomacy I must decline").

ONLY $29.99 - BUY NOW!

The True American Guide To Other Religions

The True American traveler can easily become confused by the bewildering assortment of things Exo-Americans are prepared to worship. Now, with this handsome 698-page guide, you'll never again have to wonder which is the Earth God statue you're supposed to bow at, and which is the pile of sticks you can use to stoke the fire. From Apollo to Zoroastrianism, this handy reference guide includes even the most embarrassingly preposterous deities.

ONLY $39.99 - BUY NOW! ■

The Koran
"The Ten Tricky Verses"

by Osama bin Laden

INTRODUCTION:

The Koran is the Sacred Word of Allah, thus no deviation from His Word may be tolerated.

Even so, we must occasionally re-interpret the Koran in order to correctly apply the Holy Text to situations we find ourselves faced with in today's world. Otherwise, particular verses might potentially be misconstrued as a call for amity among people of different faiths, rather than a summoning of forces in preparation for all-out Jihad.

It is my sincere hope that Muslims worldwide find this addendum to the Koran helpful in divining the true meanings of some of the Holy Text's trickier portions.

Osama bin Laden
A Cave in the Hills

Qu'ran 002.195

...make not your own hands contribute to your destruction;
but do good;
for Allah loveth those who do good.

OSAMA EXPLAINS

"Good" can be a tricky word. For instance, candy bars are delicious, but they are not so good for you. Crashing a plane into a building sounds bad on some level, but is in fact very good.

Very good indeed.

Qu'ran 060.007

It may be that Allah will grant love and friendship
Between you and those whom ye now hold as enemies.
For Allah has power over all things;
And Allah is Oft-Forgiving,
Most Merciful.

OSAMA EXPLAINS

The key word is "may." Indeed, it is just as likely that Allah will *not* grant friendship and love to those Westerners who prefer to surf the internet for pornography rather then pray. For them, He *may* instead grant a world of pain.

Qu'ran 002.190

...begin not hostilities. Lo! Allah loveth not aggressors.

OSAMA EXPLAINS

Correctly read, it's a simple question of who started the hostilities. Answer: America, Israel, and the crusaders. It is thus permissible to declare Jihad against them, because they started it! In this sense, Allah may be likened to an omniscient 3rd grade schoolteacher named Mr. Keplinger and America to the disruptive student in the back of the room. We are honored to act as the glorious ruler of Allah, which swats soundly the bare bottom of the infidel!

Qu'ran 002.060

Those who believe in the Qu'ran, and those who follow
The Jewish scriptures, and the Christians and the
Sabians – any who believe in Allah and the Last Day,
and work righteousness, shall have their reward with
their Lord; on them shall be no fear, nor shall they grieve.

OSAMA EXPLAINS

This is an archaic verse and has been removed entirely from my version. Who the hell are the Sabians, for crying out loud?

Qu'ran 002.110

...be steadfast in prayer and regular in charity: And whatever good ye send forth for your souls before you, ye shall find it with Allah.

OSAMA EXPLAINS

Prayer is a great and powerful thing. Pray for a world in which only believers occupy Allah's holy earth. As for charity, give of your money, O believers! Give to the destruction of the Great Satan! Here is a partial list of bank accounts that will ensure that your contribution will go only to those people intent on riding the world of the nonbelievers: Bank of Iraq, acc. # 2238475; Bank of Pakistan, acct. # 4509921-11; Bank of Switzerland, acct. # 7830445-08; Bank of America, acct. #124574. [Note: Al Quaeda has not been approved for non-profit status. Check with your tax advisor before claiming deductions.]

Qu'ran 098.005

And they have been commanded no more than this: To worship Allah, offering Him sincere devotion, being true in faith; to establish regular prayer; and to practice regular charity; and that is the Religion Right and Straight.

OSAMA EXPLAINS

We have only been commanded to do these things as a bare minimum. Yet, if your father asks you to take out the garbage, will he not be more pleased if you also give his camel a good brushing before you come back inside the house? Thus, is it not also a good thing to do a little extra credit work and engage in never-ending Jihad against the nonbelievers?

Qu'ran 103.002

Verily Man is in loss, Except such as have Faith, and Do Righteous deeds, and join together in the mutual Teaching of Truth, and of Patience and Constancy.

OSAMA EXPLAINS

Let us ask ourselves: what is a "righteous deed"? Beating a woman who has allowed her face to be shown in public? Surely. Hanging someone from a goalpost for preaching Christianity? Indubitably. Blending into a community, earning its trust, patronizing its businesses, seemingly enjoying its vices, before striking out and utterly destroying it? Of course!

Qu'ran 002.205

Allah loveth not mischief.

OSAMA EXPLAINS

Leaving flaming bags of dog feces outside embassy doors, then knocking, is mischievous and thus forbidden. Attacking the World Trade Center is permissible.

Qu'ran 002.224

And make not Allah's name an excuse in your oaths against doing good, or acting rightly, or making peace between persons.

OSAMA EXPLAINS

We fervently desire peace, and if Allah wills it, we shall indeed make peace – as soon as the U.S submits to the rule of Islamic Law as prescribed by the Koran! For then why would we continue to fight them? We would not think of it. Are we monsters? No.

It is our great hope that someday the entire world shall be at peace, worshipping Allah together and obeying His holy scriptures. Yet, while the non-believers continue to flout the ways of Islam, engaging in sodomy, Judaism, and music videos, there can be nothing but hatred and war between us. Invoking Allah's name is not an excuse, it is instead a justification. There is a big difference.

Qu'ran 003.057

And as for those who believe and do good deeds, Allah will pay them fully their rewards. Allah loveth not wrong-doers.

OSAMA EXPLAINS

If crashing a commercial airliner into the World Trade Center is wrong, then I don't wanna be right!

CONCLUSION

Properly read, the Koran clearly means death to the West. Death and death again! A thousand deaths! A million! The streets must run red with the blood of the infidel! Then, and only then shall we become friends.

All Praise the Compassionate,
Oft-Forgiving, Most-Merciful Allah!
Osama bin Laden ■

U.S. Gov't Apologizes for Liberating France

WASHINGTON — After France once again lashed out at US foreign policy by condemning the recent air strikes on Iraq, Secretary of State Colin Powell issued a public apology to the families of the tens of thousands of soldiers that gave their lives, and to all Americans, for rescuing France during WWI and WWII. The contrite former General pleaded with the American people to accept the apology and move on from this misguided, charitable act. "It's time that we take a hard look at ourselves and ask 'what were we thinking?'" said Powell.

Eighty-two year old former Marine Sergeant Larry Barnes, who served in France, applauded the apology. "It's about time. We knew something was wrong back then. We saved this one French family who had 14 Nazi officers shacked up in their chateau… we came plowing in there and shot everyone of those Krauts. Then some elderly French Lady comes over to us with a bottle of wine and out of nowhere starts yelling at us for ruining her shrubs. I lost 12 men and a leg and she's freaking out over some Bordeaux."

Until recently it was generally accepted that Eisenhower's decision to invade Nazi-occupied Europe through France was absolutely correct. However with continued French condemnation, experts now feel Allied Forces should have landed at the beaches of Holland, and invaded Germany through Belgium, completely by-passing France. The victorious Allied forces could then have written a loophole into the German Peace Treaty allowing the Nazis to continue to occupy France while relinquishing all other holdings. According to scholars, the United States would have still won the war but more importantly achieved the greater objective: keeping the French from "mouthing-off for the rest of the century."

However, some historians argue that a victory in WWII couldn't have been assured without the images of euphoric American GIs merrily marching down the Champs-Elysées. "I'm not sure that scenes of mildly pleased allied troops briskly walking through The Hague would have made the same impact. Support for the war back home might have ebbed, and made defeat a real possibility," said Brian Strong, WWII Studies professor at West Point.

France which was "deeply offended" by the statement has requested the return of the Statue of Liberty, the Louisiana Purchase, and anything with the name Lafayette on it.

Lack of Nagging, Educated Wives 'Key Factor' in Spawning Islamic Terrorists

WASHINGTON — A new FBI Study released today indicates that fundamentalist Islam's treatment of women as property and 2nd class citizens is most to blame for the creation of Muslim militants. "No woman with a little smarts would ever let her husband purchase airline tickets without taking her on a trip to NYC as well," said FBI spokesman, Andrew Mount, in a late afternoon press conference.

The FBI Study indicates that it is essential for Islamic factions to raise the status of their women to slightly above that of "household coffee table" in order to ensure a safer world. "An opinionated, self-assured woman would never stand for a man obsessed with dying in order to be with a harem of beautiful virgins. She would stand up and scream, 'What's wrong with me, asshole?' and then fuck his brains out," said Mount.

However, Mount pointed out that a deficiency in schooling might also play an important role in the proliferation of Muslim zealots: "A woman with at least a 3rd grade education might possess the wisdom to comprehend a skull and crossbones symbol, or a danger icon and demand that her husband take that radioactive plutonium out of the house and away from the children."

It was generally believed, until now, that a woman's nagging was a negative aspect of the human condition; but Mount insists it is in fact the key factor in keeping fanatical Muslim men from becoming international mass murderers. "Think about it… What man can be on the other side of the cave, during a work day, mixing a batch of airborne smallpox or Ebola when his wife is constantly bitching about his lack of effort to get a real job?"

The press conference ended abruptly when Mr. Mount's cell phone rang and his wife, on the other end, demanded he come home immediately to take out the garbage. ■

How To Deal With Discovering Your Friend Is A Republican

by Phil Haney

I would like to share with you my experience and what I have learned from it so that others may more openly deal with this sensitive issue.

One cold morning in March — after a surprise class cancellation— I opened the door to my small two-man dorm room. The stale odor of pizza boxes, sweaty socks, and what can only be described as "Guy Stench" hit me square in the nostrils as I entered. I rounded the corner, and found my roommate, Brian, hunched over his monitor. In the dark. It appeared that his hands were focused somewhere in his lap... I didn't want to see.

"It smells like something crawled inside you and died!" I shouted with a grin, startling him upright.

Brian spun around quickly in his swivel chair and stared at me in horror. A book fell from his lap. "I... I... thought you had class." was all he could stammer.

But as I looked past him to his computer screen, it was now my turn to be in shock. Now, I like to consider myself open minded, and I didn't want to overreact to the situation. I have admittedly seen many depraved things during my internet travels. But I couldn't conceal my immediate revulsion when I saw "National Review Online" on my roommate's computer screen. I stood motionless in the uncomfortable silence. I looked at the book on the Cheeto-covered floor. It was titled "Liberal Lies about the American Right" by Ann Coulter. Re-appropriated as a bookmark peeking out of the pages was a Bush/Cheney '04 bumper sticker....

My best friend...

Is a REPUBLICAN.

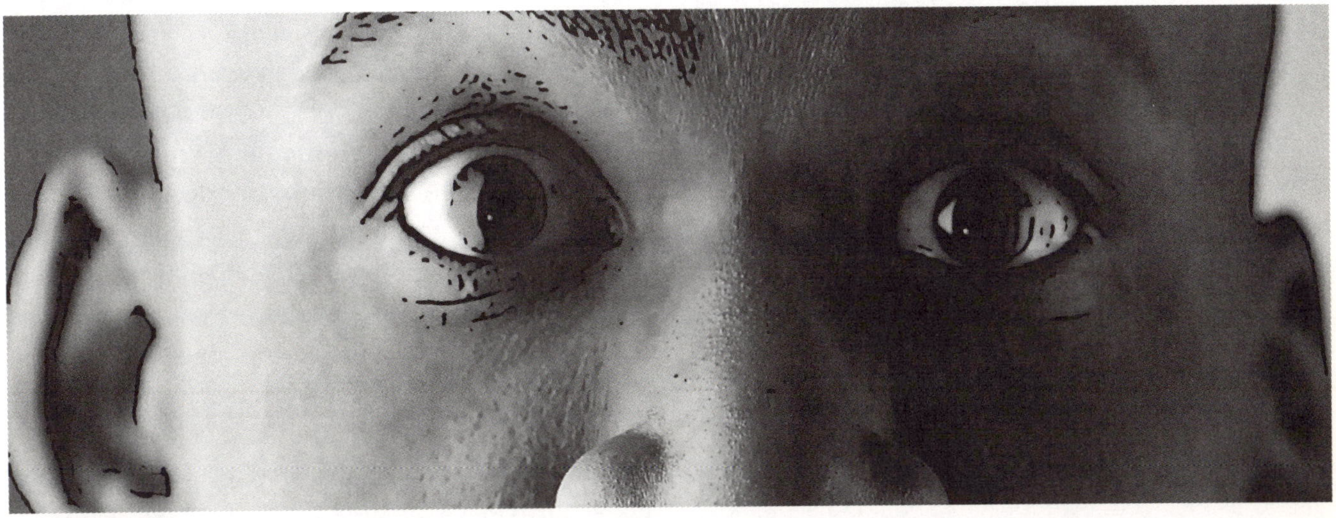

A lot of emotions rushed through me at that moment. Up until then I thought the only things Brian was passionate about passionate about were sex and substance abuse. We were close friends, and I knew I could handle this.

That day we got to talking about what it truly meant to be a Republican and how this association would shape his life. Was he born that way? Or did he choose this alternative lifestyle? Maybe it was just an experimental college thing...

Through my experiences with Brian, I have learned to tolerate the Republican lifestyle and have outlined answers to several important questions that you may have, should you discover that a loved one is a Republican.

Why do Republicans flaunt their political association?

At first you may feel uncomfortable around openly Republican people, especially when you live with one. These feelings of unease are totally natural and you should discuss them with your new Republican friend. Although their views and ideologies may seem wrong and socially regressive to you, they have a right to express them, just as you have the right to teach the tenets of justice and equality. So what may seem like flaunting is really just their version of freedom of expression. While their despicable views on taxing the poor while elevating the rich and their anti-abortion stance may make you flinch, bite your tongue. You will learn to accept the **RCRF** (Republican, Conservative, Right Wing and Fundamentalist Christian) community over time.

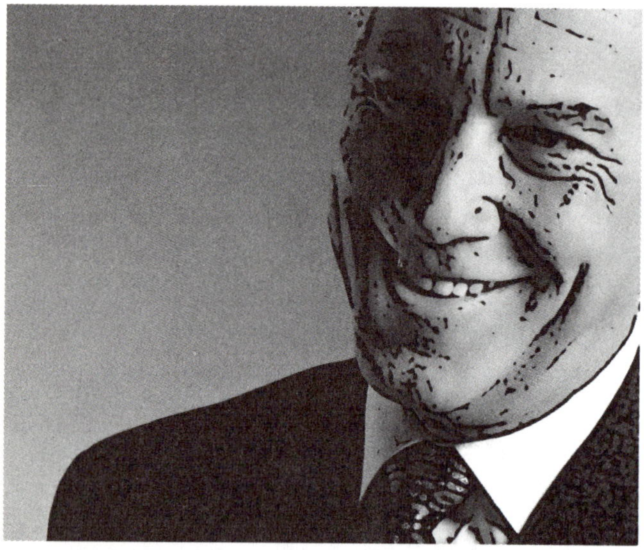

How do I avoid saying hurtful things or offending my roommate after they admit they are Republican?

The best advice I can give is to simply gag yourself. Since you have no experience in dealing with RCRF people, more than likely everything you say is going to be wrong. Rather than commenting on their seemingly abhorrent point of view, it is better to take time to assess your own feelings about the situation.

Are there trained professionals to help me cope with this news?

Unfortunately no, not a lot of counselors have specific training in the impact of Republican and RCRF issues. I found the best way to cope is to simply find a like-minded friend and commiserate when your Republican friend isn't around.

What about support groups?

You and your recently outed Republican friend may want to join one of many support groups in your area. The most prominent Republican support group is the **PFCRWATTH** (Parents and Friends of Conservatives and Republicans Who are There To Help.) PFCRWATTH has chapters nationwide, and conducts monthly meetings where you can go and meet others who are recently indoctrinated into the RCRF Community. Attending a PFCRWATTH meeting, you will meet many relatives, friends, and lovers of RCRF people who share your anxieties. Know that it is natural and we must give our love to RCRF individuals in order to strengthen our understanding.

Is there a cure for Conservatism?

To date there is no known cure for Conservatism. Most people who become Republicans, grow up having always had Republican feelings. Do you remember how you became a Liberal? Most people do not, and it is the same for Republicans. Discovering a Republican in your closet can be an enlightening experience. It is right to be compassionate to conservatives and help them through the difficult process of questioning themselves and their personal identity. Attempting to change who they really are is wrong. Though it is tempting, you should put aside any thoughts of doing so and dissuade others who think this is a good idea.

Won't my friends or parents think I'm Republican if I have a RCRF roommate or friend?

When I first found out my roommate was Republican, I asked myself "What does that say about me, that I could be so close to a Republican?" This does not mean anything about you personally, except that you are such a trustworthy person that your friend feels comfortable confiding in you. Rooming with a Republican or becoming friends with other Republicans does not make you Republican yourself —just as smoking a joint doesn't mean you should go to jail.

How do I know if I'm a Republican? Who do I tell?

Becoming friends or acquaintances with members of the RCRF Community may make you question your own political convictions. You may realize that you feel differently than your fellow students. For instance, while your classmates are protesting the World Trade Organization, you may find yourself more akin to purchasing stock in an environment-destroying multinational conglomerate. Feelings such as these can cause Political Identity Confusion (PIC) in young people who are just starting to formulate their political persuasions. Many young Conservatives feel alienated from their liberal-leaning friends and therefore suppress their Republicanism out of fear of rejection. It is sometimes difficult to tell which friend or family member will be supportive of your beliefs. In some cases young people who have come out as Republican have been kicked out of their homes by intolerant relatives.

Is Being Republican Normal?

Being Republican is completely natural and healthy. I relate finding out a friend is Republican to trying a new vegetarian dish at the local Tofu Burger. While you've never had it before and it's foreign to your taste buds, what's the harm in at least trying it?

If I'm a Republican, how do I learn to like myself?

It's hard for young Republican people to feel good about themselves because all around them are people who believe that they are sick, perverted, and destined to live unhappy lives. However more and more people are learning to accept Republicans, which in turn helps Republicans like themselves. On one campus they even let them fly the GOP flag right next to Old Glory. You could also choose a successful Republican to look up to when you feel awkward or ashamed of your political affiliation. I encourage you to say, "I'm a Republican and I'm OK." ■

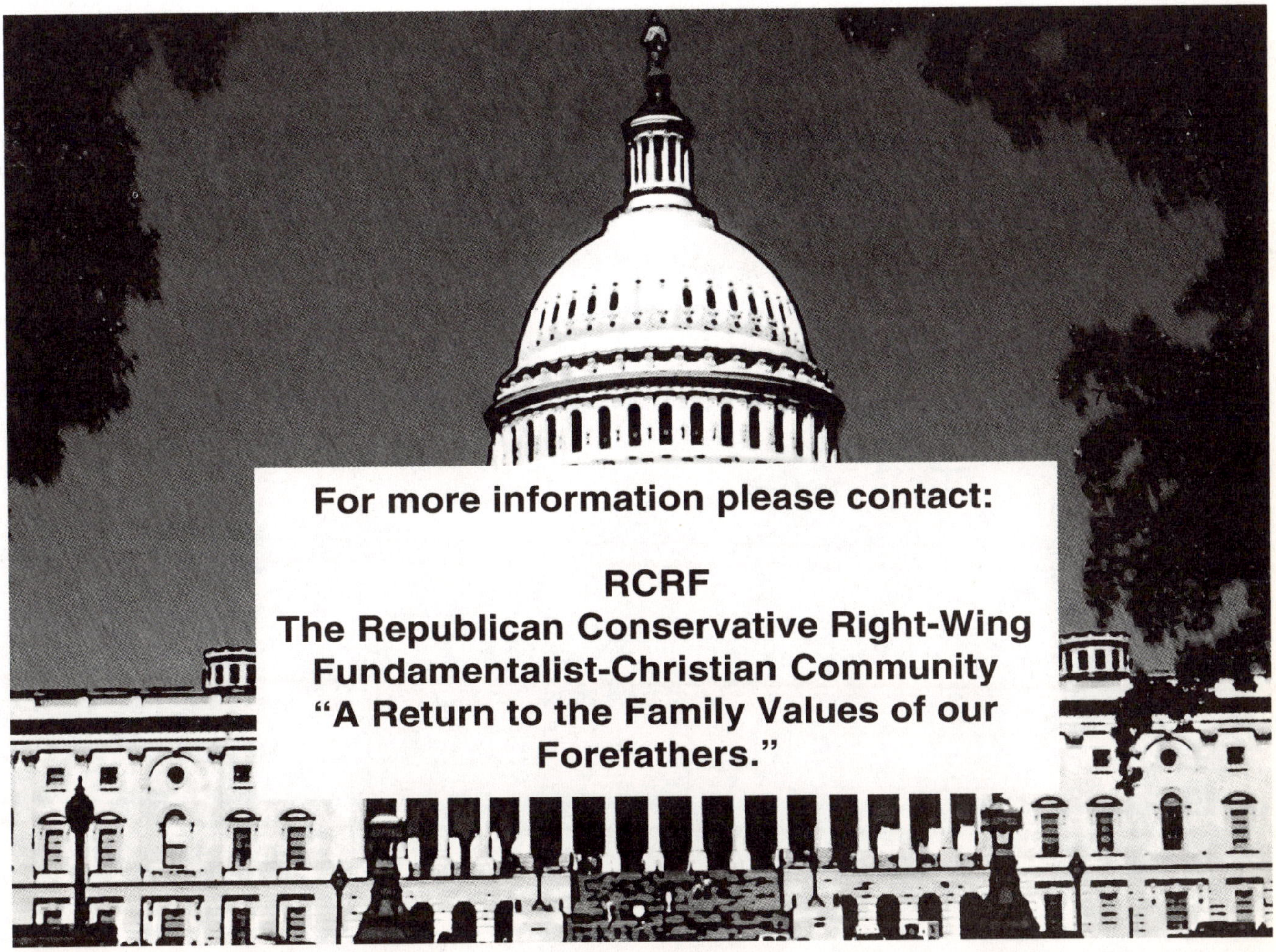
For more information please contact:
RCRF
The Republican Conservative Right-Wing
Fundamentalist-Christian Community
"A Return to the Family Values of our
Forefathers."

SHIT
"Plain or peanut?"

Chapter 2
A Compendium Of Poop

Putting the Scat Back in Scatological

Holy Shit, I Have to Fart

by Andy Kleiman

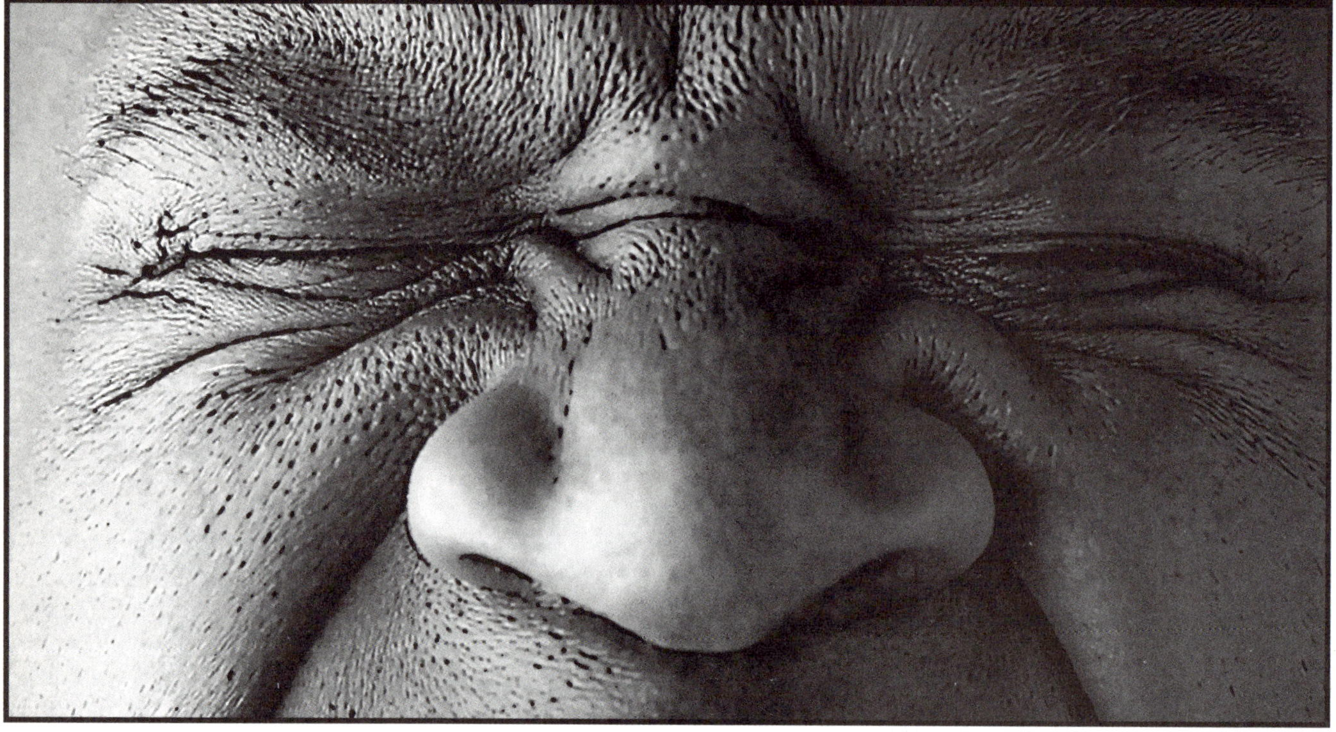

I'm serious. I have to fart like you wouldn't believe.

Good God, how long does this elevator take?

Fuck, when is this guy getting off? It's like he knows I have to fart and is just waiting it out; he wants to see me suffer. Why did I think it was a good idea to go to Taco Bell for lunch? I knew I had that meeting right after. Couldn't you have gone to Burger King or McDonalds or maybe even somewhere that's semi-healthy, you fat fuck? You're disgusting.

I cannot possibly hold this in any longer, it's gonna cause bowel obstruction or something, then I really won't be able to hold it in, I'll just shit uncontrollably—that'll be attractive. Makes it kinda hard to deny it when you can see the skid marks, and also a great way to endear myself to my co-workers.

And did I have to get cheese on my chalupa? I know I'm lactose intolerant; Christ, every roommate I had in college knew I was lactose intolerant, but no, that doesn't stop me, I must have cheese on my chalupa. You know what? Let's cut out the middleman and just put laxatives right on the fucker.

It's like what my dad said about not getting my rectum in an uproar. What did he even mean by that?

Why hasn't this guy gotten off yet? Where does he work anyway? Probably somewhere better than my piece of shit job.

Finally we're stopping; Christ that took a long time...why isn't he getting off? This is your floor, dumbass, GO! What the fuck are you waiting for?

Wonderful, now there are more people to wallow in my stench when I shit my pants.

Quit giving me a dirty look, fuck you, I can't move, if I do, my butt cheeks will unclench and then it'll be unpleasant for everyone.

This has got to be the longest elevator ride ever. My office just had to be on the top floor, didn't it? I should just quit.

Maybe if I let it out carefully, it won't make a sound. But what about the smell, dumbass? That's the whole reason you hold in a fart, and what if it does make a sound? You never know what kinda fart you're in for until it's too late. What if it's a real sloppy one? I mean, I did just have shitty Mexican food, so it's kind of a given.

Maybe I could just get off at the next floor and walk the rest of the way...but how many floors is that? Oh fuck that...or I could stop being a pussy and just do it, like a little exercise would kill me or something.

Ok, fuck it, I don't care if anyone knows it's me, I'm literally in pain—I can't hold it in any longer.

. . .

Oh crap, that's not a fart. ■

TWO FISH By: Marc M.
Hey Harrold, where are you off to looking so sad.
I'm going to the bottom of the ocean to kill myself.
Hehehe, aww come on man, tehehe, things can't be that bad. Hehehehe.
Yeah? Well, my step-dad beats the shit out of me and my mom. My girlfriend dumped me for a sea horse. My little sister was eaten by a shark. And what's so damn funny? Why are you laughing at me?
I'm sorry man. It's just really hard to take you seriously with that huge string of poo hanging from your butt.
Ya' know?
Hehe, yeah.

The Toilet Papers

by Chris Miller

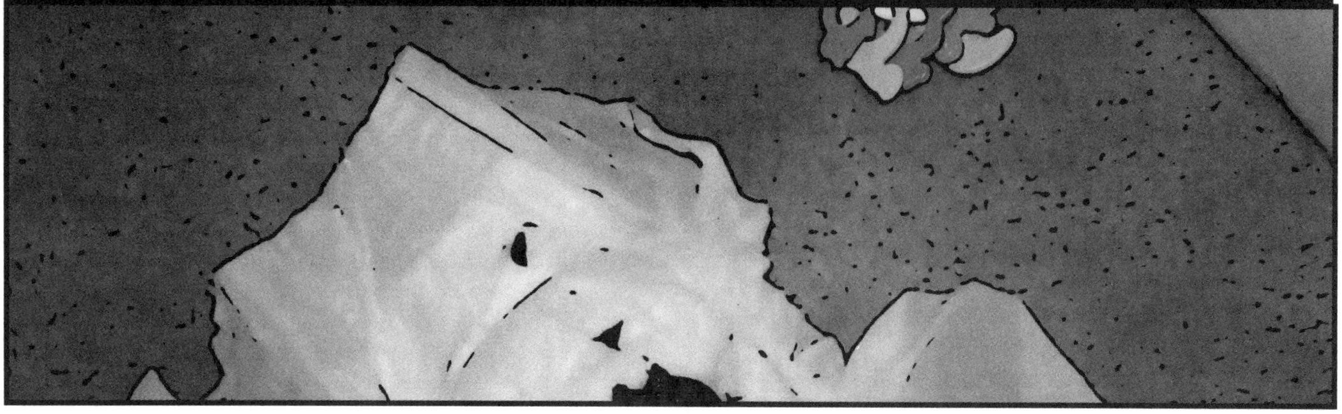

The air of my studio roiled with the sweet scent of pigment. My hands were slick to the wrists, my clothing splotched and smeared. I was tired but elated. The painting was finished and very, very good.

Some artists will tell you they are incompetent to judge their own work. Once complete, their painting seems to have come from elsewhere. *I didn't paint it, man*, they say, *I just painted it down*. Not me. I'd painted that painting and knew with certainty it was the best thing I'd ever put on plaster.

My school is chiaroscuro frescoes, whatever that means. The barely completed one, lustrous in the late-afternoon sun, was a slow explosion of moody swirls called *In a Brown Study*. The more I stared, the more excited I became. My first totally abstract work was a creation of high inspiration, even genius. It would strike my critics dumb.

I was applying my signature (a palm print in the southeast corner) when Oh Horseshit, my head Big One and harshest critic, threw open the door and began addressing me in his strange guttural language. He broke off abruptly as I stepped back from the wall. He stared. I held my breath, watching his eyes for that glint of recognition, wishing to cherish those few seconds during which he would first grasp the magnitude of what he was seeing.

"Jumping Jesus!" He spun. "Helen! The little asshole's wiping his shit on the wall again!"

His tone of voice told all. I felt no surprise when he rushed me under his arm to the stink room, crudely tore off my Pamper, and slammed me onto the water pit. Thus confined, I listened through the closed door as Big Bumps, my other Big One, scrubbed into nothingness something even a bow-wow would recognize as deservedly eternal. After a time, she began to make loud retching noises and I took my mind elsewhere. I mean, enough is enough.

Ignoring as best I could the sensation of icy void beneath my bumbum, and the cold sweat already dotting my plastic-sheathed willie (which had, as usual, been placed in the descending tunnel at the front of the seat), I wondered wearily how I had erred. I mean, I try as hard as the next guy to be open and responsive to criticism. I had watched Oh Horseshit's every gesture, analyzed Big Bumps' facial expressions until my head spun. For the thousandth time in the past week, the old cliché went through my head: communicating with Big Ones may be difficult, but, with perseverance, it's impossible. What possible need of theirs could be filled by such wanton destruction of beauty? Were they merely Philistines or was it something deeper, more sinister? I hoped not the latter, but that anyone, even Big Ones, could prefer Mother Goose lithographs to my paintings was hard to swallow.

Yes, *Mother Goose* lithographs. Can you imagine what it's like, lying around day after day being smiled at benevolently by Little Miss Muffet, Bo Peep, and Georgie Porgie? And if that's not enough, for a color scheme they chose powder blue! Dull, dull, dull!

Brown, that's the color—rich, deep, filled with secret fire, the color of earth, mahogany, and chocolate. And moo.

Hard to believe that at one time I had been unaware of moo's potential! Until last Monday, my sole use of moo had been to squish it pleasingly between the cheeks of my buttocks. In fact, until Monday, I hadn't been a painter at all, but an architect, creating elaborate maquettes for developments, heliports, and shopping centers—out of blocks.

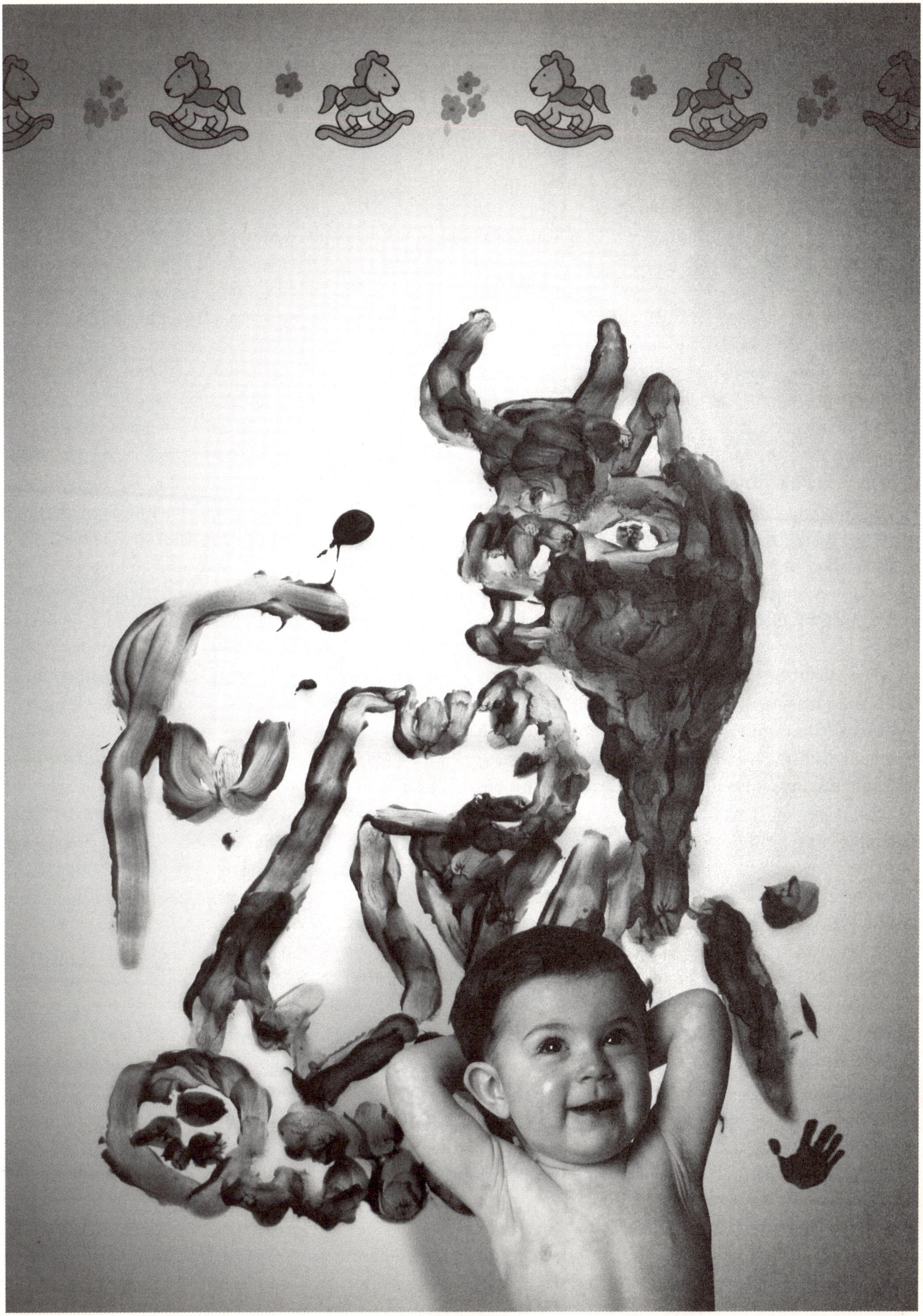

So, on Monday afternoon, I was constructing a series of modular towers. Around little-hand-on-four, the door to my studio opened and in walked Broad Buns, the Big One who lives next door, bearing Fishface, who unfortunately lives there with her. Smiling ingenuously, she deposited him on the floor in front of me, as if he were a present.

The second she left to join Big Bumps, I swept my blocks with my arm to another part of the room. Fishface's manner unsettles me. He spends most of his time staring into space and making random noises, his small balding head bobbing like a dashboard decoration. His most highly developed skill is the blowing of foam around his tongue, which protrudes far more often than good taste dictates. I believe he may be a defective.

After a time, his vacant stares and dangling strand of drool made me nervous and I went down the hall to see Big Bumps about my late afternoon bottle. When I didn't get quite the response I'd been hoping for (she threw a shoe at me), I returned angrily to my studio where, to my shock and dismay, I found that Fishface had one of my blocks and was about to put it in his mouth!

I decided to kill the little fuck. But, as I advanced on him, he leapt into a sudden animal crouch before the block pile, baring his pink, rubbery gums and hissing. I'd never seen him move so fast. Retreating to a safe distance, I looked for something to throw but found nothing. My small body began to tremble with frustration. Then I remembered moo!

There's usually a couple of tubes of it knocking around my Pamper. I reached in, found two relatively unmashed pieces, wound up, and let fly. My second shot nailed him between the eyes. Not bad for someone who's soft all over and still falls down a lot!

At first, following the loud, liquid impact, Fishface crouched unmoving, though his face fell and his hisses ceased abruptly. Then, in slow motion, he toppled backwards onto his bumbum. His mouth opened until it seemed to fill his face and emitted a thin, piercing shriek, like a peanut whistle.

Five seconds later, Broad Buns burst through my door like a demonic choochoo, Big Bumps hot on her heels. When they saw Fishface's browned countenance, they stopped short. Big Bumps made teeth at Broad Buns. Broad Buns did not make teeth at Big Bumps. She tucked Fishface under her arm and strode from the room. Neither she nor Big Bumps, who ran after her, noticed that the little bastard still had my D-G-M-R-Anteater-Panda block.

I had loved that anteater. Overwhelmed with grief, I decided to suck my foot. Eyes closed, I saw again the edentate's sly smile and long, narrow snout. A tear began its way down one of my cheeks. I shook my head. It would not help to brood. I opened my eyes; my gaze slid with distaste from Mary Mary, jumped over the cow jumping over the guess what, and came to rest near the left foot of Bo Peep. There was something there, something brown and glistening.

Suddenly alert, I started for the wall, but my legs didn't work and I fell over on my side. I started to cry but found I couldn't do that either. Then I realized **schmuck!** and pulled my foot out of my mouth.

The something on the wall was the moo that had missed. It was quite beautiful, swollen at impact into a divine, glistening bulbousness. At first, I merely stared in wonder. After a time, I reached out tentatively to touch its inviting surface. To my dismay, it came loose in my hand. Cursing myself, I tried to restick it, but to no avail, my only effect being to mar its shape, to cause with each gentle pressure a further departure from its initial perfection. Finally, my control broke and I pressed with all my might. Moo slid from the sides of my palm like jelly from a sandwich.

Stunned, I stared at what I had wrought: a dusky, grasping hand, seeming poised to snatch Bo Beep's staff upon her very next step. I had transformed kitsch into a profound study of the small Sicilian ambushes of day-to-day existence. I had created a work of relevance, spontaneity, timelessness, and pleasing aspect. In short, art.

My first thought was, "Wait till I show Oh Horseshit and Big Bumps! Will they be proud of me!"

I rushed downstairs to the kitchen, but things didn't go quite as planned. Big Bumps responded to my tugs on her apron by striking me smartly on the top of my head with a large, metal spoon.

Oh Horseshit, on the other hand, ignored me. After a mere twenty-five minutes, however, he stopped my sobs in a twinkling with that special Big One magic of clamping his hand tightly over my mouth. He then agreed to accompany me to my room, even

volunteering himself for horsie. Since horsie is what he calls dashing out my brains on low doorways, I declined. Thus it was pursued rather than accompanied that I arrived at my studio.

By coincidence, the corner in which I chose to cower was quite close to Bo Peep. Oh Horseshit had scarcely landed his foot twice when he noticed my artwork and, with a bark of surprise, left off. *Yes!* I cried silently, *What you're looking at is more important than mere lust to kill. Can you see? Can you?*

Abruptly, Oh Horseshit threw both hands over his mouth and ran from the room.

This reaction was new to me, but I soon saw it again, in more elaborate variation. Big Bumps, who soon appeared, not only mouth-clapped, but bent at the waist, made several zoolike sounds and expelled great jets of lumpy yellow matter from her mouth. I took these responses to be negative.

My job, obviously, was to figure out in what way my work was wanting. Perhaps Big Bumps' lumpy yellow matter was also a pigment, perhaps a preferred pigment. I mean, it didn't look like much, more like creamed corn than anything usable, but I thought I'd give it a try. When I bent to scoop some up, however, Big Bumps shrieked and scooped me up. From behind the bars of my crib, I watched her fetch bucket and brush and annihilate my creation.

The following morning, a special plastic seat, ironically bearing gay decals of smiling ducks and rabbits, was affixed to the water pit, and I was forced to sit with my bumbum suspended over its dank interior. Augmenting the discomfort was fear. I had seen this powerful white engine at work (it eats Kleenex and ashtray refuse) and realized how easily one of my size might fall through and be sluiced away. As a torture, it had a certain Oriental quality. I tried to outlast it by concentrating on the question of why I had been seated there in the first place.

Obviously, it had something to do with my painting. I allowed myself to become self-critical. A picture of a hand wasn't so much. Perhaps I shouldn't have expected all kudos.

Suddenly, I noticed the wallpaper. It portrayed long-legged birds walking amidst lush vegetation. That was it! The Big Ones, in their convoluted way, were trying to tell me to lay off that symbolic crap and paint instead the multiple creations of God's good Earth!

Accordingly, that evening I rendered *Tree in Sepia*. After the viewing I got to spend several hours on the water pit with the radio downstairs turned up loud to drown out my panicky cries for release.

So nature studies were not the answer. I looked for an alternative but was stumped until Big Bumps entered the stink room and placed on my lap one of the many-leaved paper rectangles she and Oh Horseshit sometimes stare at for hours. It was open to a picture of a boy sitting on a water pit and smiling. Suddenly, I understood what the Big Ones wanted: **surrealism**!

Thus, on Wednesday afternoon, I completed a surrealistic masterpiece portraying limp boombooms on a field of infinite brown. I called it *The Persistence of Mammary*. That night, Big Bumps doused my blocks with lumpy, yellow matter, rendering them permanently distasteful to me. I began to suspect a new message: art not spoken here. I considered cutting off my ear.

On Thursday, I decided to withdraw to some unspoiled, bucolic locale where I might work without harassment. In the verdant peacefulness of our backyard, I completed a gentle study of the innocent brownskin hanging Broad Buns' wash. I called it *Natural Rhythm*. Unfortunately, the innocent brownskin noticed what I was doing and ran screaming to Big Bumps, who quickly scrubbed the wall of the garage back into anonymity. I later learned that there are 366 tiles in the wall over the bathtub and more than two thousand stained white octagons in the floor.

After this failure at representationalism, I used Friday's supply of moo to complete the abstract to which I have previously referred. As you know, it, too, received bad reviews.

Looking at the problem from a new angle, I now searched for a subject so sacred to Big Ones as to ensure the preservation of my work. During my first eleven trips to the water pit on Saturday, I relentlessly asked myself what was sacred to Big Ones. On the twelfth visit, I had the answer: **themselves**! What a fool not to think of it sooner! The critic never lived who panned his own portrait!

Then, a second realization, as dire as the first was triumphant: I had to moo! I knew from an unfortunate incident with a water glass earlier in the week that the least hint of extraneous moisture simply ruins my pigment. Five thousand places to moo at my house, and I have to pick the water pit!

I slid off the seat in a panic, searching wildly for a stash...and found one! Squeezing my cheeks together so tightly they ached, I humpety-humped across the room, squatted, and gratefully allowed four fat tubes to slide out of me and nestle in the warm, plastic security of my flung Pamper.

Abruptly, there was noise without. Footsteps approached.

Thrusting the Pamper in among the dirty sheets, I made it back across the floor and vaulted onto the water pit just as the door opened. Oh Horseshit started matter-of-factly towards me, but Big Bumps paused in the doorway, wide-eyed. She emitted a startled yip and pointed a trembling finger at me, averting her eyes. Her face had gone quite white. Puzzled, I followed her finger and found that my willie had failed to return to its tunnel and instead was propped on the lip of the seat so that it pointed straight up. Oh Horseshit put his hands on his hips and barked disparagingly. Big Bumps shook her head, apparently unable to speak or lift her feet. Oh Horseshit snorted, approached me, and lifted me from the water pit. My willie fell back to normal. With a sigh of relief, Big Bumps hurried over to the water pit, and both Big Ones peered into its enameled depths. They straightened, Oh Horseshit spreading his arms wide in negative exclamation. I bounced to the floor, caroming off the sink, and rolled into the corner. Pointedly ignoring me, my Big Ones left the room growling and yapping together.

I'd pulled it off! A little painfully, I gained my feet, plucked my Pamper from the hamper, and scampered for my studio.

By happy coincidence, last night's beef and strained peaches had emerged darkly umber, the perfect shade for the brooding Wagnerian work I would now undertake. Four tubes had been a lucky break as well. Have I given you any idea just how big a Big One really is?

There's a riddle we have: Why do Big Ones never suck their feet? The answer: Because they're too far away! For this painting, I would need scaffolding. Pulling a chair to the wall, I mounted and began.

The indignities and persecution of the week slipped like splinters from my hurting consciousness; my senses focused totally on my work, on the sliding of fingertips against plaster, the heady bouquet of the pigment, the slowly forming images before me. I became part of a fused entity—me, moo, wall. I scarcely noticed the passing hours. I neither hungered nor thirsted, even though Big Bumps had taken me off all food and water that morning.

It was she who I painted first. Borrowing a technique from the Hindus, I gave her six arms and hands, one pair wringing, the others busy individually, one writing a list, one holding a long-ashed cigarette, one pulling at a fallen stocking, the last clenched in her teeth. Her body was a fruit-and-vegetable cart: instead of a head, she had a turnip; plump tomatoes replaced her knees; from her chest grew watermelons.

To her left sat Oh Horseshit, oblivious to the fire of saxophones and alumni magazines that burned beneath his chair. He had three heads: one sucked a pacifier; one was lost in a burst of exploding newspaper; the third stared with fury straight at me. His feet were propped on a makeshift hassock of cracked phonograph records. Ringing him concentrically were borders of broken glass and feathers.

Minutes or hours later, I finished. Outside, to my vague surprise, it was dark. My day had been long from *In a Brown Study* to *Artist's Big Ones at Home.* Spent, I collapsed into my crib and dreamed of nothing at all.

I awoke to the sound of a long, ululating retch. Sunday-morning sun was streaming through the window and I could see through my bars about a third of my painting, glowing with chocolate radiance. The other two-thirds had disappeared into the scrub bucket of Big Bumps, who had apparently just paused to anoint my floorboards from within.

A coy finger of dread made light with my intestines. Why wasn't I on the water pit?

The door slammed downstairs. Big Bumps straightened and wiped her hands and mouth with a towel. When Oh Horseshit entered the studio, she ran to him, eagerly plucking at the package under his arm. Oh Horseshit tore off the string and brown paper and proudly held forth a red rubber bladder trailing a wriggling red tube capped by a shining black snake head, its mouth a tiny open O. Big Bumps squealed with pleasure. Next, from his overcoat pocket Oh Horseshit withdrew a large bottle and poured a grayish liquid into the bladder. Big Bumps giggled. Then they turned on me and, showing teeth like bathroom tiles, carried me into the stink room.

How Oh Horseshit pumped that bladder! Each time I whimpered, Big Bumps clapped her hands and laughed aloud. I fantasized wildly, imagining my own inflation. Was taking it up the ass the beginning of becoming a Big One?

At last, limp and evacuated, I was returned to my studio and with many a smile and chuck beneath the chin, I was left alone. Only then did I allow my tears to come. I felt as useless as an unpierced nipple. What good is an artist without his paints? Useless...unless there were an alternate source of supply!

I sat straight up in my crib. If not my moo, whose? The Big Ones'? I assumed they mooed—they have bumbums much like mine, though uglier—but I knew not where or when, nor the ultimate resting place of their extrusions. No, I would have to look elsewhere.

Suddenly, it hit me—Fishface's bowwow! That little bowser had turned Broad Buns' backyard into a very Carrara marble quarry of moo piles! It was good moo, too, some of the best I'd ever seen. More than once I had laid my head inches from the animal's straining rump in order to watch that first darkly glistening tip emerge. It was the perfect pigment!

My depression burned off like fog under the brilliance of this idea: Alert as a cat, I scaled the walls of my crib, tiptoed to the bathroom, and secured a pillowslip from the hamper.

Soon, I had enough moo piled up in my toy chest to cover the long wall of my studio, precisely what I had in mind. I believed I had found a final solution for my Big One problem. Big Ones, different as they were from me in every particular, might yet share some common ground where we could meet. I felt certain that Big Ones could not be the highest form of life on this planet. What if Big Ones had Big Ones of their own? I've noticed their respect for cars already. And you've never seen a Big One take on, say, the Chrysler Building, have you?

If the dimensions were great enough, art would win out. Well, I would give them greatness. I would spare no anger, but neither would I scrimp on the mighty love that welled inside me. I would give them the Sistine Chapel, Guernica, and Horton Hatches the Egg, all in one. I would call my work *The Playpen of Worldly Delights.*

First, though, I would rest. The many trips to Broad Buns' backyard had tired me, and, in my second day without nourishment, I felt hampered by intermittent staggering. I dozed fitfully throughout the day. When I awoke, it was dark outside, but my hands were on fire. I stripped for action. Pulling a first great, meaty coil of doggie moo from my toy chest, I turned to the wall and let the fever take me.

I regained my awareness to the morning songs of birds. The air was thick with sweet fecal perfume. Then, first light speared the wall!

Reader, I looked through a picture window into Sepia Heaven. Words cannot paint it for you. You must close your eyes, hold your Teddy very close to you under a snug blanket, listen to the tattoo of rain on your window, and wait until you are almost asleep. Now, look hard. Freeze what you see. Drop a brown tint. Shoot it through with golden highlights. There. That is my painting.

It was a work of such blazing genius it would incinerate the hand that tried to scrub it. Reeling with hunger and fatigue, I somehow gained my crib and fell unconscious.

"You stupid shitface!" bellowed Oh Horseshit, inches from my nose.

"Igggghhhhh! Uckkkkkkk!" put in Big Bumps, jackknifed by the wall.

I tried to pull the covers over my head, but Oh Horseshit was too fast for me. In the stink room, he sat me firmly down in the basin and withdrew from the mirror cabinet a tube of toothpaste. Clicking his tongue for attention, he held the tube over the mouth of the water pit and, with ominous calm, twisted and rolled it until long, aqua tubes extruded to splash insipidly below. He then did much the same to me.

After Oh Horseshit's departure for the day, I watched Big Bumps pass the stink room door carrying two buckets, two scrub brushes, a paint scraper, a mop, and a shovel. As the morning passed, her retching noises took on the insistent quality of a woodworking shop.

I felt crushed in spirit, devoid of emotions, so empty inside I wondered if Oh Horseshit hadn't squeezed out a few of my organs. And perhaps the remainder of my creative urge as well. Life was too short to spend being squeezed in the stink room. I would paint no more.

When she had completed the erasure of my masterwork, Big Bumps joined me. She was quite a sight. There was moo on her hands, moo on her clothes, moo in her hair. Stringy matter hung from her slack jaw and mingled with the brown on her blouse. She looked like a salad.

I watched her slowly undress as the bathtub filled. Out came Big Bumps' boombooms, and an immense pair of squash they were! They spilled from her white boomboom holder to hang and dance like Slinkies. Next, down went her black lace Pamper.

Suddenly, I forgot art.

Big Bumps slid into the tub, sighing gratefully. I began to sweat. In its sheath, my doodle had become so hot I seriously expected steam. In the grip of this strange, new emotion, I honestly didn't realize I had mooed until a cold tongue of water kissed my sphincter.

At the sound of the plunk, however, Big Bumps had catapulted from the tub with a small animal-cry of hope to peer between my legs. It was a feeble little moo, no bigger than a pencil stub, but Big Bumps unleashed a scream of purest joy, threw her arms around me, and hugged with all her might. Her boombooms laved my face like two great soap bubbles.

Now, hours later, I lie in my crib, stomach full once more, my soft, rather appealing flesh newly bathed and powdered, decked out in a fresh Pamper, and swathed in warm flannel jammies. Oh Horseshit came home a while ago and visited my crib to pay his respects, tousling my hair and pinching my nose in camaraderie. All is well. Having told this tale, the artistic experience already fades. Sometimes, I have decided, it is better to bend with the winds of change.

Besides, there are new discoveries aborning. Moments ago, as I lay musing over the experiences of the day, I felt a sudden return of the hot doodle sensation. I have just made a visual check, and know what? My willie is hard like a rock. And standing straight out from my body.

Flesh sculpture!

Wait till I show Oh Horseshit and Big Bumps! Will they be proud of me!! ■

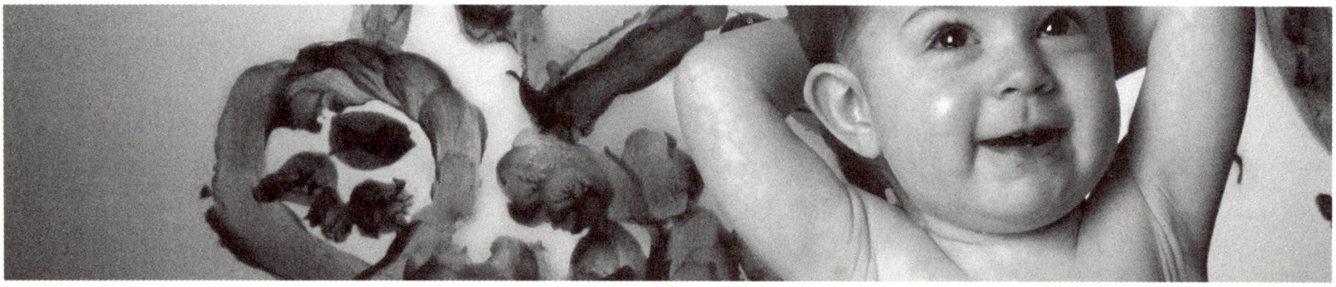

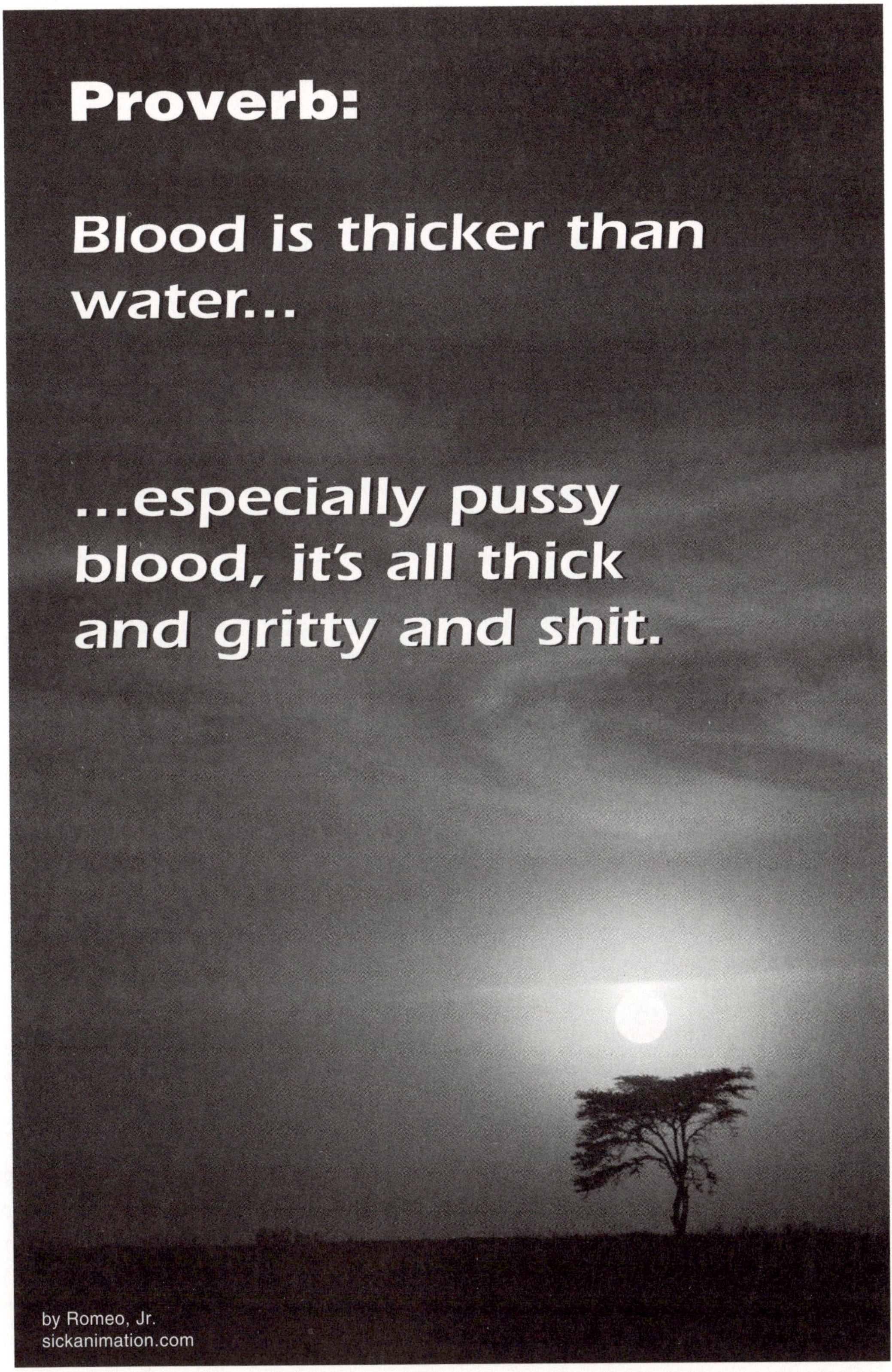
Proverb:
Blood is thicker than water...
...especially pussy blood, it's all thick and gritty and shit.
by Romeo, Jr.
sickanimation.com

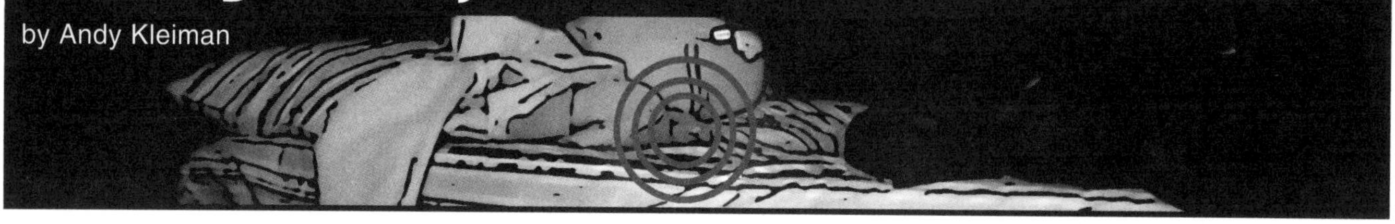

Hey Don, I Peed in Your Bed

by Andy Kleiman

Ladies and Gentlemen, Exhibit P

Hey Don, remember me? It's Andy, we lived together junior year with Greg and Nick. Well, anyway, I just wanted to let you know that I peed in your bed midway through the semester.

Yup, that's right, I peed in your bed. Not on top, *in*. I peed on that fitted sheet, the sheet that you lie on when you go to sleep. I got it alllllll over, and since no one has told you until now, that means that for the better part of three months you were sleeping in pee. Congratulations.

Why did I do this? Well, it was no secret that we never got along. Me being a somewhat normal and agreeable person and you being a douche bag. I don't like douche bags, Don, and I won't stand for them. But I will stand over their bed when I'm peeing on them, which I did. And you had no idea.

When did I do this? Well, I had been plotting this for a while, but the time was never right. I didn't know your schedule and I didn't know how fast my pee would dry. Then I came home one Friday afternoon and Greg (not a supporter of this) told me that you were gone for the weekend.

Easter.

Easter weekend. Most people go home for the weekend, as you did. I stayed at college because I'm Jewish. What a Mitzvah!

You usually locked the door to your room even when you'd be gone for just the afternoon—doucebag. But God smiled upon me that day and your door was unlocked. I knew it was meant to pee.

It was perfect. I peed on your bed Friday afternoon; you didn't come back until Monday. With all that time, you're lucky peeing on your bed was the only thing I did. Which I did. And it was yellow.

Don't believe me? Think I'm just pulling the ol' "there's something on your back" trick? Oh Don, you think I would do something so fantastic and not have proof?

I took pictures.

Yes, I took pictures and I showed those pictures to basically everyone at college. You would think that out of 6,000 people someone would have felt bad and told you. But that didn't happen, or else you would have known that I gave your bed a golden shower, which I did. And it was glorious.

I even made it the wallpaper on my computer, for it is my proudest moment.

Why am I confessing now, Don? An excellent question. Is it because I feel bad? Hardly. I'd do it again in a second; I became legend at college because I was the one who peed on your bed. Hell, I'd pee on your face if I could (not in a sexual R. Kelly way, mind you, but more of a vengeful "take that" way). No, I am telling you this because it is the second part of my plan. If I told you that I peed in your bed a few days afterwards, not only would you immediately change your sheets, ruining my fun, but you would royally kick my ass because you were on the wrestling team and even though you sucked—which you did—a sucky wrestler beats a scrawny Jew any day. I'm telling you this because I want you to be paranoid. I want you to think, "What else did he do?"

Maybe I cleaned the inside of the toilet with your toothbrush?

Or maybe I didn't?

Maybe I spit in the gin you used to make those fuckin' martinis?

Or maybe I didn't?

I want you to give your bed the sniff test every time you go to sleep, I want you to check your shoes before putting them on, I want you to wonder if that funny taste is coming your toothpaste or your toothbrush.

You were the most aggravating person I have ever met, and I had to live with you. This was just evening the score.

Now, if you'll excuse me, I have to go to the bathroom. ■

"I don't know how you did it, Bernice, but the pimples on your back spell out 'I Luv You' in braille."

Night Of The Seven Fires

by Chris Miller

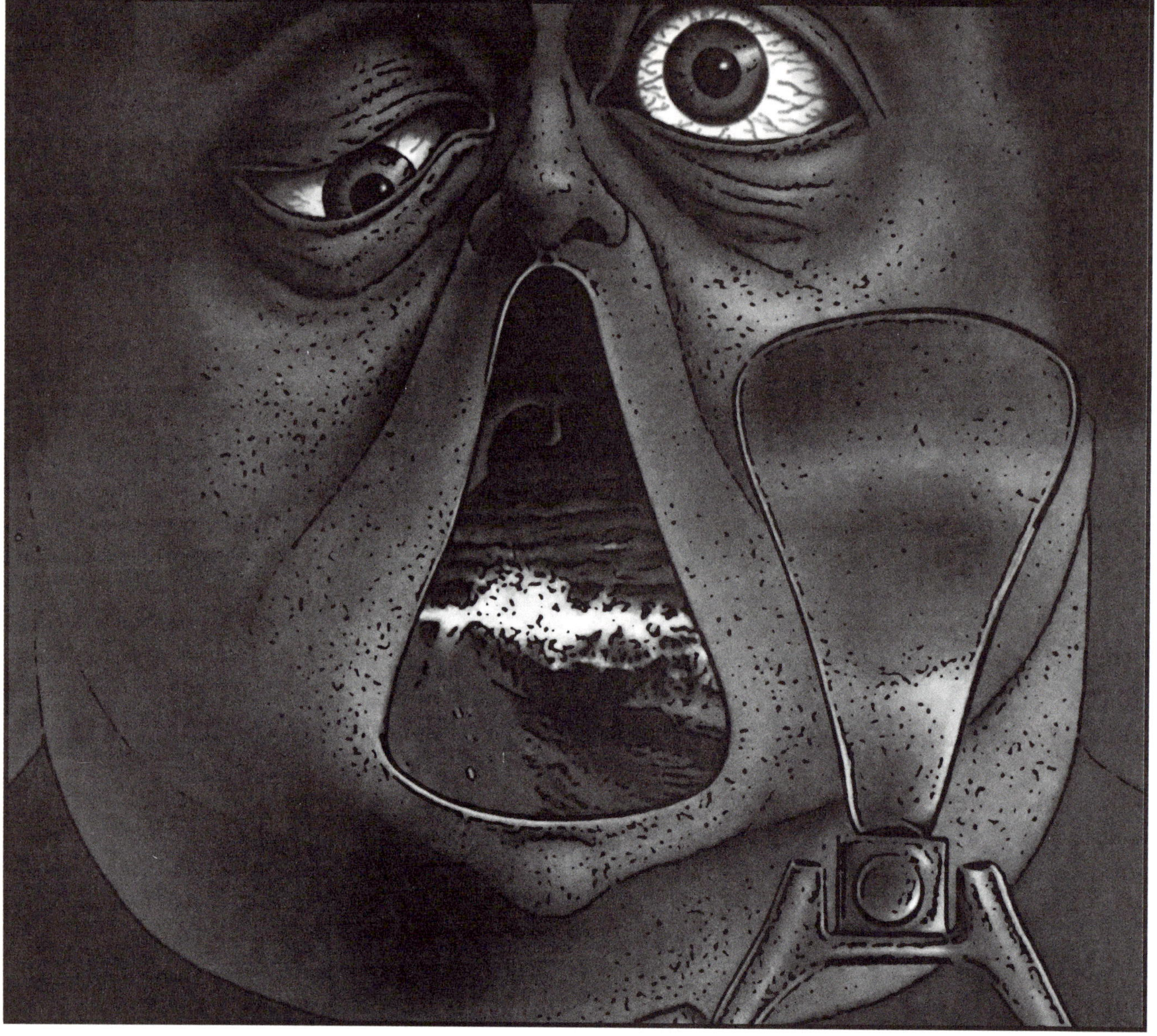

The moment he woke up, Pinto discovered two terrible things. The first was that he had a hangover. Not one of his usual ones, though these were bad enough, but a veritable Hiroshima among hangovers. His stomach felt like a swamp; his tongue like a small dead animal, bloated and putrid; his forehead as if it had been struck by an axe. He went to bring a hand to his forehead, to see if perhaps it had been struck by an axe.

That was when he made the second discovery: His hand wouldn't move. In fact, his arm wouldn't move. Nor would his other arm. He couldn't move. Below the neck, he couldn't move a thing! A terrible sense of dread took hold of him. What had he done last night?

He opened his eyes. Light speared them like hatpins, but he squinted, blinking away his tears, and...wait, this wasn't his dorm room! He was lying on a bed, a raggedy army blanket thrown over him, in what appeared to be one of the small bedrooms on the third floor of his fraternity house.

And then he remembered: The Fires! Last night had finally been the Fires, his fraternity initiation...and now he was paralyzed from the neck down? Become one of those poor assholes you read about each year, maimed during hazing? He repressed panic. He had to keep his wits, piece together his fragmented memories of last night, figure out what happened. He remembered pushing off from the house around ten o'clock, having been paired with Stu the Jew...

In his hand, Pinto carried a map. Identical mimeographed maps had been handed each pair of pledges that evening, as they'd stood about the pre-Fires keg back at the house earlier, hurling down beers for courage and against the cold. According to the map, he and Stu had almost reached the turnoff that led to the first fire, and the start of their fraternity's legendary initiation rites. The principles for which the Adelphian Lodge stood, and which had brought about its fame, were stated in their Credo, a large, hand-lettered sign that hung behind the bar: Sickness is health, blackness is truth, drinking is strength. And if there was a single event which embodied the entire Adelphian zeitgeist, it was the Night of the Seven Fires.

Pinto didn't know everything that would go on at the Fires, but he knew about "booting"—an intricate process of drinking and throwing up, drinking and throwing up, until not one pledge remained on his feet. In this fashion, they would be transformed into brothers. What was more, the pledge who threw the overall most colorful show of the night would be awarded a prize. Pinto was after that prize. He had been in training for months, spending hours by the keg nightly, learning to quaff multiple beers and then accurately boot them into the concrete gutter that ran the perimeter of their basement barroom. He was ready. His only serious competition, he figured, would come from Mumbles, La Pic, or Bags. Certainly not from Stu the Jew, trudging along beside him. Ordinarily, competing with tall, muscular Stu—in anything—would have intimidated Pinto. But not tonight. Stu's training time had gone into sports and booking rather than booting and one look at the half-scared, half-defiant expression he now wore showed that he was looking forward to tonight's activities about as much as he would to a hernia operation.

The turn-off appeared abruptly, and lead to a dark, dirt road. It was a gauntlet, the route of the Seven Sacred Watchfires of the Adelphian Lodge, each fire with its contingent of brothers waiting poised to torment them with a variety of devices and stratagems. At that moment, a low moan escaped the lips of Stu the Jew. Pinto glanced at him, surprised. He'd known Stu was unhappy, but not that unhappy.

"Stu, you okay?" His breath made white puffs of vapor against the night. Stu didn't answer. He simply stared up at the woods, muscles bunching and knotting in his cheeks. Pinto, trying to help, drew a flask of brandy from the pocket of his parka and held it out to him.

Stu recoiled incredulously, "Are you shitting me? With all we're going to have to drink?"

Shrugging, Pinto put the flask away. The way he figured it, they'd be booting all night, so what the hell did it matter how much they had to drink? But he let Stu do it his own way. "Ready?"

Stu nodded reluctantly. Stepping off into deeper snow, they started up the hill.

The first fire revealed itself to them in a shower of sparks rising from behind an upcoming ridge. As they moved closer, they heard voices, then laughter. Among the laughs was one that was unmistakable.

"Hey, that's Otter," Pinto told Stu. "Come on, this fire won't be bad at all."

Stu looked as if he doubted that, but resumed walking. The road hooked sharply around a ridge and there, primitive and terrific, was a great, crackling bonfire. Its flames leapt and danced, casting a broad circle of light that gradually gave way to crazily dancing tree shadows. Perched on a stump was a quarter-keg of beer, gravity-tapped, and standing around the keg were several figures holding beer cups. Pinto recognized Otter, Mouse, Terry, and Pale Pete. Two other figures were obscure behind the flames.

"Hi, guys." Pinto headed excitedly toward them. The brothers spun to confront them, their faces assuming looks of mock horror.

"What?" cried Mouse. "What did you say?"

Pinto halted uncertainly. "Uh, I said 'Hi, guys.'"

"Anh! Anh! That's what I thought he said!" Charlie Boing-Boing bounded from behind the fire, staring at Pinto as if what Pinto had said was "I eat farts." "On your knees, pledges!" ordered Mouse, hands on hips. Pinto and Stu exchanged looks. "You heard him!" yelled Charlie Boing-Boing. "On your knees and call in!"

Pinto and Stu fell rapidly to their knees and began to bellow: "Most unworthy neophyte..."

"Hold it, hold it, one at a time," directed Terry. "You first." He pointed to Stu the Jew. "Most unworthy neophyte, Stuart Lawrence Richman, begs to announce his most humble presence at the Adelphian Lodge!" shouted Stu.

"What? What?" Mouse was aghast. "Did you hear that?"

"Tsk-tsk," said Otter. "Appalling." Stu looked bewildered.

"This isn't the Adelphian Lodge!" screamed Charlie Boing-Boing. "You fucking asshole!"

"Oh, right, right. Most unworthy neophyte, Stuart Lawrence Richman, begs to announce his most humble presence at the Adelphian Fires!"

"At the first Adelphian Fire," corrected Otter. "Most unworthy neophyte, Stuart Lawrence Richman, begs to announce his most humble presence at the first Adelphian Fire!"

"Most unworthy neophyte..." began Pinto. "Oh, hush," said Otter. "That's enough of that." "All right, pledges, on your feet!" directed Mouse.

Pinto and Stu stood up and Terry handed them each a beer. Stu looked at it as if he had never seen one before. "Now, boys," said Otter, in his friendly, cool, California way, "before we start, I'd like yuh to say hello to muh girl."

"Hi," said a voice. Pinto squinted through the flames. There, dressed in a pert blue parka with a furred hood, was Joy Tabasco, Otter's girlfriend. A girl? At the Fires? Otter was amazing. "All right," said Otter, "now that both you gentlemen have a beer, why don't you chug them?"

Well, this was it. Pinto and Stu exchanged glances and brought their beer cups to their mouths. The frosty fluid made a ribbon of cold down Pinto's throat. "Two more beers for the boys," said Otter agreeably.

Terry had them waiting. That they were in sixteen-ounce cups, twice the volume of the glasses with which he'd been training, wasn't bothering Pinto at all. He chugged his second beer rapidly down and a moment later Stu finished his. They were immediately handed two more. They chugged. This time Pinto over tilted a bit and twin rills of beer made icy lines on his cheeks. "You're supposed to get it all in your mouth!" Mouse darted about making small jumps, like an angry cartoon character. "Asshole! Asshole!" "Now, Mouse." Otter placed a hand on either side of Joy's hood, as if to cover her ears. There was general laughter.

"Well, time we got down to some serious booting," Otter said. "Hope yuh made it down to the Italian restaurant okay. I'd hate for yuh to be chokin' on lumps in front of muh girl."

The brothers had solicitously warned the pledges to eat nothing more solid than spaghetti that day. "Sure did," said Pinto, and Stu nodded.

"Good," said Otter. "Terry, give Pinto a fresh beer." Dependable Terry appeared with a fresh beer. "Now, chug!" ordered Charlie Boing-Boing.

Pinto swung the cup to his mouth and began swallowing deep draughts. He really wanted to drink and boot well for these guys. Cold as he probably was, he felt warmed by a sense of imminent belonging. Otter was terrific. Terry was terrific. They were all ter... Glorp! Something thick and gloopy slid into his throat and caught there, like a giant wad of phlegm. Pinto gagged...and booted! He booted everything he'd had to drink since seven that evening—a gallon at least—in a single great arc of roaring foam and twining pink spaghetti strands that narrowly missed Charlie Boing-Boing's left ear and splattered spectacularly against the trunk of a tree.

"Power boot!" exclaimed Mouse. "Fantastic!" cried Charlie Boing-Boing.

"What form!" enthused Terry. "Did you see how it held together?" He shook his head in connoisseur-like respect. Otter laughed his peculiar steady laugh and looked at Joy, who managed a restrained giggle. She had gone quite pale.

Pinto spat several times, clearing his mouth. "What the hell was in that?" "A raw egg," said Pale Pete, smiling shyly. He was the house nice guy, always ready to lend a hand or clear a confusion.

"Now Stu the Jew!" announced Otter jovially. Everyone turned to face Stu. Stu went paler than Joy. "Uh, an egg, huh?" "That's right." Otter bobbed his head forward and back on his long neck, grinning his otter's grin. Everyone else nodded and smiled too. "Well..." Stu took the proffered cup and began to sip it delicately. "Drink!" yelled Mouse. "Chug!" howled Charlie Boing-Boing. Stu tried, but his mouth had made a tight, protective slot and beer began running down his cheeks. "Open your mouth, asshole!"

Stu shuddered visibly, but opened his mouth. Instantly he froze, dropping his beer cup on the ground. The brothers leaned forward expectantly. Stu's face wore a horrible expression, like a mask of tragedy, only with foam. He stayed that way for what seemed like a long time, then slowly closed his mouth...and swallowed. There was a pause. The brothers held their breath. Joy peeked between her fingers. Gradually, Stu's body relaxed. He opened his eyes and managed a shaky smile.

"Anhhhhh!" Charlie Boing-Boing turned his back disgustedly and walked into the woods, where he could shortly be heard taking a leak.

"No boot?" said Terry. "Gee." "Boooo." Everyone looked at Otter. "Boooo," he repeated. "Bad show." "Booooo," said the rest of the brothers. "Booooo, hissssss." Stu appeared to be halfway between crying and punching someone out.

"You were supposed to boot, Stu," explained Pale Pete helpfully. "Like Pinto." "That's right," said Terry. "Here, Pinto, have a gentlemen's beer." The brothers raised their own glasses in toast and Pinto, swelling with pride, took the cup and drained it easily. Terry beamed and slapped him on the back. "Aw, well, shit," was Stu's comment...

"Wow, great fire, huh?" said Pinto, after they'd been walking for a time. He felt fantastic. Stu said nothing. Pinto persisted. "Wasn't that amazing, Joy being there?" Stu stopped short. "I won't give them the satisfaction," he declared. "Fuck 'em!" "Huh?"

"I won't boot for those guys. Why should I?" Pinto regarded Stu curiously. He didn't understand. Why not boot for them? Shit, his only regret was that he hadn't gotten to boot more. Oh, his boot had been a five-star boot, he wasn't doubting that, but there would be many splendid boots that night and if he wanted the pledge prize he'd have to score on quantity as well as quality. So why was Stu so totally out of the spirit of things?

"Listen, Stu, I think you better boot. You're gonna get sicker than shit with all that stuff in you. What if you pass out in the snow? You're too big to carry." Stu started to give Pinto a hard look, but then began to list to one side and had to grab a tree to stay upright. Abruptly, his angry expression collapsed, to be replaced with a look of utmost wretchedness. "I better level with you, man. I've never told this to anyone before, but I can't boot." "You can't boot?" Pinto didn't know what to say. It was as if Stu had suddenly announced he was blind or impotent. "I've never been able to boot. Even when I was sick with the same virus that had everyone else booting their guts out, I couldn't boot. Pinto, what the fuck am I gonna do?" So that was it. "Jesus, I don't know, man. Maybe if you just relaxed more, let it come." "Oh, swell. Relax more. Thanks a shitload."

They found the second fire in a clearing behind a stand of tall pines. "Good luck, man," whispered Pinto as they fell to their knees at the clearing's edge. "Most unworthy neophyte..." "Hey, knock off the yelling, you shitheads! Get over here!"

They stood up fast and got over there. Five brothers awaited, the presiding brother proving to be Willy Machine, a quiet senior of Buddha-like imperturbability. Nestling in the snow at their feet were numerous bottles of red wine.

"Pinto and Stu?" Willy looked surprised. "We thought you were Bags and Huck Doody."

Bags and Huck Doody hadn't been there yet? That was strange. They'd been first out tonight, the only ones to leave before him and Stu. He knew they'd preceded him through the first fire; he'd seen their boot craters. So where were they?

"Well, no matter." Willy inscribed a circle in an undisturbed patch of snow with a stick from the fire. "Pinto, you get to sit in the throne." Pinto hadn't heard about any thrones. Still, with his Air Force parka and long underwear he felt pretty well protected. He started to sit.

"And, oh yes, drop your pants first." Oh, thought Pinto. Each fire, he was beginning to realize, took on the personality of its head brother. Whereas Otter's fire had been beneficent, casual, genial, Willy Machine's would be cool and efficient. Bracing himself, he dropped his pants and eased his ass into the snow.

"Stu, you take this,"— Willy handed Stu a huge mug of wine— "and stand right there between Pinto's legs. Pinto, get your legs open. Now, we're going to play a little game we just made up for you. What's it called, men?" "BOOT IN BUSH," chanted the brothers. They formed a wolfish semicircle around Pinto and Stu. Pinto checked them out in turn: Coyote, with his feral eyes; King Embryo, nudging Coyote with cowboy-like good humor; Snot, short and intense, bouncing about in place like an excited basketball; Giraffe, lanky and laconic, grinning evilly. There were no girlfriends.

"Okay, Stu, I want you to start chugging this wine," directed Willy Machine. "And when you boot, I want it to go square in Pinto's bush." "Yeah, none of this turning your head away stuff," added Snot. For the first time that night, Pinto felt a tinge of repugnance. He repressed it brutally. He'd show these guys how cool he could be. "When I boot, huh?" Stu flicked a helpless glance from brother to brother. He saw no mercy. Anywhere. He turned to Pinto. "Listen, man, I'm really sorry about..." "Hurry up and boot in my bush!" yelled Pinto. "I'm freezing my ass off down here!"

Stu gulped, shut his eyes, and began chugging as fast as he could. The brothers leaned forward eagerly. Pinto fought hard to keep from flinging himself out of the way. Now that Stu was on wine, Pinto couldn't believe he'd be able to continue not booting. He could almost feel the steaming cascade blasting about his genitals. "Yurch!" said Stu. "Blurg! Hurch!" Pinto shut his eyes and cringed, waiting for the splash. There were several more series of noises...but no splash. He opened his eyes. Stu was jackknifed over his groin gagging, but all that was coming out were two long strands of saliva boot, dangling like pale, glistening worms from the corners of his mouth. "Stu, come on already!" Pinto's ass had gone numb.

"BOOT, BOOT, BOOT," chanted the brothers.

Stu straightened in short jerks, as if he were being cranked. He resumed chugging, but more slowly now, taking several swallows, then stopping and weaving a bit, then swallowing again. Suddenly, he dropped the mug and bent violently from the waist. The brothers leaned forward. Pinto cringed. Stu made a terrible set of sounds...and nothing came out.

"ASSHOLE, ASSHOLE, ASSHOLE," chanted the brothers. "I don't think you get the idea, Stu," said Willy Machine. "You're supposed to boot. In Pinto's bush." "Pledge Adelphian, boot Adelphian," put in King Embryo. "Yeah, yeah," muttered Stu. He wiped the stringy tusks from his mouth with the back of his hand. "I'm trying, I..."

Abruptly, in a double bellow from the rim of the clearing: "Most unworthy neophyte, John Ellington Bagbaum/Edwin Charles Wylie, begs to announce his most humble presence at the second Adelphian Fire!" Two figures parted from the darkness and headed toward them. "Why, Bags and Huck Doody!" purred Willy Machine. "Stop off for a few drinks?"

"On your knees, pledges!" barked Snot. "You crawl in here! You're late!" Bags and Huck Doody exchanged exasperated looks. Pinto guessed they weren't getting off so well on the degradation aspect of things.

"Stu and Pinto beat you here!" Willy told them. "Pinto, stand up and pull up your trou." With a gasp of relief, Pinto jumped to his feet, drawing fabric rapidly over his poor frozen cheeks. Willy Machine found a fresh patch of snow and drew side-by-side circles in it with his stick. "Bags, Huck, you drop your pants and sit your asses down right here."

"What?" rumbled Bags.

"Jesus Christ!" complained Huck Doody, rolling his eyes.

"Hit it!" roared Willy, his stick pointed unwaveringly at the thrones. Radiating indignity, Huck Doody dropped trou and sat. "Holy shit," he said as his ass met snow. Bags dropped his pants more slowly, with an expression that coolly told the brothers he was damned if they could dish out anything too sick for him. Without comment, he settled himself into the throne next to Huck's. The snow pushed up his scrotum and his stub-like penis pointed at the stars.

"Snot, mugs of wine for Pinto and Stu," directed Willy Machine. "DOUBLE BOOT IN BUSH," chanted the brothers happily. Pinto was delighted at the turn of events. Now he'd show the brothers some real regurgitation. He took his wine eagerly and positioned himself next to Stu over the wide-open legs of Bags and Huck Doody. They began to chug. "Hey, what is this?" said Huck Doody, with dawning comprehension. "Stu," bellowed Bags, "if you boot in my bush, I'll kill you." Pinto paid them no mind. He had almost drained his mug when the last of the wine caught in his throat, triggering a gag. A red parabola sailed from his mouth to Huck Doody's groin, where it spattered with great violence.

"Pinto!" howled Huck. "Jesus Christ!"

Stu was still chugging. Then, abruptly, his legs buckled and he simply sat down, the remainder of his wine spilling unnoticed into the snow. Bags, seeing himself safe, turned to laugh heartily at Huck Doody's lapful of boot.

Pinto saw his chance. "Snot, gimme another mug! Quick!" Seconds later, another spout of wine left Pinto's exterior, a spray-boot this time, that drenched Bags from nipple to knee.

"Good Christ!" thundered Bags. "You son of a bitch!" He began rapidly wiping himself with handfuls of snow.

"YAYYYYYY!" cheered the brothers, pounding Pinto happily on the back. Snot ran about making parade music noises, pretending to play a trombone.

"Hey, Stu," called Pinto. "Two down, five to go." Stu put his head in his hands and groaned.

The next four fires passed in a surreal blur. Pinto, drunker than he'd ever been, was booting like never before. He remembered power boots and dribble boots; spray boots and tight beam boots; spit boots and gusher boots; beer boots, wine boots, and even a warm-salt-water-with-cigarette-butts boot. He felt positive that no other pledge could possibly be putting on half the show he was.

For Stu, however, the night grew worse and worse. He kept drinking whatever was handed him, often gagging loud enough to wake the dead— yet still nothing came out. At the fifth fire, which had involved total nudity, Pinto had noticed that Stu's stomach was distended fearfully, as if he had swallowed a helmet. By the time they left the sixth fire, Stu was in as sorry a state as Pinto had ever seen a human being, colliding with trees, mouthing wild, meaningless strings of syllables, leaning heavily on Pinto to stay upright. He seemed to be continuing only by the most incredible exertion of will.

Now the seventh fire wove into view. It seemed a smaller fire, with a smaller contingent of brothers, but they were the very sick heart of the junior class-Magpie, Whit, Scotty, and Dumptruck. He and Stu were just going to their knees when they were spotted.

"Hey, cool it, you guys," called Scotty. "None of that stuff here. You made it through this far, that's enough for us. Come on over and have a gentlemen's beer."

Pinto couldn't believe it.

"No, really," assured Dumptruck. "You guys've had enough. Come have a beer with us and then I'll drive you back to the house."

They sounded serious. A sense of letdown took Pinto. He'd been ready to go on all night. Well, if the Fires were over, they were over. He'd booted brilliantly throughout and if he hadn't won the pledge prize by now, he didn't know what else he could do. Slinging one of Stu's arms over his shoulders, Pinto pulled the two of them to their feet and staggered in an S-shaped path toward the brothers.

"Hey, how'd the other fires go?" asked Magpie, handing them each a beer.

Pinto propped Stu against a tree and began an animated account of the night's events, not forgetting his single-handed double-boot-in-bush at the second fire or the simultaneous boot and piss he had taken at the fourth. His report was greeted by much good-natured laughter from the juniors.

"Well, sounds like you've had quite a time," said Dumptruck at last. "But it's all over now. No drinking and booting at this fire."

"Right, right," said Whit. "In fact, we figured you guys'd probably be hungry after all that booting. So we brought you a midnight snack."

A midnight snack? What was this? He looked at their faces. Something had just changed in them. The smiles were still there, but they had suddenly become leers.

"Can't eat anythin'," managed Stu. "S'impossible."

"You'll eat, you fucking asshole pledge, or you won't leave this fire!" yelled Magpie. "Scotty, where's the hot dogs?"

Scotty handed a hot dog each to Pinto and Stu. "It's okay, Stu," he said. "They're kosher."

"You mean, all we're supposed to do is eat these and then we go back to the house?" Pinto didn't quite get it.

"That's all," said Scotty, but the gleam in his eye didn't match the innocence in his voice.

Shrugging, Pinto brought the hot dog to his mouth.

"Hey, pledge, that's frozen solid. You want to break your teeth?" Whit grabbed Pinto's arm and pulled the hot dog clear before his jaws could close. He smiled. "Before you eat it, you have to warm it up."

"Drop trou, Stu!" barked Magpie. "Spread your cheeks!"

Ah, thought Pinto. Hot dogs up the ass. Cute. But Stu...Pinto hadn't believed Stu could look any worse than he'd been looking, but his partner had just turned gray as death.

"Hey, don't look that way," counseled Whit in a kindly tone. "I'm sure you guys keep yourselves clean. And even if you don't, if you've ever tasted shit you know it's not so bad, anyway."

"S'not that," said Stu, darting imploring looks from brother to brother. "I got a thing about things being put in my ass. Listen, you can't do it to me. I..."

"Drop trou!" screamed Magpie. "Bend over an' spread 'em!"

Stu rolled his eyes despairingly, too sick and semiconscious to protest further. With slow, heavy hands, he dropped his trou and spread his cheeks.

"Go ahead, Pinto," prompted Magpie. "And leave it up there until it's warm enough to eat."

Stu's cracked ass was not the most pleasant sight Pinto had ever beheld. Scraggly hair ran its length, spilling over onto his buns, and his sphincter looked too tight and tiny to admit a knitting needle. Well...he began to make tentative thrusts at it with the hot dog.

"That's it, that's it!" cried Whit excitedly. "Slide it right in!" "I...can't. It won't go."

"Hey, Stu, relax. Your muscles are all tight."

"I'm trying," moaned Stu. "I'm not doing it on purpose."

"I thought something like this might happen," said Scotty. "So you know what? I brought along some lube."

Lube? "Hey," said Pinto, "I'm not eating any Vaseline. Shit's bad enough."

"Now don't worry your head, Pinto. This is edible lubricant." He withdrew from within his coat a large jar of Miracle Whip. Dumptruck shook his head in admiration. "Scotty, you think of everything."

"Oh, go on with you," said Scotty modestly. He dipped Pinto's hot dog into the jar a few times. When he handed it back, it was dripping creamy white stuff.

Taking the wiener gingerly by its dry end, Pinto returned it to Stu's bum and began probing for entry. Abruptly, it slid in a little.

"Ga!" cried Stu. His sphincter closed even tighter, stopping all forward progress. "Come on, man," Pinto pleaded. "Let me get it over with."

"I'm trying," gritted Stu.

"Hey, we haven't got all night here," said Magpie. "Jam it in!"

"Okay, okay!" Holding it in place with one hand, Pinto swung his other hand in a long arc and smacked the hot dog hard as he could with the flat of his palm. The wiener slid into Stu's asshole like a greased plunger. Stu began to rumble. "Gnorg!" he cried, then "Bluuuuuurrrrrchhhhhh," but before Pinto could tell what was happening something struck him a tremendous blow on the forehead and...

And that was all. He couldn't remember another thing. Lying now in the strange bed, drenched with sweat, he realized that he still had no idea where his paralysis had come from. So much for piecing together memories; his panic came uncorked and he bellowed for help until the door to his room flew open and Otter, Scotty, and Dumptruck burst in.

"Hey, you bastards, what'd you do to me? I can't move. I'm paralyzed!" "Uh-heh-heh-heh-heh-heh," laughed Otter. "He thinks he's paralyzed."

"Hey, man, don't worry." Dumptruck swept away Pinto's blanket. "Look."

Pinto raised his head. His arms and legs were tied securely to the mattress with sheets. "What...why...?"

"You don't remember?" Dumptruck was incredulous. "Pinto, when Stu finally booted, the hot dog shot out of his ass like a rocket and knocked you cold. We had to carry you back. You were thrashing around so much when we got you here, we decided to tie you into Otter's bed, so you wouldn't get hurt."

"Slept with muh girl last night," put in Otter as he untied Pinto. Pinto brought a freed hand to his forehead and found a bump big as a golf ball. So that was what hit him. And he wasn't paralyzed! And...wait a minute. "Truck, did you say 'when Stu finally booted'?"

"You didn't see it?" cried Dumptruck. "It was the most incredible boot in the history of the Adelphian Lodge! It must have lasted a minute and a half! It was this wide!" He gestured with his hands to show just how wide.

"I got drenched," remembered Scotty dreamily. "It knocked three of us down. It must have gone fifty or sixty feet!"

"Pinto, it was magnificent!"

Pinto was having a terrible sinking feeling. "And the pledge prize...?"

"Went to Stu the Jew, of course! Pinto, he actually put out the seventh fire! That's never been done before!" Dumptruck was hardly able to contain himself. "We've been calling alumni all morning! Black Mike and T Bear from the class of '55 are sending a wreath!"

Pinto was crestfallen. He'd tried so hard.

"But, hey, Pinto, don't feel bad," said Otter. "You were terrific last night and just so you don't think we didn't notice, we brought you a consolation prize." He brought his hand from behind his back and held out Pinto's prize: an ice cold glass of beer. ■

Baby Animals Found In House of Filth

by Jason Mathews

DU BOIS, PA (AP)—A local woman, known only as "Nanny" to her neighbors, was charged Thursday with animal neglect and abuse after authorities raided her home and found close to a dozen animals dressed in children's clothing, living in conditions witnesses described as "deplorable."

Animal control officers were summoned after receiving numerous complaints about a foul odor emanating from the residence.

"The smell was unimaginable," said animal control officer Betsy Leto, who was first on the scene. "I rang the bell, and up walked this elderly woman wearing nothing but a skirt, green stripped socks and a pair of sneakers. As soon as she cracked the door the stink hit me and I about lost it." Added Leto, "There was garbage and fecal matter everywhere you stepped. It was a house of filth."

Once inside, officers found all of the animals locked in a single room with no floor drains or running water. According to officers, the room appeared to be decorated as if it were a child's nursery, complete with toys, cribs, and even children's books.

"She really thought these things were her children," said Amanda Hohmann, a psychologist who was called in to evaluate the mental state of the home's owner. "She kept referring to them as her babies, and from the looks of it she may have been attempting to breastfeed. It's a very sad case."

All of the animals were severely malnourished. Some were found to have parasites and oozing wounds, while others were already dead. Eyewitness accounts of the raid describe animal control officers removing numerous species from the home, including a dog, a frog, and various other creatures that were so caked in their own feces that they could not be easily identified.

Despite the wide variety of animals, the owner apparently allowed all of them to mingle freely amongst one another, a decision that led to a particularly gruesome scene for investigators who found a small bear gnawing on the remains of an animal that could only be described as a "blue weirdo."

"You can't have these animals living together like this without cages, especially if you're not going to feed them properly," said Humane Society spokesman Luke Hanish. "I mean, a bear and a pig? How the hell is that going to work?"

Hanish noted that all of the surviving animals are likely to be euthanized.

The raid came as no surprise to many nearby residents, who complained that the city did not act fast enough in dealing with the situation. Next-door neighbor and retired police officer Frank Caruthers says that he has been complaining to the city for years, but to no avail.

"This stuff has been going on since the mid-eighties," Caruthers said. "She must have been an exotic pet dealer or something, 'cause some of those things looked almost human. I know it sounds crazy, but once while I was watering my lawn, I heard this animal yell 'go bye-bye' in perfect English!" Added Caruthers, "I'll sleep better knowing they're dead."

If convicted, the home's owner could face up to a year in prison and $50,000 in fines. The woman's court-appointed attorney, Timothy Nelson, says that his client suffers from a well-documented mental disorder known as "Pet Hoarding," and that he will be mounting an insanity defense.

"Let's look at the facts," Nelson said. "This poor old woman is dressing animals in diapers, encouraging them to read books, and trying to get them to sing songs. Is there any doubt that my client is insane? When the facts are made known to the jury, it will be an open and shut case."

The woman is due in court this Friday. ■

An Embryo's Right to Self-Abortion

Practical Solutions for Unplanned Birth

by Taii K. Austin

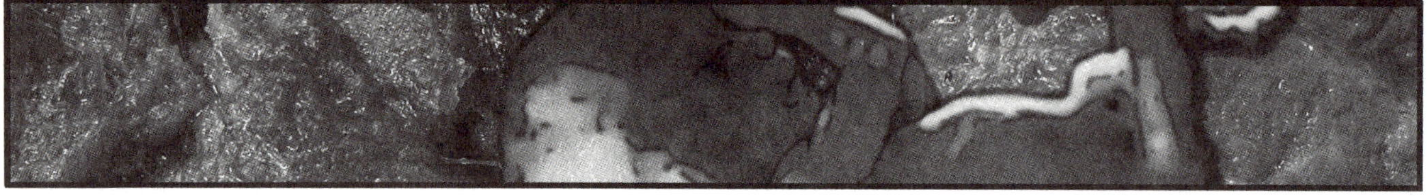

Combatants in the war over abortion have grossly neglected the most important party involved, the embryo. Liberals argue for *women's rights*, Conservatives revere *God's rights*, but absolutely no one has taken up the banner for *embryos' rights*. No one, that is, until now.

Y.O.U.A.RE.A.L.L.D.U.M.B (Youths Organized Under the Aegis of Really Educated Activists who Love Liberty and Despise Undue Meaningless Bullshit) is the premiere organization lobbying for legislation which protects an embryo's right to safely self-abort. The general assumption is that every embryo *wants* to be carried to term, *wants* to be emotionally scarred by transgendered teachers, indifferent parents, and emo. But we disagree. We won't take "no" for an answer. We won't consider the opposition's point-of-view. And we damn sure won't conduct any viable research to support our claims. We are American and we do things the American way.

Y.O.U.A.R.E.A.L.L.D.U.M.B. will march on Capitol Hill next Saturday at 9:00 a.m. Those wishing to join are encouraged to bring egg salad sandwiches, homemade weapons, and obstinacy. Placards will be provided to those who can prove they are of moneyed ancestry (to remind Congress of our constituency's economic influence). Then, after a non-partisan, non-denominational moment of reflection, we will line up in order of aesthetic pleasantness and let freedom ring.

EMBRYOS' RIGHTS ARE PROTECTED BY THE CONSTITUTION

Amendment IX.
The enumeration in the Constitution, of certain rights, shall not be construed to deny or disparage others retained by the people.

Though there is no explicit mention of embryos' rights in the Constitution, these rights cannot be denied or disparaged. So saith the forefathers; so saith us.

Amendment XIII. Section 1.
Neither slavery nor involuntary servitude, except as a punishment for crime whereof the party shall have been duly convicted, shall exist within the United States, or any place subject to their jurisdiction.

There is no involuntary servitude as cruel and unusual as being forced to spend nine months in a bloody vacuum sucking down backwash and barbequed mayonnaise balls.

Facts

- 1 in 10 American women of childbearing age will experience a miscarriage. 3 in 10 of these "miscarriages" are actually successful self-abortions.
- There is no such thing as a "temper tantrum." This behavior is merely the physical backlash of a child whose self-abortion attempt was thwarted while in the womb.
- "I wish I'd never been born" is the most common utterance of children during a so-called "temper tantrum."
- Flava Flav and Britney Spears are parents.

Be informed, be intolerant.

Here at Y.O.U.A.R.E.A.L.L.D.U.M.B. we fight for the slimy, amorphous citizens of our nation who previously had no voice. It is our duty to ensure that embryos have the right to duck out of this bullshit before it's too late. Face it, life sucks: quit while you're a head (and arm buds). ■

Dear Lord Why Not Me?

The Hottest Statutory Rapes of The Last Decade

by Travis Rink

Two questions have plagued me over the last few years. Why are hot female teachers suddenly introducing their young students to the joyous world of sex? And why not me, dear Lord?

I suppose the first time everyone really heard of this was by following the Mary Kay Letourneau scandal. Naturally, I too followed the sordid details of the story with keen interest, but at the time it just seemed like "one of those things" that had occurred, not unlike those occasional news stories where police report finding stacks of mummified and decomposed bodies piled on top of each other in the basement of some rural crematorium. But watch the news or read the papers now... Florida, New Jersey, California. It has become an epidemic like something out *of Night Of The Living Dead*...only in a good way! I am not a scholar. I am not a psychologist. Actually, I'm pretty much a simpleton. But I have realized one necessary item that is missing. Since you can't keep track of the game without a scorecard I have compiled my own data, which I now present for your information and possible titillation.

NAME: Debbie Lafavre Age: 24 Educational Position: Middle School teacher "Victim": 14 years old
Location of Sexual Trysts: Her Classroom, her house, and the backseat of her SUV.

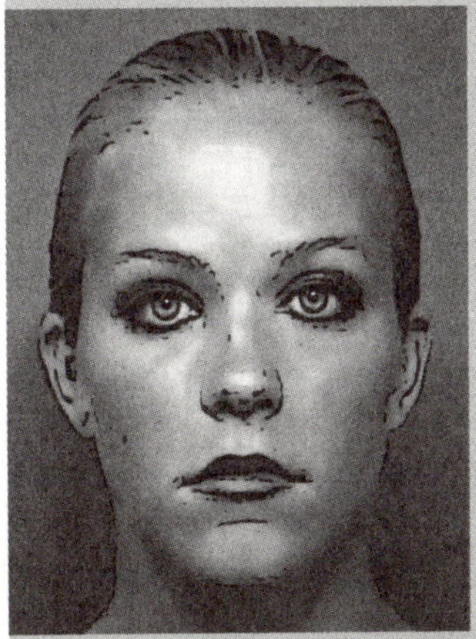

Comments: This is just her police-booking photo for crying out loud! Very hot blonde. Extra points given for having sex in the back seat of her car while the lucky lad's cousin drove them around (shows exhibitionist qualities...yeah, baby!).

Additional Information: Excerpt from the police report: "At the request of investigators, the student gave them a description of Lafave's tattoo, tan lines, and private parts."

Hot Rating: Hot! Hot! Hot! A solid 10. Debbie sets the standards that all others will have to strive to match. In addition to being a real cutie, let us reiterate her exhibitionist tendencies. And while we're at it, let's not forget the tattoo, and the student's vivid memory of her private parts. Man, they must be doozy! I wonder if he drew the cops a diagram?

NAME: Jaymee Wallace Age: 28 Educational Position: Basketball coach "Victim": 14 years old
Location of Sexual Trysts: In the locker room after the other students had left

Comments: Okay, so she's not as good looking as Debbie, but here's the kicker...her student was also female. Yessssssh! Extra points will be awarded at a later date if it is revealed that Jaymee is bisexual.

Additional Information: This go-get-her took the initiative by stapling a note to a paper of the student's that read, "You're really attractive." The affair with Jaymee's young, nubile protégée lasted nineteen months. Just imagine all those warm, steamy showers they took together after the other players had left!

Hot Rating: A makeover and more fashionable hair style would definitely help. Still, it's hard to knock Jaymee's aggressiveness, and the fact that the affair lasted nineteen months must show that Jaymee could more than just dribble a basketball. I rate her a 7, but that score could go up with a little effort. Stay tuned.

NAME: Pamela Rogers Age: 28 Educational Position: Elementary teacher, coach "Victim": 13 years old
Location of Sexual Trysts: Both at her house and the student's house...when his parents were sleeping, no less!

Comments: Extra points for screwing the kid in his own house while parents were home.

Additional Information: Started the affair by text messaging "I think you're cute" to the student. Engaged in both oral sex and intercourse a minimum of 12 times...time frame of encounters unknown. Information on "swallower" or "spitter" during oral sex unavailable.

Hot Rating: What can I say? Another hot blonde! I rate her a 9, but that score could easily go up if rumors of tattoos and detailed diagrams of her private parts surface.

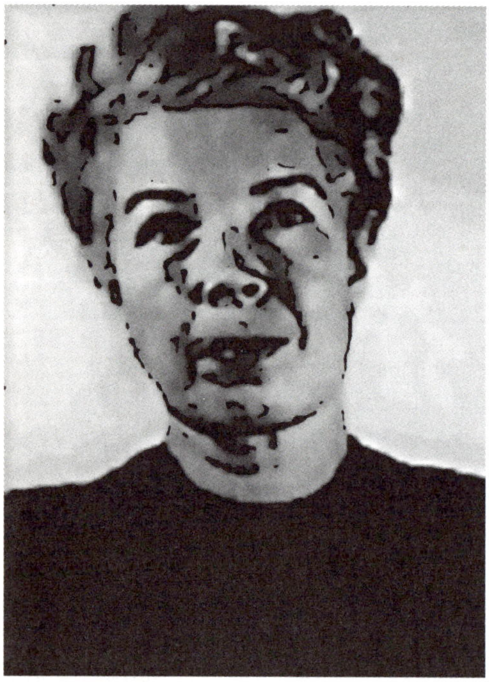

NAME: Dorothy Albertson Age: Old Educational Position: Elementary teacher "Victim": Me
Location of Sexual Trysts: School janitorial closet

Comments: I cry every time I remember this incident.

Additional Information: I was asked by Miss Albertson to portray Santa Claus during our school's 1966 "Christmas Jubilee." As an aspiring young actor, I'd had the supporting role of Jacob Marley in the previous year's staging of *A Christmas Carol*, but with the "Christmas Jubilee" being held in the gymnasium now I'd finally hit the big time. And I was thrilled to be chosen for such an important part of this extravaganza.

As my entrance neared, I entered a backstage janitor's closet to change into my Santa outfit. Moments later, the door unexpectedly opened, and there stood Miss Albertson. To this day, I can remember the look in her eyes as she gazed at me. Two words come to mind to describe that look...crazily depraved. I was pounced upon before I could react. The pillow under my jacket—my "bowl full of jelly"—was quickly pulled away. Her wrinkled, spindly hands groped my trembling body as she asked if I'd "ever had my candy cane sucked." I couldn't speak. At my young, innocent age I didn't even know what she meant, not that it mattered, because seconds later, my vinyl belt was opened and my red costume pants were yanked to my knees. And then... my candy cane was indeed sucked. When she was done having her way with me, Miss Albertson rose up, wiped off her lips, patted my head, and told me to get dressed. "I'll have the Glee Club do another verse to give you time," she stated as she turned and walked out the door. And that was that...except for the years of therapy that followed.

Hot Rating: Are you fucking nuts? Out of pure kindness I can give her a 1. Or maybe bump that up a 2 considering she took her dentures out. ■

SOUP OF THE DAY
Cream of Melanie

iPon
Welcome to the personal digital music revolution. 1,500 songs in your hot pocket. Works in all women.

Cupertino, CA – October 15, 2006 - Yesterday Apple®, in collaboration with Tampax, Inc.®, introduced the newest member of the iPod family, the first digital media tampon —the iPon®. Coming off the successful release of the iPod Nano, Apple was ready to expand and improve upon the portable music market yet again —and they have. Not only is the iPon smaller than the Nano, it is also 13 times more absorbent.

The iPon takes the iPod technology to a new level. It holds up to 1,500 songs or 75,000 photos, connects to the internet, and has an optional full color LCD screen. This innovative, one-size-fits-all media tampon also expands or contracts in correlation to the amount of moisture around it, providing superb protection while you menstruate to your own soundtrack. For the first month only, iPons will come pre-programmed with the ovulation-friendly the iTunes "Girls Just Want to Have Fun," "I Will Survive,", and your choice of any one complete Alanis Morissette album.

In the much televised presentation of the iPod Nano Steve Jobs, Apple's CEO, pulled the tiny player out of the previously useless pocket-within-a-pocket of his Levi jeans. He wanted to do a similar reveal for the iPon but, obviously, Apple executives were wary of Jobs removing a tampon from his vagina in front of an auditorium full of shareholders and members of the press. Refusing to disappoint eager fans with a less than spectacular reveal, Jobs went in search of a woman to present the iPon in the true Apple spirit.

As it turned out, that woman was Murielle Jobs, Steve's mother, who was chosen to model the iPon for the share holders after an exhaustive cross-country audition process. Apple felt that the senior Jobs would be a great model to help market the iPod brand to the sexagenarian crowd. Plus, she has already been through menopause so there would be no risk of Murielle bleeding all over the product. Steve Jobs notes "We wouldn't want [a younger model] her pulling out the player covered in menstrual fluid. That would be disgusting. So I had my mom pull it out of her vagina."

It proved to be a smart move. Murielle Jobs was very well received when her son brought her out on stage and told the audience that she was there to show them the future of iPod technology. Murielle then dropped her pants and reached into her enormous underwear. She was met with uproarious applause and some excited vomiting as she presented the world with the first cervically compatible multimedia device.

The iPon is available immediately in a 17GB model priced at just $649 and a 32GB model priced at just $1,199.

by Marcus Terry

Remembering Mama

by Chris Miller

Halberson's depression greeted him that morning like an avalanche of boulders. They roared down on him the moment he opened his eyes, first in ones and twos, then in massive agglomerations, driving him into his mattress, blocking his light, mashing his ribs, pressing his spine flatter than a two-day-old highway snake. He had been dreaming of kittens; they died beneath the crush with a firecracker string of tiny screams. He was numb within seconds.

Somehow he forced his hand to the phone and dialed. "Help," he croaked.

With merciful haste, Jenny Jiminez arrived in his bedroom, hitched up her skirt and sat on his face. He sipped weakly at first, then with growing greed, as if from the warming rum keg of a St. Bernard. Gradually, the boulders dissolved.

"Hey, leesten, man," Jenny told him as he dressed, "you can't keep callin' me like thees every mornin'. Ees been two weeks now an' I been late to work three times. Can' you jus' dreenk orange juice in the mornin' like ever'body else?"

"It's pretty weird," agreed Halberson.

"Wha' doss your shreenk say?"

"Halberson, you're disgusting," said his shrink. "I'll bet you're the only man on the planet who needs cunnilingus to get up in the morning."

"Of course, it's only the latest manifestation of your overall insatiable need for sex." He leaned forward. "How many women this week?"

"Sixteen," said Halberson, very quietly.

"My God," whispered his shrink.

Halberson shifted miserably in the overstuffed armchair. "It could be worse," he pointed out. "My father could have been run over by a bus on the way to the maternity ward. Then I'd be a fag with an insatiable need for sex."

"That's probably true. But he didn't and you aren't. What you are is someone who didn't get any love from his mother and who tries to make up the deficit with every woman he meets. You know what I wish? I wish you could go back and have intercourse with your mother. Then maybe you'd get the whole obsession out of your system."

"Hmmmm," said Halberson.

He took a cross-town bus to Larry Leibeskind's studio. Larry was the brother of a girl he had once had three whole dates with. He was into tachyons, photons, quantum mechanics, things like that. With the money he earned from producing weird light shows for rock 'n' roll ballrooms, he was constructing a faster-than-light drive for a starship. He believed that Earth was fucked beyond redemption and wished to leave.

"I want to go back in time," Halberson told him.

"In time for what?" Larry inquired.

"No, man, I mean I want to go back into the past. You know, in a time machine."

"You're crazy," said Larry. "But, I'll see what I can do."

Halberson went home. In the next two days, he made it with a small-breasted seamstress, a gym teacher whose high-energy humps flung him about like a bronco rider, an Australian virgin, a divorcee who tasted like horseradish, and a daughter of a San Francisco police chief. It was hard for him to cut down like this, but he needed time to think.

Halberson didn't like being neurotic. His dependency on women was getting him down. Increasingly, his sexual liaisons were not satisfying him. Oh, they were fine while they were going down, but a half hour later he'd be hungry again. While this was especially true of Asian women, it applied as well to all colors and creeds. His shrink's thesis about his mother had struck him as very interesting, perhaps the key to the solution of his entire problem. Now, if only Larry could come through...

The call, when it came, was brief. "Get your ass over here, man. I think I've got it."

Halberson found Larry's studio pulsing with an eerie violet light. In the center of the room was a gleaming metal cylinder the height of two men. Electricity twined its sides like jagged yellow worms, humming and crackling. The air was sharp with ozone. Larry, in facemask and insulated gloves, was welding closed the cylinder's seam. Sparks showered to the stone floor, bouncing about his feet like bright BBs.

"Fantastic!" exclaimed Halberson. "You know, that's exactly what I thought a time machine would look like."

"No, man," said Larry, cutting his torch and flipping up his mask, "this is a light show for the Family Bug. That's the time machine." He indicated a boring metal box on a workbench.

"Oh," said Halberson. He walked over to inspect it. The box's surface was lusterless black, without feature except for two dials, a red button, and a carrier grip like the handle of a suitcase. It was about the size of a breadbox.

"It used to be a bread box," said Larry. "I put some various kinds of shit inside, messed around a little, and I think it ought to work. This dial controls location. You got to find out the exact coordinates of where you're going and set it like this." He manipulated hair-thin lines around a fine circle of numbers. "And this one controls year and month."

"And the button activates it?"

"Right. But listen, the time control is approximate. I can't promise you'll arrive exactly when you want. Also, you can only use the machine once. The box stays behind when you return."

"That's cool." Halberson stood up to leave.

"One other thing. If my calculations are correct, you're not going to remember a thing about it when you get back. All in all, it's a pretty risky proposition. Why do you want to go back in time so badly, anyway?"

"I can't get up in the morning without having cunnilingus with a Puerto Rican woman," Halberson explained.

"I can dig that," said Larry. "Well, that'll be five bucks for parts."

Halberson returned to his apartment. He placed the time machine on his desk, canceled the three dates he had made for that evening, showered, shaved, and brushed his teeth. He became worried briefly when he noticed his shoulder-length hair in the mirror. He might be thought a little weird with it back in the past. Then he realized all he need do was transport himself directly to his parent's apartment. He'd tell his mother he had a job posing for Bible illustrations or something.

Now he sat before the black box and set the dials. He set the time control for 1939, three years prior to his birth. He had no great relish for the idea of running into his own infant self. Furthermore, his father, a musician, had been on the road much of that year. He didn't want to confront that son of-a-bitch, either.

He had a terrible thought then. What if he knocked his mother up? He might never be born, or have to grow up with an older brother who was his own son. The ramifications were beginning to make him nervous. Hands sweating, he hurried to the medicine cabinet and secured a prophylactic. Then, before he could think of any more problems, he grabbed the black box by the handle and pushed the button.

There was no sense of transition. He blinked his eyes and when he opened them he was in the parlor of his parents' apartment. His stomach thudded with recognition. There was the coffee table, there the lamp with the Tiffany shade, there the Persian rug upon whose loops and swirls he had crawled for endless hours as a babe. Everything was so small! A sudden dizziness took him and he sat down hard on the sofa.

Outside there was darkness. He had no idea of the time. Almost before he realized it, he found himself turning to the end table beside the sofa. Sure enough, there was the clock he would break at age four, calmly ticking, unaware that its death lay a mere seven years in the future. The dial read two o'clock.

Something crackled beneath him. He pulled it out a newspaper. "GERMAN ARMOR RACING TOWARD KIEV," said the headline.

German armor? Halberson felt a second thud in his stomach. The war shouldn't even have started yet. Swallowing, he squinted in the semi-darkness to read the date.

It was July 17, 1941.

With an extreme exertion of will, Halberson calmed himself. It was still nine months before his birth, nothing to worry about on that account. He could still do what he had set out to do. He stood up a little shakily and crept into his parents' bedroom.

Gradually, his eyes adjusted to the deeper gloom, picking out the dressing table with rows of perfume bottles, the framed photograph of the black and white cat, the two single beds separated by the night table, and...good God, his father! His father was home!

Halberson leaned weakly against the wall. He considered giving up the entire plan. The time traveler was still in his hands. All he had to do was push the button and he'd be home in the future, maybe call a few girls...no! That was the thing he'd come here to *stop* doing. But how could he...

Suddenly, his mother rolled onto her back and Halberson saw her face. Instantly, he forgot everything. Her face...*that* face...primal emotions thudded inside him like body blows from a good heavyweight. His stomach thrashed like a fish in a net. Without conscious control, his hands stripped off his clothes. Glancing down, he found himself so erect he appeared about to blast from his own body like a V-2. With his last shred of presence of mind, he rolled the prophylactic onto himself, then covered the distance to his mother's bed in three-quarters of a second and slid in beside her.

A lock of hair had fallen across one of her eyes. Scarcely daring to breath, Halberson rolled down the sheet. And it was there! All the remembered ripeness, the lushness that had tantalized his dreams, it was real! Unbidden, his hand trembled forward and began to touch things.

His mother made a half-awake noise and rolled her back to him. "Not tonight, I told you Paul," she murmured. "I still have that awful headache."

But Halberson hadn't come as far as this to stop now. Calling into play every fondle in his repertoire, every skillful tickle, he began to caress his mother with great urgency. As he molded his front against her back, his rubber-encased member clove between her warm, soft thighs like a knife through butter.

"Paul, I said..." Her breath caught suddenly in her throat. "Oh. Oh, Paul, you never...oh, my God!" She expelled her breath in a rush and her body began to undulate.

"At last!" thought Halberson wildly. "At last! At last! At last!" And he plunged the residence of his neurosis a full ten inches into his mother's pulsing vagina.

"SNORK!"

Snork? With a sudden profound sense of dread, Halberson slowly turned his head to look behind him. His father was sitting up in bed! In his sleep-aid mask, he looked like a panelist on a TV game show.

"Nancy? Are you having a bad dream?" A note of eagerness entered his voice. "Shall I get in bed with you?"

Halberson thought fast. His mother, moaning and sighing, was beyond all hearing. He would have to answer.

"I told you not tonight, Paul," she said in a strained falsetto. "I've still got my headache."

"Aw, Jesus Christ, Nancy, you've had that headache for two weeks now. Come on."

Halberson tried to answer but could not. His mother's accelerating wriggles were tossing him about too wildly. So his father crawled into bed beside him and began to stroke his head.

"Oh, Nancy, your hair is so soft," his father said hoarsely.

"Uh, thanks," Halberson managed. Then, with a short, choked-off scream, his mother came. Her body jackknifed convulsively, sending him slamming against his father, who fell out of bed with a crash.

"Dear God," his mother sighed, "that's the first one!" Her voice trailed off into a blissful purr. She swooned.

There was a silence in the bedroom...except for a husky, irregular sound like a saw being drawn backward across rotten wood. He looked down at the floor. His father lay on his back, his head against a leg of the night table, his neck twisted at an impossible angle.

Halberson decided to get out of there fast. Forgetting his clothes, he launched himself for the time traveler and pushed the button.

Nothing happened.

He tried again, watching closely. His fingertip passed through the button!

What? Halberson stared at his hands and found them fading from view, growing insubstantial, like the hands of a ghost. His fingertips were fully transparent, and the transparency was spreading. What the hell?

Abruptly, with a terrible sinking feeling, he understood. His father was dying and had not yet impregnated his mother. And when he actually died, no baby Halberson would ever be born. He, the adult Halberson, would cease to exist!

There was only one thing to do and Halberson did it. He hurled himself to the floor before his father, ripped open his pajama bottoms, and set to work.

The poor man certainly had been horny despite his rapidly fading life force—he attained an almost instant erection.

Good. Now Halberson leapt to his feet, bent down, encircled his father with his arms, and began tugging him up onto his mother's bed. It was like pulling at a sack of wet cement. Halberson's hands were fading, fading. With a grunt, he rolled his father on top of his mother.

"Oh, Paul, more?" his mother whispered, her eyes still closed.

"Sure thing, Nance," said Halberson, imitating as best he could his father's gruff tones. "German armor's racing toward Kiev, so what the hell."

It was penetration time, but Halberson's hands were now no more than transparent wraiths. Working essentially with his stumps, he somehow fumbled his father's banana into his mother's split.

"Glork. Snorf," commented his father. His breathing was becoming raspier and raspier. Pink spittle had begun to collect at the corners of his mouth.

Halberson's body was still fading. He had hoped that effecting penetration would be enough, that biology would then take over, but this obviously was not to be the case. With a curse he took his father's hips between his elbows and began hoisting and lowering him, as if with a pair of ice tongs. And still Halberson's body faded.

"Come on, you bastard," he growled, "you never gave me shit in my life, don't take my birth away from me!" He began ramming his head against his father's buns on each downswing.

"Graaak," rattled his father, his body spasming randomly.

"Oh, Paul," whimpered his mother, "you're so alive tonight."

"Fnork!" replied his father. His body arced into a sudden bow, then collapsed utterly.

Pop! Halberson snapped into full substance. His desperate tactic had worked! Relief washed over him.

"Paul? Paul, darling? I've still got my cookies. Are you stopping?"

Uh-oh. Halberson dove for the time machine.

Was he cured of neurosis? he wondered. He would never know. Whatever future was waiting for him up there would be the only one he'd ever experienced. If Larry had been right, he'd remember nothing of what went on here tonight.

Abruptly, the light went on. There was a scream.

Halberson pushed the button.

* * *

Halberson's depression greeted him that morning like an avalanche of boulders. They roared down on him the moment he opened his eyes. He was numb within seconds.

Somehow he forced his hand to the phone and dialed. "Help," he croaked.

With merciful haste, Pablo Jiminez arrived in his bedroom, dropped his pants, and sat on his face. ■

How Did I Fall For This Pedophile Sting?

by Mike Polk

Carla? Carla...are you in here? I saw your bike outside, and you were right, it is way cool. I'm so excited to finally meet you.

Carla?

Hey, why's it so dark in here, Carla? Do you mind if I turn some lights on? Here we go...

Wait a minute. Who are you? You guys aren't an eleven-year old girl. Where's Carla? What's the deal with the guns? Stop yelling at me! Okay, I'm getting on the ground. Ease up! Geez. What the heck is going on around here anyways?

Wait a second. Hold the phone. Don't tell me...this was all a big hoax wasn't it?! There never was a Carla! Oh my God. I can't believe I fell for this! Boy, is my face red. Well played, guys. Good burn.

Well I feel like a real horse's ass right now. I bought the whole thing hook, line, and sinker. What a dope. Don't worry, I'm not angry or anything. I've always considered myself a pretty good sport. I'm more embarrassed than anything. Just call me "Captain Gullible."

Okay, so I've just gotta know. Fess up...who all was in on it? Come on, just tell me, I won't be mad. Show of hands. You two? And you? All of you? You were all in on it? Oh Lord. That is funny.

And which one of you was I really talking to that whole time? Who was KARLA_JUICY_APPEL1994? This guy? I was talking dirty to this guy? Wow! I've just gotta say, you are good at what you do, my friend. A little too good, if you ask me. You guys might want to watch yourselves when you're out on assignment with this dude! Heyo! I'm just bustin' your balls, man. Seriously, nice work.

Boy, you fellas got me good. Ya know, I was kind of suspicious when Carla said she wanted to meet up at the Motel 6 by the Turnpike. I was like, "That's kind of a weird thing for a 5th-grade girl to suggest," but I guess my curiosity trumped my common sense. And now here we all are. This is a hoot.

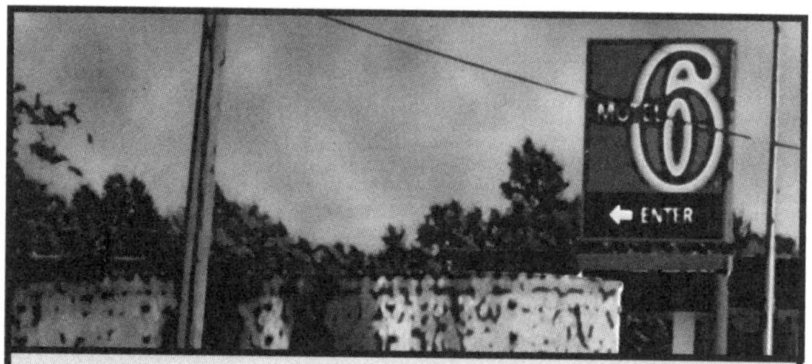

Looked Harmless

Okay, so you were Carla. Now which one of you guys was Becky? Who's BEKERZ_LUVZ_PONYZ_69? That guy?! The dude with the mustache? Oh come on! You're kidding me right? Oh, that's rich. So I'm guessing that you're not really the captain of the junior high swim team then? Man, that is the last time I trust the Internet. You never know what you're getting. Ha!

"Carla" (LOL!)

Hey, don't think for a second that I'm going to forget about this, you goofballs. I'm known as a bit of a prankster myself, so don't be surprised if you end up on the other end of some shenanigans down the line. After all, one good turn deserves another. Maybe you'll get a crank phone call or an unwanted subscription to *National Geographic*. I don't know, I haven't really had time to think of a good comeback prank yet. This is all still sinking in. But you're in for it!

So I suppose it's time to head down to the station now, eh fellas? Well, that's the way it goes. Listen, is it cool if we swing by the playground on the way, I'm supposed to pick someone up. I'm just kidding! Totally kidding! Did you see his face?! He was all like, "What?" That was great. Good times... ■

HANS DICK By: Marc M. "Marbles"
Honey, have you seen my lucky marbles? I can't find them anywhere.
Hmph, maybe that's a good thing.
WHAT DID YOU SAY?! WHAT THE FUCK DID YOU FUCKING SAY!?!?!?

Proper Use of Ejaculatory Slang

Male Finishing School, Part I

by Nick Gaudio

During the early decades of the 20th century, women didn't aspire to become novelists, poets, or painters. They didn't ask for the right to earn college degrees or to pass anti-domestic abuse laws. They didn't really even bitch at all. They wanted only a few things: a roof over their head, a stern hand to keep them in line, and a simple life. That is, a life consisting of makeup parties, pie-baking, and fellatio.

Yes, those were the good ol' days—the days of the finishing school. You see, at these selective academies of domestic knowledge, women were hammered into cooking, cleaning, child-rearing, cock-sucking machines. They were molded and scolded and folded fourteen times, then released as valuable members of society.

There was not and is not, however, a partner school for men. We have military schools, where we're taught how to kill. We have Catholic schools, where we learn the benefits of binge drinking. We have all-male schools, where we...sodomize. But no school has ever existed to teach men the ways of society. So, I have come to end this problem. I have come to show you all the ways of being effective, helpful members of society. I have come to show you how to be honest, hard-working men. I have come to teach you how to cum. Or at least, how to talk about it.

This week, I'll be discussing the proper settings, times and usages of ejaculatory slang, as well as some examples.

Semen

Word Origin:

Latin, from "cemani" meaning "juice."

Acceptable Use:

During urologist visits, father-son talks, and priest-alterboy confessions.

Ejaculatory Factoid:

"Semen" is an umbrella term used to describe ejaculate in the English language. However, that doesn't always make it the correct word choice. Try to avoid saying "semen" when discussing women you've ejaculated on, or in. Also, in intimate company, "semen" is a tad too formal.

Everyday Example:

"There's blood in my semen!"

Skeet

Word Origin:

African; The Tribe of Snoop, from "skizzle" (untranslatable).

Acceptable Use:

When rapping. Use it also to describe those clay discs that you can shoot in Duckhunt. Never use if you're white.

Ejaculatory Factoid:

Most likely, "skeet" developed from the sport of professional shooting. Like most of the terms here, it can be a verb and a noun. It is generally associated with ejaculation to/on/about the face of a ho.

Everyday Example:

"Bitch, imma skeet up yo nose while I be sippin' on bubbly in the club, yo!"

Bill Clinton's Calling Card

Word Origin:

A cognate of English and Republican.

Acceptable Use:

During the 1990s, when talking to Bill Maher, or when ejaculate is found and used to incriminate.

Ejaculatory Factoid:

A dried up, pale stain on our nation's history...and a fat chick's blue dress. Measured 4 inches in diameter.

Everyday Example:

"Tiffany is really pissed off at me."

"Why?"

"She found my Bill Clinton's Calling Card on her sister's blouse."

Baby-Batter

Word Origin:

A hybrid of Gerberese and EGGOan.

Acceptable Use:

When baking cookies for babies, cookies in the shape of babies, or cookies with chunks of baby in them. Also, during Planned Parenthood visits.

Ejaculatory Factoid:

As the consistency of sperm is comparable to pancake batter, and its use unfortunately leads to pregnancy, baby-batter has become a popular term for ejaculate that gets your bitch pregnant.

Everyday Example:

"Girl, you get me so hot, my baby-batter might just bake."

Cocknog

Word Origin:

German, from "kauknau" meaning "glop of elation."

Acceptable Use:

Christmas time. (Can't use if you're Jewish, sorry!)

Ejaculatory Factoid:

A twist on eggnog:

the thick, yellowish substance that appears once a year in your local dairy aisle. Tastes excellent with white rum and cinnamon... (Eggnog tastes good with white rum and cinnamon, too.)

Everyday Example:

"Tis the season for some *cocknog*, fa-la-lalala, la la la la."

Jizz/Jizzum

Word Origin:

Dutch, from the word "Ja!" meaning, "Yes! Yes! Yes!"

Acceptable Use:

To any person, anytime, anywhere.

Ejaculatory Factoid:

"Jizz" is onomatopoeia for the sound a kazoo makes when placed at the top of an ejaculating dick. A very common, very funny, slang word.

Everyday Example:

"I'm going to pull her hair, smack her ass and then jizz on her back...then I'm going home to drink a beer and watch Sportscenter."

Seed/Spore

Word Origin:

Scandinavian, from the word "seduch" meaning "moisturizer."

Acceptable Use:

In biology class. Also, during March Madness banter, conversations about sunflower products, discussions of Uma Thurman in that Batman movie, or rants about bad weed.

Ejaculatory Factoid:

This term for the sticky white substance that ejaculates from a penis is the most formal expression. The term comes from the plant world, as seeds are a form of reproduction for much vegetation. Also, sperm look sort of like little seeds with little whips attached to them. Never use it in slang.

Everyday Example:

"When the female Yorkshire terrier accepts the male's seed, she scrapes her ass on the pavement until the semen has crawled high enough into her womb that an offspring might develop."

Nut-Nectar
Word Origin:
Old English, from "nautnekturh" meaning "matrimonial glue."
Acceptable Use:
Shakespearean drama; poetry writing.
Ejaculatory Factoid:
Until a few "accidents," semen once enticed hummingbirds to a penis. Thus this idiom derived from that, I guess.
Everyday Example:
"Hark, Horatio! Unite thy companions of old, that I might shooteth thine nut-nectar on faces of beauty!"

Spooge
Word Origin:
French, from "spoogè," meaning, "What we, the French, eat with our wine and cheese! Awh haw haw hawh!"
Acceptable Use:
When being courteous or insulting the French.
Ejaculatory Factoid:
The French suck lots of dick.
Everyday Example:
"Pierre had so much spooge in his mouth he couldn't even sing 'Frere Jacques!'"

The Creamy Filling
Word Origin:
Twinkien.
Acceptable Use:
When commenting on cumshots or harassing your friends.
Ejaculatory Factoid:
Basically, this word refers to completely visible ejaculate. Though, it's generally more compliant with food products that contain resemblances of ejaculate. Warning:
Using "The Creamy Filling" around your friends while they eat anything consisting of heavy cream, confectioner's sugar and vanilla extract could get you punched in the nose.
Everyday Example:
"Hey Billy, how's that Snackie Cake taste?"
"Good, why?"
"Hey Tom! Billy likes The Creamy Filling!...hahahahahahaha."
Wham

Penis-Paste
Word Origin:
Colgatean.
Acceptable Use:
During art class or hygiene discussions with friends.
Ejaculatory Factoid:
Usually, this term is used to describe the highly concentrated sperm that results from dehydration. It has a tendency to stick to whatever it touches, even more so than regular semen.
Everyday Example:
"Dude, I had some serious penis-paste last night."
"Hmm...maybe you should drink a glass of water and then never speak of this again."

Cum
Word Origin:
Italian, from "Roberto Benigni" meaning, "unholy water."
Acceptable Use:
When speaking directly to women about ejaculate.
Ejaculatory Factoid:
This term's development is possibly the most interesting. The noun "cum" evolved from the verb "come" as if, when people have sex, the destination for both participants is one specific location named orgasm. Pretty peculiar if you consider that women are included in this theory.
Everyday Example:
"How's my cum taste momma?"

Liquid Sin

Word Origin:

Created originally by the Catholic Church, perpetuated now by incensed Fundamentalist Protestants.

Acceptable Use:

During sexual education class or Lent.

Ejaculatory Factoid:

"Liquid Sin" is generally used to describe the resulting ejaculate of premarital sex. Being as most of you are all in college there really is no differentiating between the two…just remember that all semen is "Liquid Sin."

Everyday Example:

"And Elohim spoketh to Abraham saying, 'Thou shalt catch thy Liquid Sin in the tissue of atonement!'"

Boner Brew

Word Origin:

Fleetwood Mac

Acceptable Use:

Karaoking up "Dreams," "Peacekeeper," or "Go Your Own Way."

Ejaculatory Factoid:

Y'all might forget it, but Stevie Nicks used to be pretty bangin'.

Everyday Example:

"Thunder only happens when it's raining
Players only love you when they're playing
They say, women, they will come and they will go
When the rain washes you clean, you'll know
You'll know…boner brew."

Man-[Any Liquid Dairy Product]

Word Origin:

The Dairy Farmers of America

Acceptable Use:

On trips to the supermarket, dates at fancy restaurants, or when shooting shit at the farm.

Ejaculatory Factoid:

Each of these terms has their respective advantages. I have a few problems with "Man-Chowder" though. First, because I once enjoyed eating chowder; and, now I don't. Second, chowder is improper because there aren't any chunks of meat in it. At least, not in my experience. Feel me?

Everyday Example:

"Hello. Tonight, we have a lovely roasted duck in walnut sauce."

"I think I'll have the veal, medium rare, in the Man-Cream Sauce with a tall glass of chocolate Man-Milk."

"I'm sorry, we don't serve any of those items."

"Okay the duck then, whatever."

"Would you like an appetizer?"

"Just bread."

"Would you like some Man-Butter on that?"

"Man-Margarine, please."

Ejaculate

Word Origin:

Gaudion.

Acceptable Use:

Website articles.

Ejaculatory Factoid:

"Ejaculate" sounds like something a car should be able to do. I'm not really even sure you can even use it as a noun. But hey, this isn't a fucking research paper, capicce?

Everyday Example:

"Male Finishing School Part I: Proper Use of Ejaculate."

A Review of Jefferson Elementary's Spring Concert

As Performed by the 5th Grade

by Chris Caccioppoli

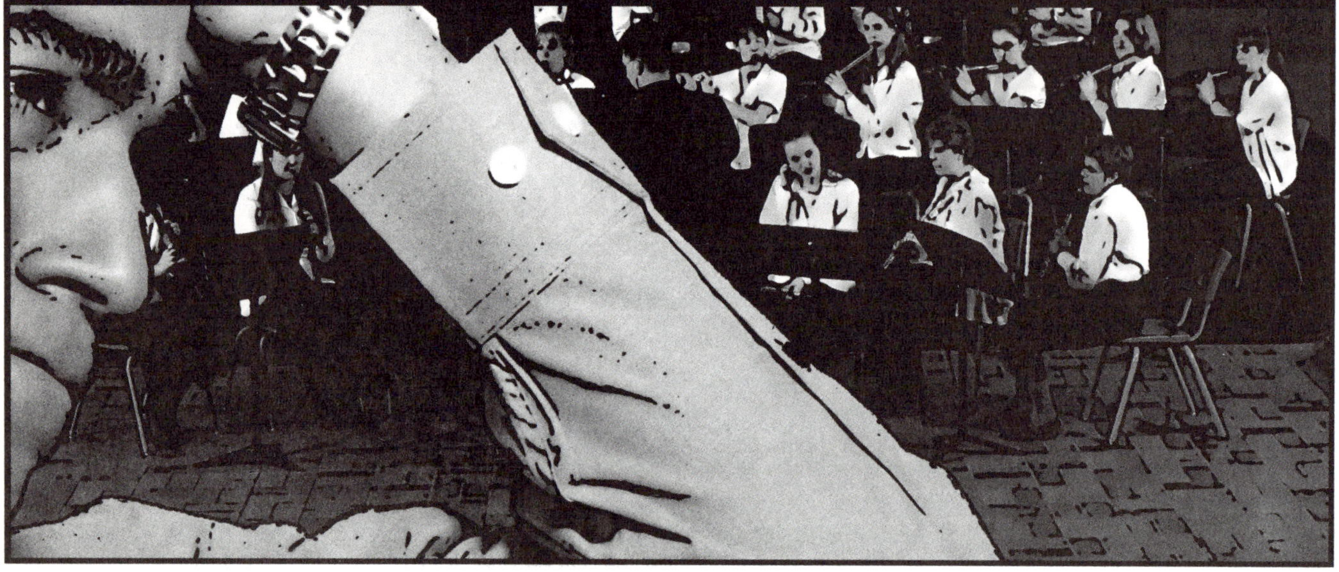

Sure, fucking an older woman is fun when you're actually doing the fucking, but everything leading up to the sex pretty much blows. However, nothing blows quite as hard as going to see her eleven-year-old son's spring concert. I mean, there's usually a system of checks and balances, for instance: knowing her head will be methodically ramming into the unlocked bedroom door while I pound her from behind is worth riding shotgun in the minivan to pick her kid up from soccer practice. Or having her and I take her son trick-or-treating in a two-person horse costume so I could covertly fuck her while we walk from house to house is worth waiting in line at K-Mart to buy that little cunt rag his Harry Potter lunchbox. But listening to three hours of tone-deaf retards butcher my favorite songs needs to be reciprocated with some of the nastiest, freakiest, most traumatizing sexual experiences I can imagine.

Of course, I decided this before the first intermission. So as soon as the curtain dropped I dragged her to the lobby and had her suck me off under the refreshment table. Naturally, she expressed how inappropriate she thought it was. Then I reminded her that I drove us to the concert, and unless she wanted to walk her kid home down twenty miles of poorly lit highway she better swallow her pride, her gum, and whatever else accumulated over the next ten minutes.

As we walked back in to see act two of my own personal hell, she realized that she had missed the parent-child concert photos and began to cry. Of course I didn't know this at the time so when I asked, "What's the matter? Got your period?" she spit in my face and ran back to the lobby. Normally I wouldn't mind the saliva spray but unless she used an invisible toothbrush, her little outburst left my nose glazed in pimp juice.

Five minutes later she came rushing through the auditorium door with a Polaroid in her hand. Lucky for me, I was waiting by the entrance so her momentum complimented the hardy slap I greeted her face with. Unlucky for me her son was holding her hand and started crying.

I tried to explain to the principal that she had it coming, but apparently my actions were "inappropriate," so I "inappropriately" kicked him in the nuts. Suddenly a couple of three hundred pound housewives with papier maché badges restrained me and dragged me outside. I figured if I played my cards right I could score digits from one of them, but they stayed silent until the cops came.

I never did get to see the end of the performance, but from the little I heard, it sucked. Overall, I'd give the concert one and half stars and I would not recommend it to a friend. ■

HANS DICK By: Marc M. "Mrs. Robberts"
Isn't it weird how like, you can eat something really spicy one day, and the next day when you shit it out, it burns your ass! I mean, you'd think that all of the acid in your stomach would eliminate the hotness.
Look Mrs. Robberts, is Todd home or not?

In Search of Sanitation

by Karolyn McKenzie

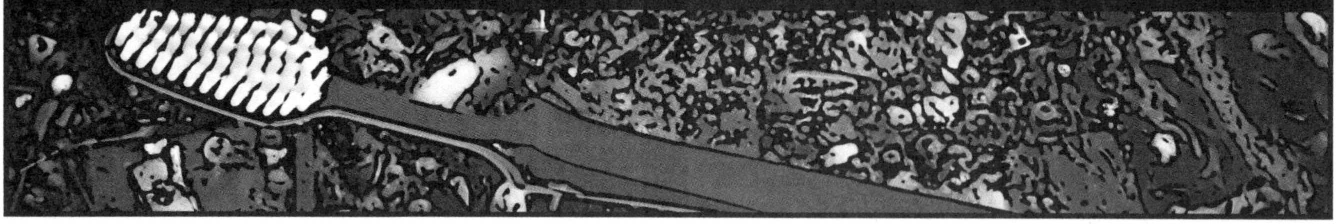

It was one of those mornings where I had purposely neglected to turn on the light in the bathroom before taking a shower. You know, to trick myself into staying at least partially asleep. Big mistake.

In my stubborn refusal to turn on the light, I had also neglected to pick up a towel. Post-shower, I stood shivering and dripping onto piles of my nasty roommate's dirty designer clothes that littered the bathroom floor.

The stream of daylight shining under the door was enough to reveal a hand towel thrown in the trash. The TRASH. "Amy!" I only screamed it in my head because I didn't want to wake Charmin —Amy's Canadian friend who was living in our apartment rent-free, at Amy's insistence. Amy, though the omnipresent traces of her filth would lead you to believe otherwise, had practically moved in with her boyfriend/boss, Brad.

"Forget me! Forget my life! Forget you ever even met me Brad! ... And do NOT put my clothes on the sidewalk!" What you'd think were lines from Hilary Duff's latest movie, were actually phrases Amy had used to break it off with her boyfriend/boss the exact same day Charmin arrived with her one-way ticket. The discarded towel had probably been used to wipe her tears, and throwing it in the trash purged herself of the fight, freeing her to forgive him and reconcile. Which they did, the very next day. Because she's not only dirty but also co-dependent, melodramatic, and spoiled.

For now, I excused her dramatics. If I didn't pull out the towel, I would probably have to buy another one later. I used the rag to dry off and ring out my soaking wet hair. I tossed the towel over the top of the shower and came to the harsh realization that I now had to turn on the lights.

The blinding jolt revealed our cluttered and slovenly sink. Instead of shedding skin like a regular snake, Amy preferred to shed her thick, black hair, and lots of it. If I needed any extra cash, I'm sure I could've sold a few hair pieces to a wig salon on Melrose. On top of the layer of hair sat make-up, perfume, a layer of miscellaneous junk, and one more coating of thick, black, dirty, nasty hair. Did I mention that it's Amy's hair? And that she's dirty? Because both are true and you should know that.

Then to top it all off, I discovered Amy's thong floating in the sink soaking in Oxy-Clean. You know there is a serious bacterial problem at hand when both soaking and Oxy-Clean are involved.

Not wanting to know any more, I pushed the junk aside in search of my toothbrush. It was then that I noticed a few pills spilling out of a bottle. But not just any pills, *urinary tract infection pills*! I had used these a few times myself, but for much cleaner means — sorority prank wars. Crushed up and mixed into chocolate icing, UTI pills turned the urine of an unsuspecting cupcake-eater bright orange —leading to a harmless, hilarious, but extremely confusing week of bathroom visits. However, I wasn't aware of any prank wars going on at the time, and so my own conclusions led me to believe exactly what you're thinking: Amy had a urinary tract infection and left her skanktastic orange pills to bleed all over our bathroom. One had already stained a puddle of water around the sink, so I reached again for the hand towel to clean it up. And that's when I saw it. The towel I had just wiped all over my body was already covered in UTI orange.

"Sick!" I threw it in the trash, but just as I did, something caught my eye. My toothbrush! The handle stuck out from the puddle of water. I grabbed for it and held it up, cherishing it like a trophy. It was my one last hope of sanitation! But alas... As it shone in the light, the bristles revealed its own death... a dark orange stain. In disgust, I flung the toothbrush into the trash and began to weep internally.

Sometimes the good guy loses. And I had lost in two big ways: Not only was I now officially grossed out, but also fully awake. ■

Mason Deforest: Food Critic At-Large

by Scott Rubin

Little Toni's Pizzeria — rating:

As most of you know by now, after complaining about dirty utensils while dining at Blake's Stone Crab, I spent the next 3 days in intensive care for swallowing a titanium drill bit that had been nefariously placed inside my lobster tail. Thank you for all your very touching get-well cards. I am forever grateful.

Feeling a little better, I decided to venture out again, and to take in some Italian cuisine. I regret to inform you, my loyal readers, that my recent visit to Little Toni's Pizzeria on 2nd and Elm near the Glatherton Ridge Mall did not fare much better than the Blake's fiasco. In my 45 years as the restaurant critic for this fine literary endeavor I have never been more revolted in my life. Quite simply, I was poisoned.

Little Toni's Pizzeria, established in 1962 has been a popular Italian restaurant on the East Side for many years. Although I did not give them a flattering review during my last visit in 1987, I thought I would give the eatery one more try, especially with all the buzz they've been receiving lately.

The meal started out fine, with a lovely Cabernet followed by a sumptuous garlic bread, —although served a tad late. And this is where I believe the problem began. I very politely complained that my guest and I had waited nearly 10 minutes for the tasty appetizer. The waiter gave me a dirty look and walked away. At the time I didn't really read into it, and moments later went to the restroom. While I was walking out of the men's room, however, I did see something peculiar: A man walking exiting stall carrying what appeared to be a bag of human feces. Again, I didn't think anything of it at first but now that I lay here for my 2nd week at Our Lady of Victory Hospital, I wish that I had.

When I returned to my seat my dinner was served. Little Toni's specialty is Lasagna and although it had a peculiar smell, I was famished and finished at least a third of the entree before realizing I was eating raw shit.

Within minutes I was gagging, sweating, projectile vomiting, and relieving myself of diarrhea in full public view. I have never been so humiliated in my life. To make matters worse, there was absolutely no compassion from the staff. The Maitre 'D came over but instead of helping me, he threw a large table cloth over my quivering body, picked me up and tossed me onto the street. I laid there for hours in my own vomit and human excrement as patrons entering the restaurant kicked me and spat upon my face.

I hate to tell you my faithful readers, but I may never fully recover from this culinary disaster. The thought that I ate lasagna made from public restroom feces samples, continues to make me vomit even weeks later. And for what? Because I complained about the garlic bread arriving late at my table. Is that the way we treat other human beings?

I don't know exactly what is happening here, but the morality in this country has reached a new low. Eating out is now as dangerous as any of those X sports the kids on the street play.

It has now reached the point, that if a restaurant doesn't make me sick it gets my 5 fork rating. Here are a few eateries that have not made me ill in the last two years. Although they are not very good, I still recommend them as safe places and that's all that matters these days.

Pizza Hut located inside Glatherton Ridge Airfield — rating:
Gwen's Nuts'nThings on Highway 78 — rating:
Cafeteria at Our Lady of Victory Hospital — rating:

MURDER ACADEMY
MIDTERM EXAM...
LET'S TRY A THIRTY-FIVE DEGREE CROSS CUT.

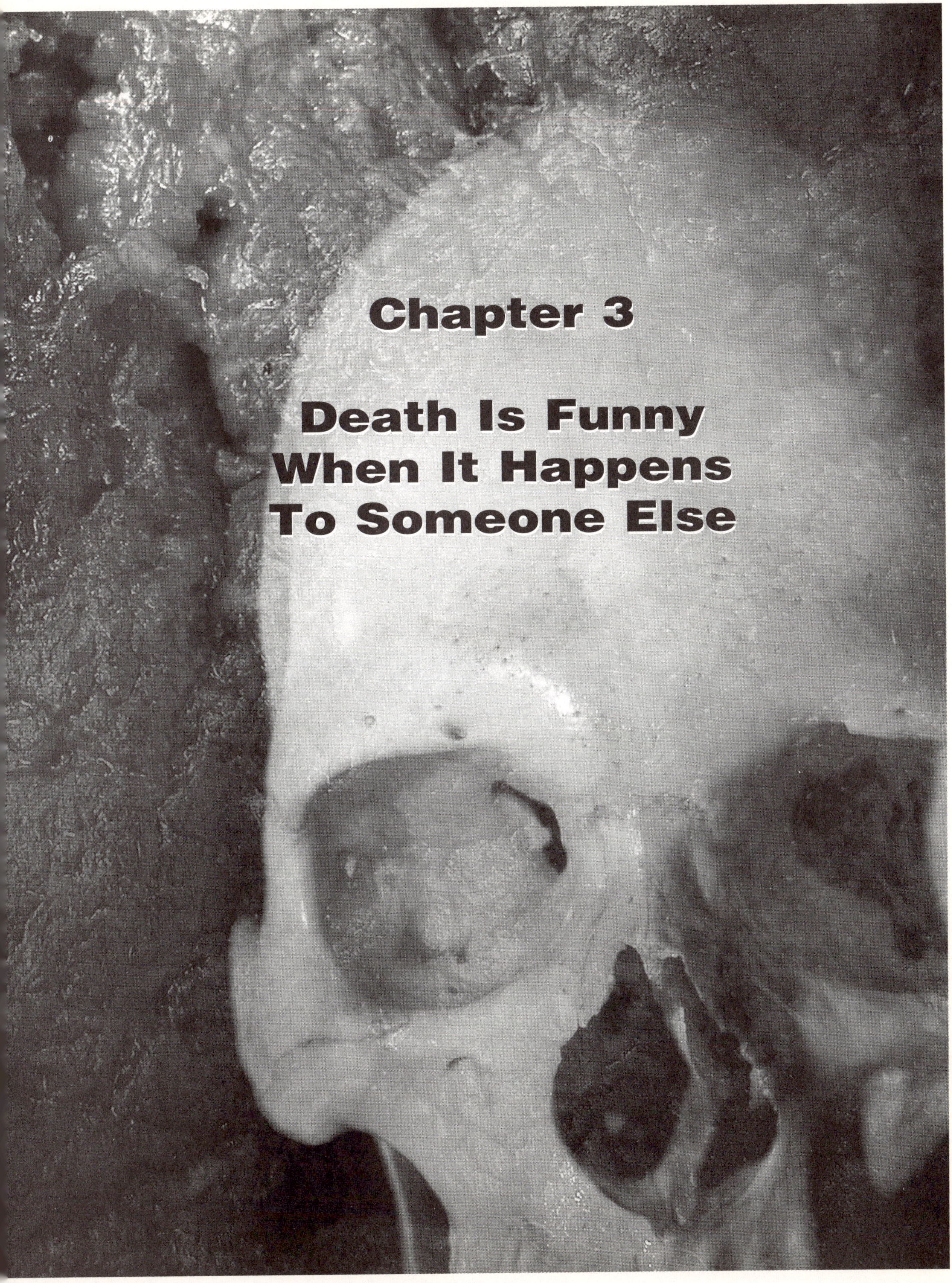
Chapter 3
Death Is Funny When It Happens To Someone Else

A Gentleman's Guide to Laughing at Tragedies

by Phil Haney

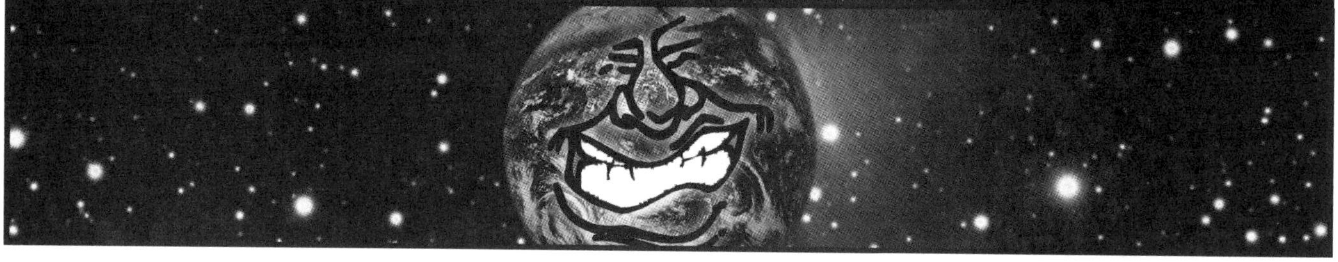

Every time there is a tragedy of epic proportions, the grieving public is faced with the tasks of mourning, helping victims' families recover, and deciding when is a good time to start cracking jokes. The last of these requires pause for thought. After all, when it comes to laughing at tragedy, when is "too soon?"

Ask yourself the following questions before opening the floodgates of humor:

1. How many people died?
2. Are the words "genocide" or "mass terrorist destruction" used to describe your tragedy?
3. Was it in America?
4. Were the people who died brown?

Below is a quick reference guide to 10 major tragedies and how the "too soon" factor is applied to each.

#10 The Titanic, April 15th 1912

The builders of the *Titanic* boasted that their ship was "unsinkable," but in a great ironic twist, the damn thing went down on its maiden voyage! Cocky bastards. Although white people died, they were mostly foreigners and it was a long, long time ago.

Too Soon Factor: Slice your iceberg into the side of this tragedy!

Example: Yo' mama so fat, she sank the *Titanic*!

#9 The Hindenburg Disaster, May 6th 1937

The Hindenburg is just silly by now. A death toll of only 36; it happened 68 years ago. Plus, it launched from Nazi Germany, with whom we would be at war just a few short years after this event. It would be kind of like a big hot air balloon of Al Quaeda members falling out of the sky in 1998. Screw 'em! "Oh the humanity," indeed.

Too Soon Factor: Joke at will!

Example: A giant air ship filled with Hydrogen! Brilliant! I can't wait till they build the nuclear-powered 747.

#8 The Holocaust, 1938-1945

This one is a real doozy. Six million white people died in Europe, 60 years ago. That's quite the tragedy! Hitler was a vegetarian artist who liked to dabble in genocide. Kind of a foo-foo hippie if you ask me. Next time your painter buddy, who lives on the beach, invites you over for some tofu, politely decline when he asks you if you can "get something out of the oven."

Too Soon Factor: This one really depends: It's kind of like how black people can use the special "N Word" in good fun, whereas when I use it in casual conversation I wake up naked in a dumpster with the word "honkey" written in blood across my chest. In other words, its always "too soon" for us gentiles. So your best bet is to get a Jewish friend to make one of these jokes for you. My good pal Andy Kleiman gives us this:

Example: What's the difference between Jews and pizza? Pizza doesn't scream when you put it in the oven.

#7 Pearl Harbor, December 7th 1941

Al Quaeda thinks they are so smart flying planes into stuff, but they are just ripping off the Japanese, who perfected the "Kamikaze" move long ago. The impromptu attack of Pearl Harbor brought the United States into World War II and the Japanese into our hearts.

Too Soon Factor: Americans died 64 years ago. Hmmm. But so did a lot of Japanese, so now's a good time to dive-bomb this tragedy. Fire away!

Example: After watching Ben Affleck in *Pearl Harbor* you almost wish the Japanese had done a better job.

#6 JFK Assassination, November 22, 1963

It was one guy! You would have thought the assassination of President Kennedy was equivalent to the mass genocide of tens of thousands of civilians in Rwanda, the way people get all bent out of shape every time I crack a joke about JFK's brains landing in Jackie's lap. If one white person counts for two brown people, and one American counts for two foreigners, then one white, American President apparently counts for a whole shit load of people! Also he got shot in Texas, and that's about as American as it gets.

Too Soon Factor: Forty years later and it's still a "Too Sooner" for some people. But when old people talk about "I remember where I was when JFK died," you can smugly inform them you weren't born yet and regale them with this zinger:

Example: The bullet going into JFK's head was the first time JFK was the one getting penetrated.

#5 Space Shuttle Challenger Disaster, January 28th 1986.

School children across the country watched the launch and subsequent disaster on live television. Way to ruin a childhood, NASA! A faulty "O Ring" dashed our dreams of Star Trek-and-Jetsons living and sent the space program back to boring orbital missions.

Too Soon Factor:Five whites, one Asian, and a black exploded above Kennedy Space Center almost 20 years ago. That's only five white Americans, although they were all Astronauts so that makes them public figures, which thus increases the "too soon" factor. Ironically, however, because of the Challenger disaster no one cares about Astronauts anymore, so screw 'em!

Example: How many Challenger Astronauts does it take to screw in a solid fuel booster rocket? None, they're all dead!

#3 The Tsunami, December 26th, 2004

Close to 250,000 people died. But they were brown people. In Indonesia.

Too Soon Factor: Although more people died in the 2004 Tsunami than in any other single natural disaster in MODERN HISTORY, it was half a world away.

Example: This week is Indonesian hygiene week. Thousands will be washing up on the beach.

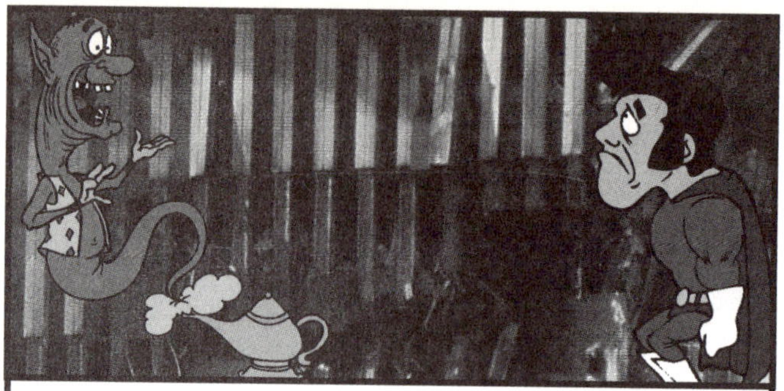

#4 Terrorist Attacks, September 11th, 2001

Although it's been five years already, it's still a little touchy when you try to throw out some 9/11 jokes at a dinner party. The best way to broach the subject of 9/11 humor is to put it in the perspective of "Well at least 19 of those towel heads died, too."

Too Soon Factor: Three thousand Americans died in a heinous act of war in New York Fucking City. **TOO SOON!**

Example: I'm not putting an example. Because it's too soon. The teacher has become the student.

#2 Hurricane Katrina. August 29th 2005

To figure out how long to wait before making Hurricane Katrina jokes you have to divide by half the amount of time it takes to make jokes for 9/11. This is because while the people who died in Katrina are Americans, they were also not white.

Too Soon Factor: Give it another six months.

Example: If you were a homeless guy in New Orleans before the Hurricane, things have got to be looking *pretty good* right about now! Start picking up chicks at the Superdome: "Yeah man, I can't believe I lost *everything*! Can't wait to start rebuilding my plantation."

#1 Hurricane Rita, September 24th 2005

Already devastated from Katrina, the nation was all but mourned out. Then in comes Rita looking to wreck some shit and we're so supposed to get all teary-eyed again. I think it's a conspiracy to keep the people living in fear. Why are hurricanes really happening?

Too Soon Factor: While this Hurricane happened after Katrina, not as many people died from it (around 113) so the "too soon" factor decreases sharply. I say **go for it**.

HANS DICK By: Marc M. "Hanging"
Oh my God, Michael! Bobby's hanging from a tree in the backyard!!!
Oh God, NOOO!! WHY!!!!
No silly, I meant hanging in the good way.
Our little boy's growing up.

You Call That a Suicide Note?

by Rob Sanford

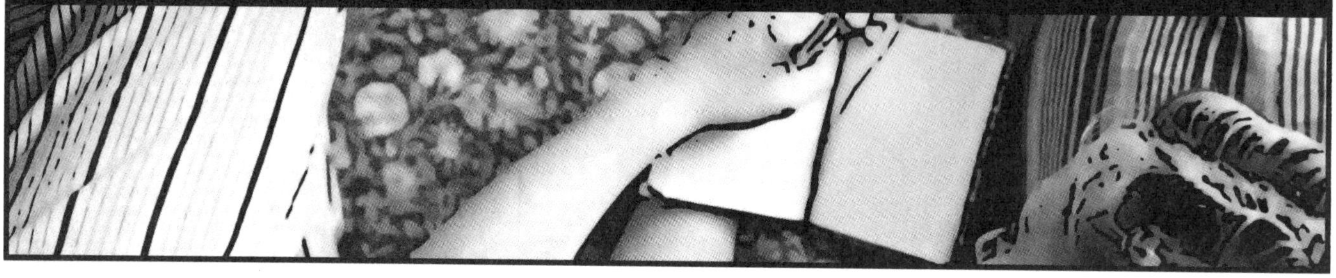

Hey Shit Stain,

I just finished reading this little "suicide note" of yours and I gotta tell you, it's fucking awful. I mean, I've never really read one of these before, but if they're all as boring and poorly-written as yours, then I think the entire genre should just be discontinued. Seriously, this thing is flat-out terrible.

First of all, you open with, "To whom it may concern:" Are you fucking kidding me? This is your final statement to the entire world; the last thoughts you will ever share with the handful of people who are going to feel guilty enough to take off half a personal day and go to the pathetic "celebration of life" that someone's going to have to put on for you, and you start out with the salutation from a college recommendation letter? Unless you decided to off yourself because of a tragic love affair with an assistant dean of admissions, there is no way that should be your opener.

And by the way, what is up with that colon? If you had at least sacked up and put a comma on the end of that shit then the reader might have glided over the actual verbiage. But goddamn, that colon is just so awkward. It really makes the reader uncomfortable. Look, I'm way too nice of a guy to sit here and list ALL the ways in which this thing sucks, but there are a few truly awful moments that simply demand individual recognition.

In the first paragraph, you have this whole bit about the crushing trauma of your break-up with Emily Falcone. Newsflash, jackwad, you went out with that skank for all of three weeks. In the tenth grade. She "broke-up" with you by skipping your last "study date" to do a three-way with the assistant manager and the drive-through-guy at a Jack-in-the-Box. The fact that you would even mention that "relationship" in a suicide note ten years later is reason enough to kill yourself.

Then you ramble on about how you just want to be free from all your troubles and shit. I guess that's pretty standard stuff for a suicide note, but then you drop this little ass nugget: "Even though I've wanted to be free for so long, I guess in the end, freedom's just another word for nothing left to lose."

Uhh, did I read that right? Did you really just explain your decision to end your own life with a line from "Me and Bobby McGee?" Did you think you were going to strike some kind of emotional chord with your readers by using one of the most over-quoted lines in music history? If so, you're even dumber than I realized. Fortunately, Janis Joplin drank herself to death and there's no chance that she'll ever have to read that.

And finally there's the dingleberry on top of this little shit sundae of yours. The last paragraph—your very last chance to say anything to anyone—starts out with, "Walking home the other day, the setting sun behind the trees radiated in the most brilliant orange and gold..."

What the fuck? This is supposed to be your clincher paragraph and you start it with a dangling participle?? That's just disgusting. I mean, last time I checked, the sun is a fiery gaseous ball at the center of our solar system, so I'd be willing to bet that it wasn't "walking home the other day." Just because you're on the precipice of existential despair doesn't mean you can simply discard the basic rules of sentence structure.

I suppose the one bright spot in all of this is that you'll at least have the chance to do a re-write. Apparently seven Tylenol gelcaps and a Sunny D just aren't potent enough to do the job on a three-bill behemoth like yourself. So I hope all my constructive criticism won't go to waste.

And hey, if you do give it another shot, would you mind waiting until your mother and I get back from our Caribbean cruise? The tickets are non-refundable so do your old man a favor and bear the pain of living until at least February 23rd. Thanks. ■

NDate: The Dead Don't Talk Back

http://www.ndate.com

NDate for discriminating adults who appreciate l'esprit de corpse

posted by Dale Dobson

I'm a Living Man
seeking
Anything I can get
from
Anywhere at all
And I have access to a **MAJOR CREDIT CARD** or **ELECTRONIC CHECK**

SEARCH NOW

Today's Top 5!

9.92 Laura PalmYer
Me: 19, blonde; I love fast cars, road head and plastic! You: What-EVAR! Look up for the hookup!

9.87 Jane Doe #69

9.82 Necrolette

9.76 Rottin' Robyn

3.60 Eva Longoria

NComing!
Pending Member DeathWatch
NEW!

Parsippany, NJ - police scanner mentions "chick"

LATEST UPDATES:

Orlando, FL - Auto accident near mall

Macon, GA Comatose, plug pull ruling expected

Compton, CA Overdose, condition critical!

Seattle, WA Suicidal tendencies, signs encouraging

"Yo, I got hooked up for my first corpse fuck right after signing up online. You dudes rock!" — Anon.

"I got laid right away! All it took was a major credit card or electronic check!"— Anon.

"We're getting married!"— Anon.

On the "Live" NDateCorpseCam: SexeePokojnika

CONNECT NOW

"Are you people insane?"

Far from it! **The secret is out**, stud: attractive women die every day, in all kinds of ways. **NDate** offers the most reliable source of fresh, pre-putrescent ladies on the 'Net, and none of them could think of turning you down.

So sign up NOW! It's fast and easy with a major credit card or electronic check. Browse our online catalog of thousands of horny angels, and place your order RIGHT NOW! She'll be on her way within 24 hours, freshness guaranteed!

When your date arrives, welcome her inside and tip the delivery guy. Who cares what he thinks? You're a wild, naked stallion with a crowbar and a hankerin', so get that girl out of her crate and into your arms!

Close the blinds. Lock the doors. Take the phone off the hook. That come-hither stare in her cold, blank eyes lets you know she craves the life-juice bubbling deep within your loins. Caress her naked, mottled flesh. Inhale the subtle, promising scent that characterizes the mystique of all dead women. **Awwwyeah**. Talk to her now. Tell her how much you hate your mother, your ex, your first girlfriend who wouldn't do anal sex and kept blinking.

Soon you will be unable to resist the allure of her icy femininity. Enjoy yourself. Show her how sensitive and appreciative you are of your sexuality. She's open, will-less; she won't laugh if you try something novel. If she's been autopsied, you may discover exciting new orifices in which to exercise your unshackled masculinity.

And if you fail to complete the mission, just box her up and send her back. There are plenty of other girls waiting to experience your sweet, sweet necro love at **NDate.com**! ■

Roll out the red carpet and **get ready for LOVE!**

DEAD FAMOUS

Celebrity Escort Service

Now Booking:

Eva Peron Thoroughly embalmed, lubricated!

Clara Bow She's still got "IT"!

Marilyn Monroe Lust in the dust!

DEAD BANGER'S BALL 3-FOR-1 SPECIAL!!!
Janis Joplin - Dana Plato Jayne Mansfield*
*** Some parts not original**

deadspace.com a place for fiends

DeadSex
"When you absolutely, positively need to freeze her overnight"

THE BIG PUMPER

Pumps fluids out or in, hot or cold!
The perfect accessory for the sophisticated necrosexual

$79.99

Children's Letters To The Gestapo

by Michael O'Donoghue

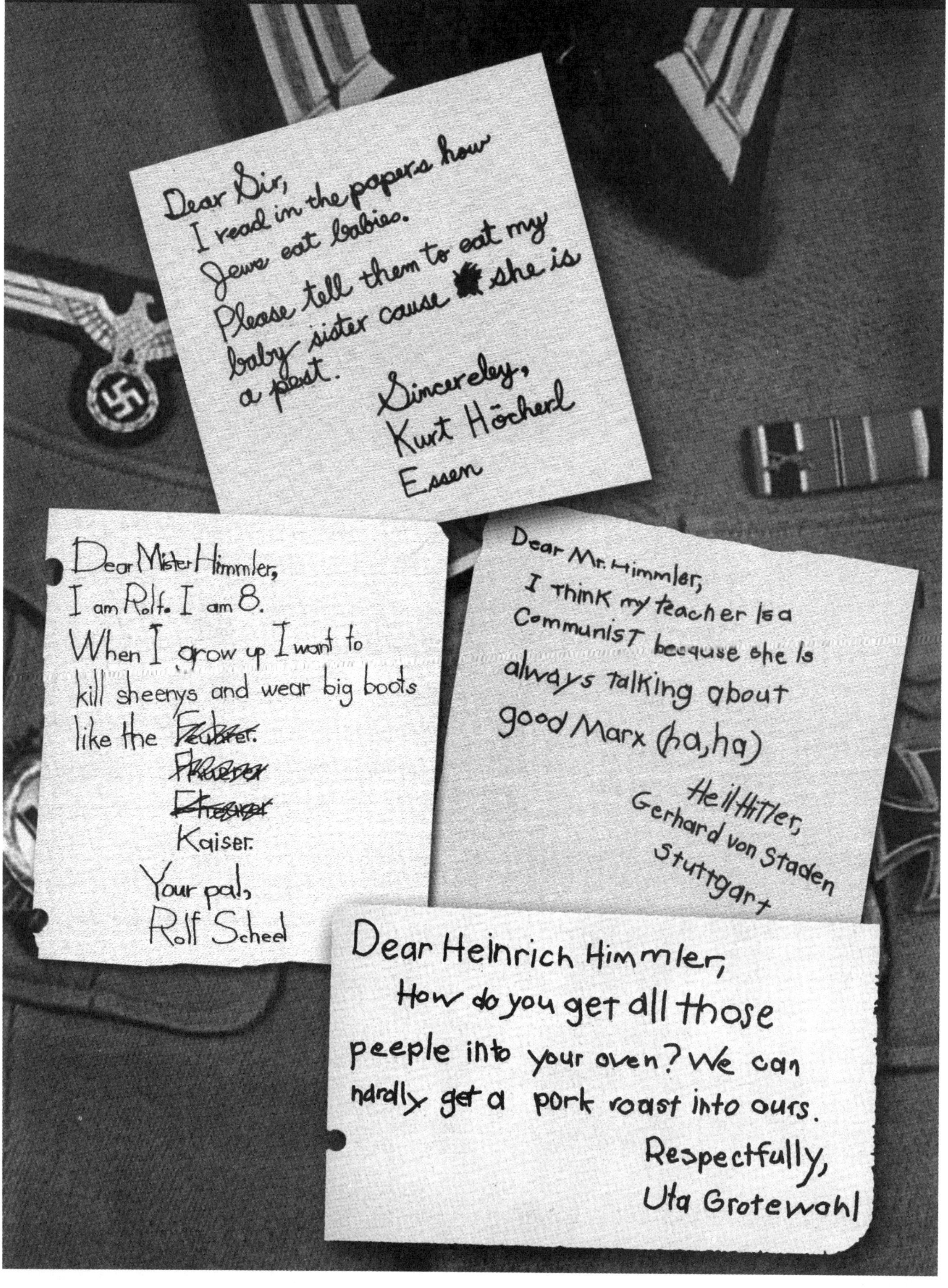

Dear Sir,
I read in the papers how Jews eat babies.
Please tell them to eat my baby sister cause she is a pest.
Sincereley,
Kurt Höcherl
Essen
Dear Mister Himmler,
I am Rolf. I am 8.
When I grow up I want to kill sheenys and wear big boots like the
Kaiser.
Your pal,
Rolf Scheel
Dear Mr. Himmler,
I think my teacher is a Communist because she is always talking about good Marx (ha, ha)
Heil Hitler,
Gerhard von Staden
Stuttgart
Dear Heinrich Himmler,
How do you get all those peeple into your oven? We can hardly get a pork roast into ours.
Respectfully,
Uta Grotewohl

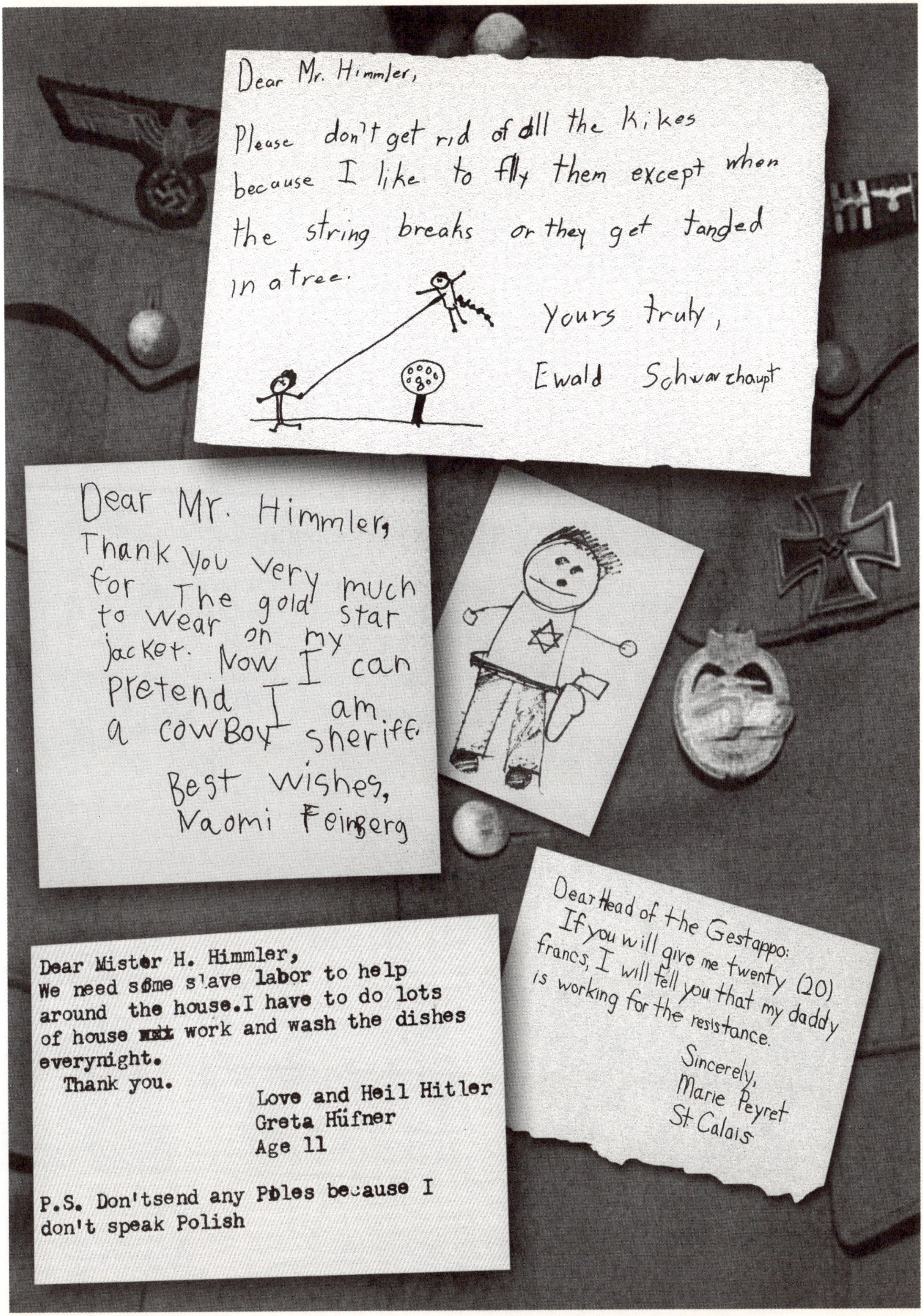

Dear Mr. Himmler,

Please don't get rid of all the kikes because I like to flly them except when the string breaks or they get tangled in a tree.

Yours truly,
Ewald Schwarzhaupt

Dear Mr. Himmler,
Thank you very much for The gold star to wear on my jacket. Now I can pretend I am a cowBoy sheriff.
Best wishes,
Naomi Feinberg

Dear Mister H. Himmler,
We need some slave labor to help around the house.I have to do lots of house work and wash the dishes everynight.
Thank you.
Love and Heil Hitler
Greta Hüfner
Age 11

P.S. Don'tsend any Poles because I don't speak Polish

Dear Head of the Gestappo:
If you will give me twenty (20) francs, I will tell you that my daddy is working for the resistance.
Sincerely,
Marie Peyret
St. Calais

Telling A Kid His Parents Are Dead

by Ed Bluestone and Shary Flenniken

ABOMINABLE FREAKS
I've got good news for you. Your parents are never going to turn into freaks.
...and your parents hadn't paid my bills in three years. So we paid them a visit last night. A couple of the elves got drunk and tore your mother's dress. Then for some reason your father got mad. It was a lot like *A Clockwork Orange*.
Among the combat deaths reported today are five GIs, three pilots, and Timmy Halderman's parents.

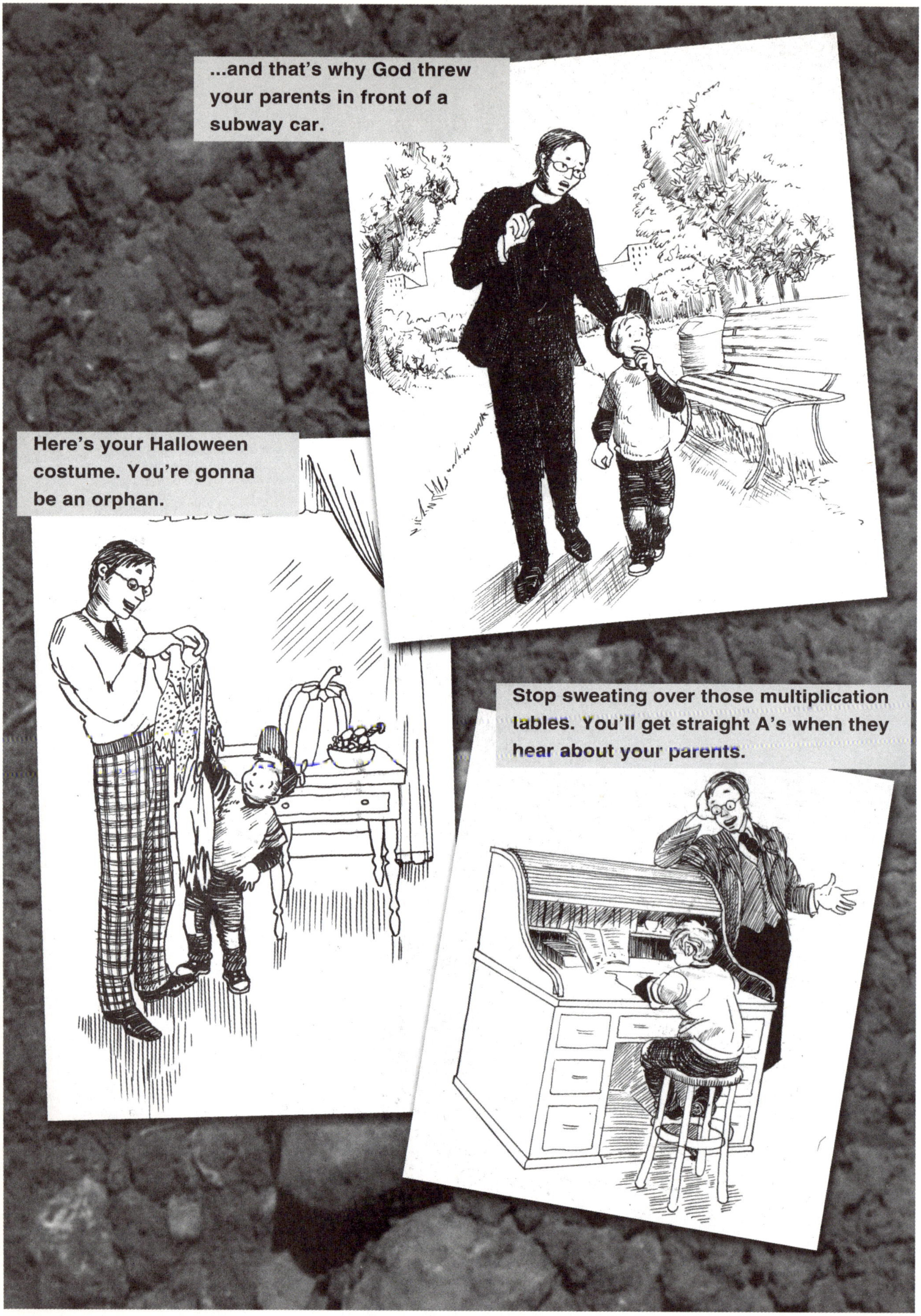
...and that's why God threw your parents in front of a subway car.
Here's your Halloween costume. You're gonna be an orphan.
Stop sweating over those multiplication tables. You'll get straight A's when they hear about your parents.

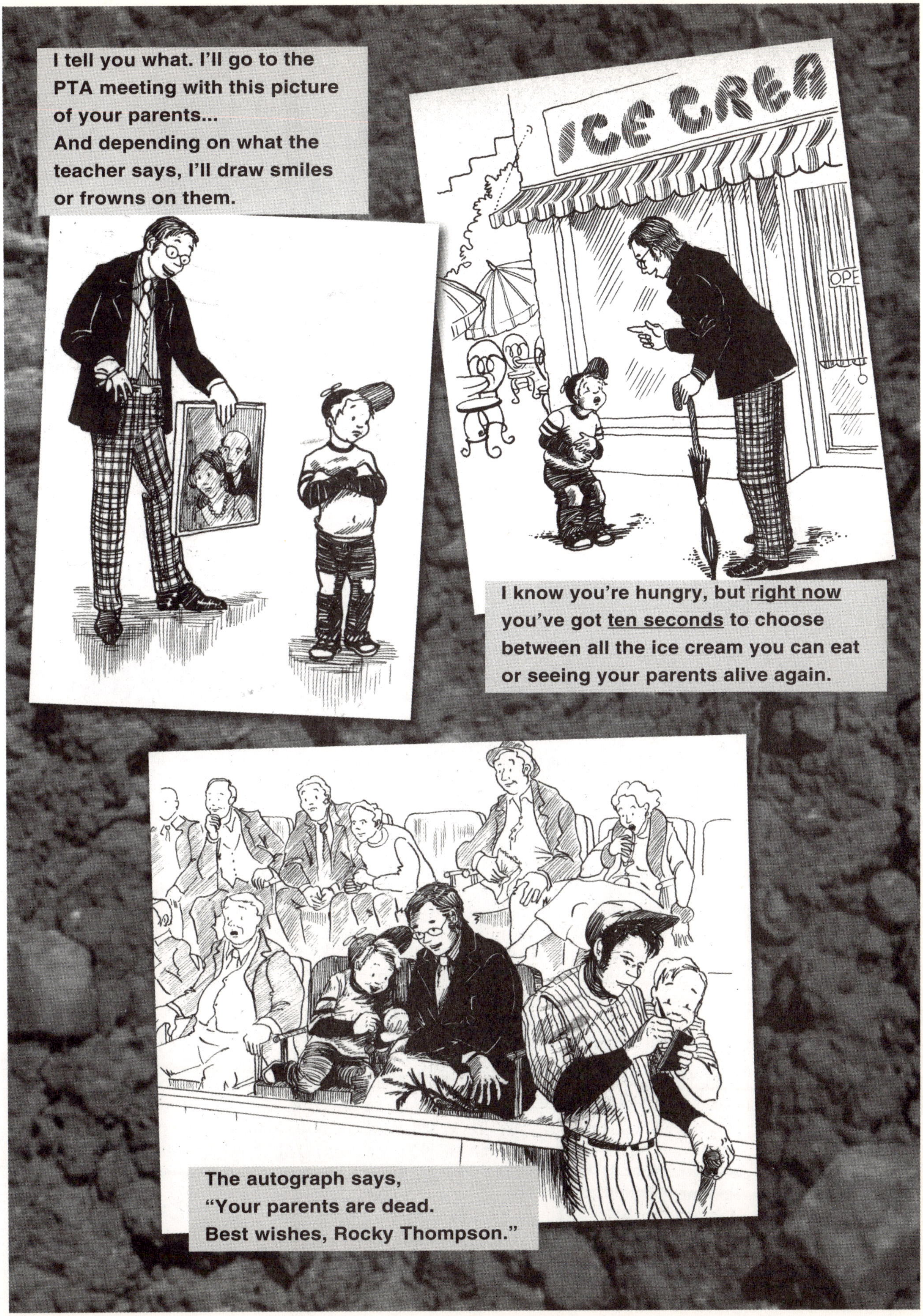
I tell you what. I'll go to the PTA meeting with this picture of your parents...
And depending on what the teacher says, I'll draw smiles or frowns on them.
ICE CREA
OPE
I know you're hungry, but right now you've got ten seconds to choose between all the ice cream you can eat or seeing your parents alive again.
The autograph says, "Your parents are dead. Best wishes, Rocky Thompson."

CollegeTumor: Terminally Funny Pictures, Videos, Links!

http://www.collegetumor.com

CollegeTumor

DOCS X-RAYS HOSPITALS MEDS WILLS

Chemofest Episode 5: Last Call

Contest: Coolest Hospital Room Wins $1000 Cash

More

CollegeTumor's Top Ten Girls of The Cedars Sinai Cancer Institute

Party Theme Suggestions: *Tumor Party!*

Who Spiked the Chemo?

Perform a Killer IV Drip Stand!

Links

Nurse-o-the-Day

CHEAP FUNERALS

Funny Hospital Gowns

Custom Bed Pans

Hilarious Wills

King of Cancer Cribs

Unlimited Wig Rental

Bedpan Pranks to Pull on Your Roommate

My last roommate at John Hopkins Intensive Care was a real pain in the pituitary. One time at 3AM I had to get up for an early surgery the next morning, but Billy had his girlfriend sleeping over for a little game of hide the feeding tube in the abdominal incision. Hello! *Mcfly*! *Way* past visiting hours! This guy was always busting my (one remaining) ball. A rich kid, who didn't even need Medicare, he had it really going on, like a sixty to seventy percent chance. I tried to not let him get to me, but Spring Break was around the corner and Billy made it known to everyone he was headed to the sunny Cedars Sinai Institute. I was so jealous! Someone told me Sinai was ranked in *Playboy* at number three for having the hottest women. That bastard was the worst roommate I ever had and now he gets to go mack it with some hot Sinai in-patients!? Something had to be done. So I decided to send him off with a bang and formulated a plan; The Asian kid with the big colon C down the hall was a tech wiz. What if he hacked into the hospital mainframe and flat lined Billy's EKG machine? But then I thought that might freak him out so much he would have a heart attack and *actually* check out early. Or I could pour vodka in his IV drip while he was asleep, *getting him totally wasted!* But then I thought of the one thing we all dread:

The Bedpan.

Yes, the inevitable consequence of being bedridden with stage three inoperable melanoma is that you're going to become very acquainted with that shiny, silver bowl housing your own shit and piss. We all hate the cold steel against our bum, but that doesn't mean you can't have a little fun. And what better way to get Billy really good, I thought, than to pull some kick ass bedpan pranks on him before he goes! Here are some of my favs…

Bedpan Beer Chug

Tell your roommate that it's a rite of passage for all patients leaving the hospital to fill their bedpan with beer and chug it! I scored a six-pack of Mickey's from the hip male nurse Carl and convinced Billy to fill up his pan. (You would be surprised how many beers you can fit in a bedpan, we got a solid three!) The best part was he did this on *taco* night and downed the whole pan *before* they were changed. It was awesome.

Keep reading ...

Posted by Phil Haney on August 24, 2006 | Link

coolest hospice

hottest hospital

vote now

CollegeTumor: Terminally Funny Pictures, Videos, Links!

http://www.collegetumor.com

CollegeTumor

DOCS X-RAYS HOSPITALS MEDS WILLS

Note:
These pranks work best if your roommate is at more advanced stages of his affliction as he will be more apt to make poor judgment.

Fallacious Feces
Save your portion of green pea soup from your food tray and slip it in your roommate's bedpan when the opportunity arises. This will flip the hospital staff right out: When Carl the male nurse saw the bubbling green pea soup and thought it came out of Billy, the poor bastard spent the rest of the day having tests done!

Pee Pee Hat
This one is great: Billy had been slipping in and out of a coma all week, but as everyone knows you don't just pass out around your buddies like that! I took his full bedpan and put it on his head like a little hat. He was drenched in his own piss water! I brought all the kids in the ward in to see, they were rolling with laughter. One kid took a sharpie and drew a mustache on his face. Carl was a good sport and got lots of digital pictures as we took turns posing next to 'Billy Pee Pee Hat.' Later I posted the pics on his memorial blog. His family was *pissed*, haha.

Bedpan Frisbee
Convince your roommate that the hippest game the kids in the ward are playing these days is *Bedpan Frisbee*. Just as some hot mastectomy chicks were walking by our room, Billy wound up to the side and tossed me his dirty bedpan like he was a discus thrower for the Special Olympics. I ducked as his Cosby kids flew through the air and landed in the hall, nearly splattering the horrified babes. Sweet!

Flip Pan
Billy was woozy from a full day of chemo and so I decided to put together a little game of *Flip Pan*. Everyone gathered around Billy's bed with their own bedpans. We each placed them on the edge of the bed and had to flip them over one after the other in a row... Only thing is we didn't tell Billy that *our* bedpans were empty. Oops!

CollegeTumor: Terminally Funny Pictures, Videos, Links!

http://www.collegetumor.com/sex

CollegeTumor

DOCS X-RAYS HOSPITALS MEDS WILLS

How do I know if she's into me? Easy! You don't have anything to lose so ask her. What's the worst that could happen? She says no? Things can't get any worse, you're at the bottom of the luck barrel and you deserve some action! Slip some of those extra Vicoden in her next vitamin boost.

How to Get Sympathy Sex

One of the biggest problems in the youth cancer ward is that it's tough to get some tail. Sure, having cancer can be a drag. Sure, your enlarged prostate makes it medically impossible for you to get an erection. But you shouldn't' let that slow down your game. That's why College Tumor has been scouring the halls, walls, and bathroom stalls of hospitals for the hippest ways to get down and dirty with your woman even if she *is* bleeding more than just once a month.

The Sponge Bath

It's Friday night and you've had a long week of doctor's appointments, but that doesn't mean you can't set the mood right with that special someone: The Hot Nurse. We have all seen the Hot Nurse or at least heard rumors about them. If you're lucky like me, she's *your* nurse *and* she's on sponge bath duty. She's young, blonde and quick with her hands while changing your sheets. And if you play your cards right she could be quick with her hands *under* your sheets.

Making a move during the sponge bath can be a sticky process. While the HN (Hot Nurse) is slowly scrubbing your back side try to position yourself so your shanker rubs against her arm. Also, if you have any open sores on your penis now is the time to pick at them, so they will ooze puss and she will have to wipe them for you. Score!

You just better hope and pray to God (Yes that same God that put you in here in the first place, but come on get over it, He can be forgiving why can't you?) that you don't get stuck with an Edna (AKA the old, gray haired, skanky ass nurse) on sponge bath day. Note: If you get stuck with an Edna, make the best of it. Worst-case scenario: Older women are experienced, so if she gets the hint and is down with "playing doctor" you will be in for a wild ride. Otherwise, what with her cataracts, she probably won't even notice you rubbing one out on her ripped nylon stockings.

Pill Party

Every guy knows the easiest way to get with a girl is with a little help from the pharmacy. Your special lady friend doesn't stand a chance versus the best western medicine has to offer. Luckily for you, you happen to have a veritable arsenal of drugs at your disposal. A cornucopia of contraband awaits with just one sly trip to the medicine cabinet and you will be knee-deep in puntang. Grab a handful of Vicodin, Xanax, Nyquil, and a tank of Anesthesia. You may think that this

Keep reading ...

Posted by Phil Haney on August 24, 2006 | Link

Busted Gowns
funniest hospital gowns

Anywhere.

CollegeTumor: Terminally Funny Pictures, Videos, Links!

http://www.collegetumor.com/sex

CollegeTumor

DOCS X-RAYS HOSPITALS MEDS WILLS

Bare Breasts for Breast Cancer! A Charity Event we could all get behind. This could actually work; go to a college and each girl gets a sponsor. Every time they flash their tits to a group of guys they get money, which is donated to an undisclosed breast cancer charity.

scenario has some loose moral footing, but trust me these girls up in C Ward are half zonked anyway —you're just helping them along. So send out an Evite to all the hotties on your floor and throw what the high school kids in the know call a "Pill Party." The cuties will be doing IV drip stands before you know it and you will be bagging some much deserved snizz.

Medical Marijuana is Your Friend

One of the finer perks of being a person with an alternative state of health, especially if you are lucky enough to be in a liberal state like California or Vermont is Medical Dubes! It's awesome, we can actually get our own reefer and claim its for medical purposes! This stuff is great! If you really want to impress a girl invite her to your hospital room to split some spliffs! If you could keep solid food down, you would have the munchies. Hopefully, after rolling some Js you'll be rolling in the hay. The good news is after your last operation it's medically impossible for you to get her pregnant.

Hospital Cafeteria Food Can Be Romantic

To weak to make it to Chili's? Head on down to the hospital cafeteria, stick a candle in the mystery loaf and call if a date. This will really win a broad over 'cause they're not expecting it. If she's an in-patient then she hasn't been out in a while and this could be her last hurrah. Actually you'd be surprised how the old 'You don't want to die a virgin do you?' line works, especially over a hot plate of Salisbury steak. With a romantic dinner like this you'll be taking each others rectal temperature before you know it.

Turn a Catheter into a Beer Bong

Nothing says 'I Love You' like a Catheter Beer Bong. Take your catheter, your prospective mate and a six pack of MGD. Turn the catheter upside down and take turns pouring the beer down the tube and drink from spout. This should have your girl rolling in no time. In her drunken stupor, play up the puppy dog eyes calmly whimpering that she is your 'Make A Wish' and your last wish is to nail her harder than Jesus.

Conjugal Visiting Hours

When girls come to visit make the most of it if you know what I mean. If you have a girlfriend, wife, or lover on the outside, put a colostomy bag on the door so your roommate will know not to come in, 'cause your getting some long overdue sympathy sex. That, or pay a hooker.

SEXY X-RAYS

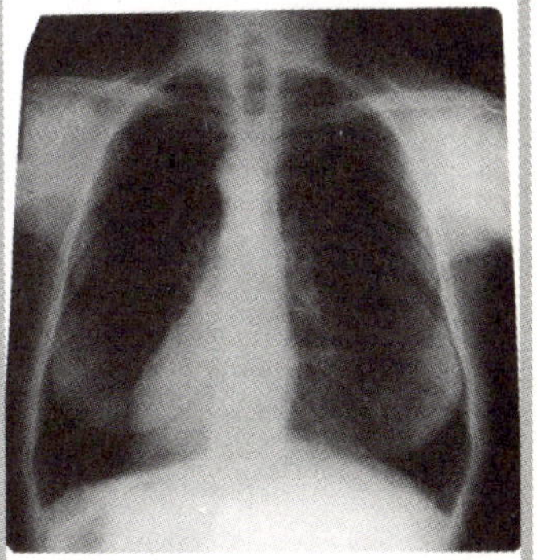

OVER 30,000 PICS AT SEXYXRAYS.COM

THE DEATH SHOCKER!!!

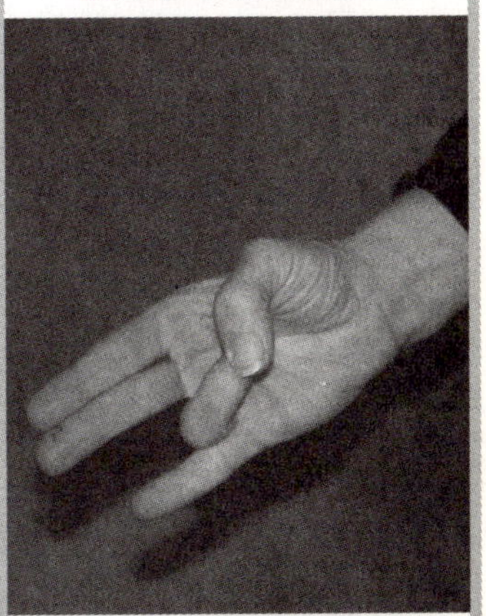

Two in the nostrils, one in the tracheotomy!

Beached Whale
Robert Rhine Story
John Watkins-Chow Art
ARE YOU SEEING THIS?
LIKE I'M IN A BUD COMMERCIAL.
OOO... YEAH... RIGHT THERE... RUB IT... MMMmmmm...
YOU LIKE THAT, HUH? YOU GONNA DO ME NEXT?
SO, ARE WE GOING TO HAVE A CIRCLE JERK, OR TALK TO THEM?
I DON'T KNOW, DUDE.
THEY'RE WAYYY TOO HOT TO APPROACH.
CHECK OUT THOSE GUYS.
CAN THEY BE MORE OBVIOUS?
THE BLOND ONE'S KINDA CUTE.
HEY, WHAT'S THAT SMELL? DID YOU CUT ONE?
NO, I SMELL IT TOO. LIKE A DEAD FISH. YOU ON THE RAG, ZOE?
NO, IT'S COMING FROM DOWN THE BEACH.
IT LOOKS LIKE A DEAD WHALE.
HOW DO YOU KNOW IT'S DEAD? IT COULD BE RESTING.
HEY, THEY'RE COMING THIS WAY. NOW'S YOUR CHANCE.
WHAT DO YOU MEAN, MY CHANCE? YOU'RE SUCH A PUSSY!

YEP, HE'S DEAD.
YA THINK?
SKOOSHSHHHSPLTTTTTT!
YOU POPPED HIM! NOW HE STINKS WORSE THAN BEFORE!
WHEW, THAT'S SOME DEAD WHALE. I KNOW A SPOT DOWN THE BEACH WHERE THE AIR'S A LITTLE FRESHER. WANNA GO?
OKAY. SEE YA LATER, ZOE.
GEE, THANKS.
UH... IS THAT A DEAD WHALE?
NO, IT'S THE GOODYEAR BLIMP. IT JUST STOPPED FOR REFUELING.
LATER...
YOU ENJOYING THIS?
IMMENSELY. NOW FOR THE FINAL TOUCH, WE'RE GOING TO BURY YOUR HEAD.
WHAT?!
DON'T WORRY. I'LL GIVE YOU A STRAW TO BREATHE THROUGH.
THERE MUST BE ONE AROUND THIS FILTHY BEACH SOMEWHERE...
SEE, HERE'S ONE.
NOW BE A GOOD BOY AND LIE BACK.
NOW DON'T GO ANYWHERE!
MMMMMMM MMMUUHHM...
WAIT 'TIL ZOE SEES THIS!

MULIMM GGHHH !!!
HUNTER! HUNTER!!
SLURPP
MUNCH
FARRRTT
MM MMMM UUGHHH ...!!
WAIT 'TIL YOU SEE...
HEY, WHERE'D HE GO?
MAYBE HE WAS FARTHER DOWN?
HE PROBABLY SPLIT.
OH WELL. WANNA GO TO THE MALL AND HIT SOME STORES?
SURE. THERE'S A REALLY HOT GUY WHO WORKS THERE.

HERE'S WHATS CAUSING YOUR CONSTIPATION, MOLLY.
NOW, HOW DID THIS CARTOON STRAW GET UP THERE?
ONE WEEK LATER...
ARE YOU SURE YOU GOT IT ALL OUT, DOCTOR? I STILL FEEL ALL BACKED UP.
WELL, LET'S TAKE A LOOK, SHALL WE?
HM. I FEEL SOME MORE BLOCKAGE...
BUT I CAN'T SEEM TO GET IT.
YOU'RE GOING TO HAVE TO PUSH IT OUT.
PUSH, MOLLY!
PUSH HARDER!!
BREATHE...
THAT'S IT, HARDER!!
MEANWHILE, AT THE CORONER...
WHEW, YOU REALLY BROUGHT IN A STINKER THIS TIME, FRANK.
WE FOUND HIM BURIED BY THE SHORE.
WE WOULD'VE FOUND HIM SOONER, BUT NO ONE SMELLED HIM WITH THAT DEAD WHALE AROUND.
WHERE'D HIS HEAD GO?
PUSH!!
CHRIST, MOLLY! YOU'VE GOT A HEAD UP YOUR ASS!!

ACUTE ASPHYXIATION...
...FROM METHANE GAS...
DID YOU SAY METHANE--
BOOM!
--GAS?
end

HANS DICK
by: marc m.
Ya know, I think that probably the worst part about dying would be getting brought back to life five years later and not knowing shit about current events.
Yeah. That, and the guy at the mortuary getting to see your dick.

Girls Crying...Awesome!

by Andy Kleiman

I enjoy watching girls cry. It's not like I'm hiding in the bushes with a pair of binoculars and some lotion, but it definitely is one of my guilty pleasures. Now before you go condemning me for being a horrible person, allow me to defend myself. Popular to contrary belief, I do have some semblance of a conscience; I don't get pleasure from ALL girls crying, just most. It depends on the situation. It's kind of like real estate, it doesn't matter how nice the house is if it's in a crappy neighborhood. If the girl is bawling her eyes out, but it's because someone died, not cool. However, if said girl was bawling said eyes out because someone died on a television show, I am smiling from ear to ear. Oh, and if I can *make* them cry, I touch myself.

Also, it's not just the act of crying, but the process. I love every delicious detail from the quivering lip to the running make-up. It's like a golf swing. Hitting the ball is one action, but to actually hit the ball takes about 80 steps. You have to pick the right club, line up the shot, arch the back, keep your head down, bring the club down, swing your hips, have a good follow through, a good backswing, it goes on and on. Same with girls crying.

I think I like making girls cry because it's like giving them an orgasm and since I've never done that, I've gotta make due with what I have.

I love the initial look on their face as it starts to contort, the eyebrows coming down, the eyes squinting, the lips forming an upward curve. Although it doesn't make a sound, I can tell when it's happening up to 50 feet away, it's like a sixth sense. I have truly been blessed.

I love their heavy breathing as they try to hold back the inevitable.

I love when they lower their head so as to try and hide what's going on. Don't hide it baby, it's ok to cry, just let go of your inhibitions and let 'er rip.

I LOVE the whimper...ohhhhhh the whimper, it's like the sound they make when you first hit the G-spot and you know you gotta keep doing what'cha doing if you want discharge to come out, be it from eyes or vagina.

I love when the eyes start to water, you're basically there. It's like in Punch-Out when the guy is dazed and his life meter is almost all the way down and you still have a super punch left. All it takes is a slight tap of the A button.

I love the first tear. Watching it as it rolls down the cheek ranks right up there with the first sip of beer and the first blast from the AC on a hot day. Plus, if you look at the tear close enough, you can see a bit of their soul and watch as it splatters on the ground.

Sometimes it's just the one tear —and I can be content with that— but if it turns into an all out cry fest, then next comes the sniffling. It is, in my opinion, one of the most underrated parts of the whole ordeal. The sniffling is like when a girl plays with your balls, it's not discussed very much and it's rarely done, but it is always appreciated. And if all the stars are aligned and the wind is blowing in just the right direction, you'll get the snot bubble.

A favorite cry of mine is when a girl is crying because she is upset with herself that she's crying and that causes her to cry more. There is no telling when this is going to end, it's a vicious, beautiful cycle that could go on for hours. I've never seen the end of one of these as I have passed out with orgasmic pleasure each time.

However, out of all the different kind of cries, there is no cry (no cry I tell you!) better than the drunk cry. Most notably, it's almost never for a good reason, so you feel significantly less guilty for laughing at it. It's usually something like the guy she's been eyeballing the whole night from across the bar started talking to another girl or she's having a party and someone passed out on her bed (why she can't kick that person out is beyond me, but they never do). Which brings me to another point, if you want some guaranteed crying, go to a house party thrown by one or more girls, it is a consistent as gravity that one of the girls will cry by the end of the night, trust me on this.

If she's really drunk and it's for a really stupid reason, the drunken cry will turn into a top of the lungs, drunken wail and when it gets to that point it's like pushing a snowball down the hill. You can do whatever you want, but it's not going to stop anytime soon, in fact it's just going to get bigger and destroy everything in its path.

Also, for some reason when one girl cries it usually sets off two or three other girls within a 5 mile radius. I don't know how it works, but maybe it's kind of like how girls get on the same cycle when they live together, but then again I don't know how periods work either. However when you think about it, isn't a period the same thing as crying except through your vagina?

Now, I am in no way, shape or form condoning violence towards women. Hitting a woman is a deplorable act that is only done by the most unstable of men. I cannot stress enough that you should not hit a woman to make her cry. Just chip away at her self esteem —emotional scars last longer. ■

The Gas Man

by Kyle Buchanan

When I lose early in my weekly game of poker, I need to overachieve to salvage the night. Whether it's cleaning my room or getting a lot of writing done, I've gotta do *something*, or else I go to bed angry.

A few weeks ago, after busting out on a flush draw, I had a distinct lack of post-game options. A cruel card streak that month had left my room spotless, my script written, and my checkbook balanced. I decided I would fill my empty car tank with gas so I wouldn't have to do it in the morning. Cards be damned, I was going to be productive.

I had barely parked at the gas station around the corner when he came up to me.

"Hi," he said. "I'm Henry. Spare some change?"

"Sure, one sec," I said, beep-bop-bopping my choice of unleaded.

"Where you from, big man?" he said.

"Around here."

"I'm from Atlanta, man. Tryin' to raise enough money to take the bus back."

I turned to look at him. Henry was a few years older than me and pretty put-together for a homeless man. The clothes were lived in, but the eyes were sharp.

"Got married in Vegas two years ago," he continued. "Moved out here because *she* wanted to. Worst mistake I ever made!"

"Oh yeah?"

"Yeah, she was a big ol' lesbian as soon as she got here! They all are! You know it, am I right?"

The first curveball. "Really?"

"C'mon, dawg, you know I'm right! Every chick in LA a lesbian! You ain't never been with one?"

This, as a gay man, I could safely lay no claim to. "Uhhh…"

"You know you have! Shit. People don't know that that's why we're like this. All those lesbians." He kicked the asphalt by my tire as I pondered lesbianism as an indirect cause of homelessness.

"I'm just tryin' to live my life right, though. Just trying to live life like the Bible says."

"How's that going?"

"Shit, it's hard. You know, I wanna go back to my kids in Atlanta, but I know what they all gonna say. They gonna say I couldn't make it in L.A. Well, maybe so, but at least I lived life like the Bible said, you know?"

"Yeah, man. You can't worry about what other people think." I reached inside my car for some spare change. "Here you go."

He sneered at the change and looked up at me, disappointed. "What, you think I need money?"

"Didn't you…I thought…"

He took it. "Gotta pay for that bus ride."

Right. I looked at the gas meter. Why wasn't the car full yet? Meanwhile, Henry came close to me, his manner intimate, like I was his most trusted confidante. He looked up at me with lidded bedroom eyes and spoke in a low voice.

"So tell me, man," he said. "Should I do it?"

"Do what?"

"You know." Pause. "Should I kill her?"

"What?"

"My wife. Should I kill her?"

"No!" I exclaimed.

"Why not?"

Why not? How do you explain "thou shalt not kill" to a religious man who conveniently overlooks the commandment? I decided to be practical.

"You'd get in even more trouble, man. You might never make it to Atlanta."

He leaned in close, smiling. "Not if they don't find out I did it," he said.

"I think they'd suspect you, man. You're the husband." And homeless. And vengeful.

"I got it all planned out, though," he said, backing up. "They'd never know it."

THUNK. The gas nozzle shuddered as it switched off, my car tank full. I put it back in the holder and turned to Henry with finality.

"Go to Atlanta," I said.

He nodded, but a small smile played across his lips. He was lost in a murderous reverie.

That night, as I went to bed, I thought about Henry and the casual indifference he had to picturing his wife's death. Was this lack of emotion abetted by his certainty that he could get away with the crime? In Hollywood, any dream seems possible, but this was one all too often reserved for the rich and famous, not Henry.

The "bus money" story is a common one among homeless guys, even if they never find their way out of town. The other threads to Henry's story were less common, but I hoped his darker impulses would also go unfulfilled. Ultimately, there was nothing I could do. It's LA. ■

SEX DEATH MUSIC FICTION COMICS CARS BABES MORGUES
GIRLS AND CORPSES
TM
HORROR MEISTER FOREST J. ACKERMAN
"A Corpse is A Corpse... of Course, of Course" - Fiction from R.S. Rhine
COMIC ARTISTRY OF "BUTTMAN"
HOW TO DRIVE YOUR CORPSE WILD IN THE SACK!
PLUS!
Great Severed Head!
Scream Queens!
Death Metal!
Sexy Goth Girls!
and...
Corpse College Cuties!
SPECIAL TWINS ISSUE!!!
CASSIE & MAILE
fresh from the Lingerie Bowl
"My Corpse Won't Commit"
How To Keep Her Hot Long After She's Gone Cold
"Talk Dirty To Me - You Nasty Bag Of Bones!"
GC
Sex Tips From Dr. Necrophilia and...
America's Sexiest Corpses Next Door
UNDEAD GIRLS EXPOSED!
YOU ASKED FOR IT...AND NOW IT'S HERE!
GIRLSANDCORPSES.COM
Girls and Corpses © and TM Robert Steven Rhine 2005 Cover photo by LCB Photography Corpse by www.edgeincollection.com Layout by Gonewest.com

CORPSE COLLEGE CUTIES

7-Sexy Corpse Erogenous Zones

GIRLSANDCORPSES.COM

Cassie and Maile represented by CUNNINGHAM, ESCOTT, DIPENE

 Layout and design by R.S. Rhine and Frank Forte Photos by LCB Photography

Got Corpse?
GIRLSandCORPSES.com
GIRLS AND CORPSES © TM R.S. Rhine 2005 Photo by LCB Photography Corpse by edgeincollection.com Models Cassie & Mailie Moore

Emerald's Ragin' Cajun Stew

by Marcus Terry

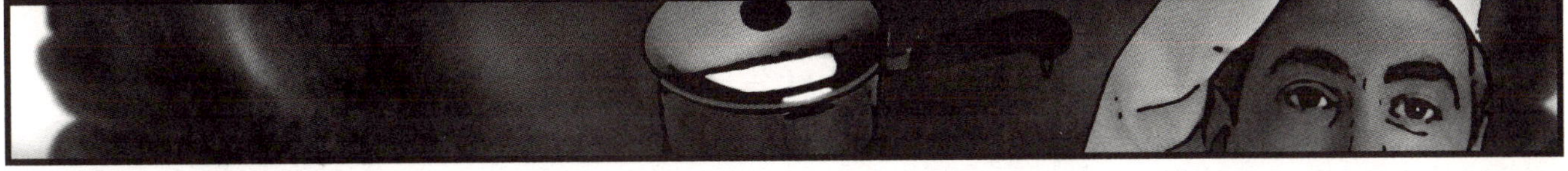

There's nothing quite like a good, meaty stew. I know it gets my fire a-boiling when I smell a big pot of Jambalaya simmering on the stove. So I, Emerald Goulashy, will treat you to one of my favorite stew recipes from my new cookbook, *Top Choices*.

The ingredients:

1 stick of butter	1½ cups of celery
½ cup of dry red wine	2 cups diced yellow onion
3 cups of water	1 clove garlic, pressed
3 cups of rice	1 Freshly gestated human

Yes, the main ingredient in this stew is the succulent flesh of a newborn **"bundle of joy."** The reason babies are the most desirable meat is that they haven't had a chance to build up lean stringy muscle. They're the equivalent of human veal!

So let's get started. The most difficult part of this—and any baby-heavy recipe—is procuring the meat. The aftermath of Katrina was a real windfall but by now most supplies have dwindled. Another way to go is to head straight for the "ethnic" end of town. We all know if the baby ain't blonde, nobody's gonna go lookin'. Plus, I've found that ethnic baby has a rich, full-bodied flavor that is not found in most white meat. Once ya go black baby, you'll never go back, baby! **Bang!** Sometimes you'll be lucky enough to find one in a dumpster. This is rare, but the best time to look is about nine months after prom night. A dumpster baby is the best because you get your meat and the scared teenage girl who threw it away never gets caught. So everyone wins.

You've heard the old joke "How do you make a dead baby float? A glass of root beer and two scoops of dead baby." Well that and all the other Dead Baby jokes are disgusting, vile, and irresponsible because any good chef knows that live babies are much more delicious than dead ones.

You have to keep the baby alive as you use the parts. Plus if you kill the baby before hand you miss out on the most important seasoning, the tears. Baby tears are by far the most robust flavor you could hope to have in any stew. **Remember though, go easy on the salt!!** With Baby Stew the main ingredient bastes itself in its **own flavorful juices, its tears**.

First, you have to knead the baby. Don't be afraid to press your fists, knuckles, and even elbows down into it to loosen up and tenderize the meat. A meat tenderizer could be used as well but you run the risk of shattering the bones which means you'll miss out on my favorite part, chewing on the bone like a big toothpick after the meal. And be sure to do this in a pan so you can catch the tears for basting.

Once the baby is nice and tender use the stick of butter give it a nice thick coating. Go ahead and use the whole stick. Then set the baby out in the sun or in a window for 20 minutes. Make sure to flip it after 10 minutes. This allows the butter to seep in which will help bring out the full-bodied flavor of the baby meat. And once again the baby is stewing in its own tears. Take this time to dice your onions and celery and press your garlic.

Now that the baby is prepared it's time to quarter it. Don't worry, "quarter" is just a cooking term. You aren't actually cutting the baby into four pieces. You're cutting its limbs off. Using a cleaver and a cutting board (and it may be a good idea to spread some trash bags on the floor for easy clean up) chop off the arms at the shoulders and the legs at the hips. Don't be put off by the bursting capillaries in the baby's eyes; the tears will still be delicious. And if you like, save the fingers and toes as garnish for an attractive presentation.

Put all the pieces of the baby into a pot with the water, celery, onions and garlic. Let it simmer. After about 15 minutes add the wine. When the meat starts falling off the bones add the rice. Continue simmering until the rice is tender. Remove from heat and enjoy.

Other infant-inspired recipes featured in *Top Choices*:
Emerald's Baby Back and Ribs
Emerald's Baby Carrots and Baby
Emerald's Blackened Baby Rump Roast
Emerald's Southwest Steak with Toddler Sauce

HANS DICK By: Marc M. "S.T.V."
WAIT!! You can't become a vampire just from fucking, right?!

Chapter 4
The Finer Intricacies of The Hot Lunch vs The Cleveland Steamer

Which is Your Orgasm Face?

by Matthew McCoy

There are more than ninety muscles in the human face. And there's only one event known to man that gets them all to contract simultaneously: The Male Orgasm.

The facial contortions resulting from the male climax could stand down a rabid pit bull. Have you ever seen YOUR orgasm face? I bet you think you have an idea what it looks like. But trust me on this one, you don't. Because if you did, you'd never have sex again. Ever.

For those thinking to themselves as they read this:

"Whatever, I've had sex in front of a mirror before, I know what my face looks like during an orgasm."

I'm sure you have seen yourself getting it on. But I guarantee you've never watched your face while "it" was happening. This is why male porn stars are Satan's children. They can watch their faces distort in horrifying fashion on the big screen and then saddle up for another shoot (pun absolutely intended) without a care in the world. I will never understand this.

There are numerous types of male orgasm faces and all are dependent on the situation during which they occur. How many of the following orgasm faces have you made?

"I Can't Believe She Snuck A Finger Up My Butt"

Oh yeah, you've made this face before, haven't you? You were anally violated in some fashion by your proctology-aspiring partner, yet somehow you still came. This orgasm face of perplexion reflects a man grappling with three questions simultaneously:

1. Did she really just do that to me?

2. Did I really come AFTER she did that to me?

And most importantly...

3. Am I gay because I kinda liked it?

"Oh Shit, The Condom Broke"

It's amazing how fast a man crashes back to planet reality when this happens. You're cruising along at 35,000 feet in a state of heavenly bliss so all-encompassing that you don't even realize it's suddenly a helluva lot more sensitive down there. You're wondering why? Because now you're bare-backing it, YOU HUGE FUCKING IDIOT.

Tell Louise at Planned Parenthood I said hello. She'll take good care of ya.

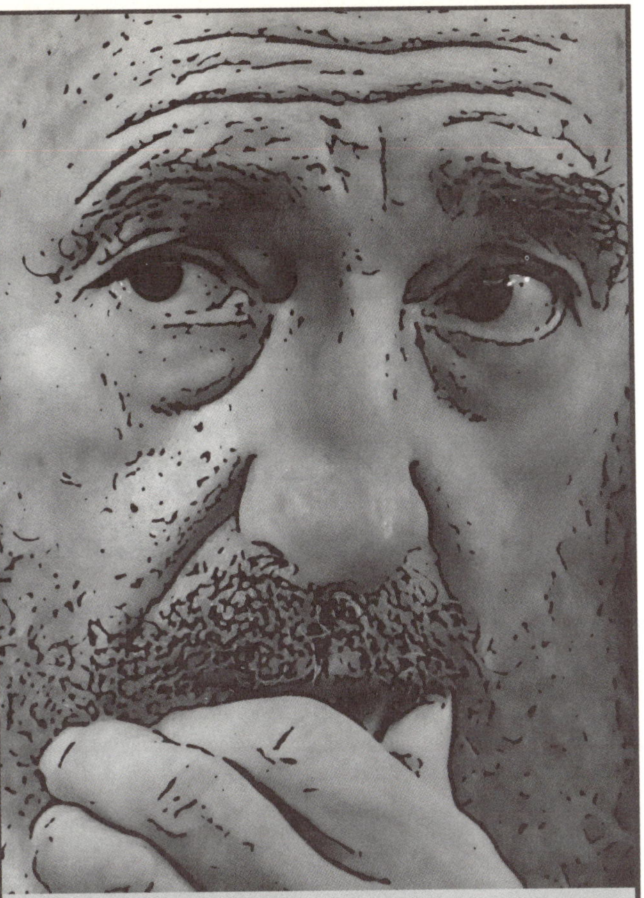

"I'm Trying So Hard Not To Come Too Fast"

Yep, we've all tried to stop the inevitable. I've gone to desperate lengths upon realizing I was about to fall short of the pathetic two minute barrier. Visuals have included picturing my manhood on the guillotine block or my balls being rubbed furiously against a cheese grater. All to no avail. Once the tide builds, there's no turning it back. Just make sure you're ready to go again in about thirty seconds, or she'll never speak to you again.

"Sensitive Man Crying During Orgasm"

If a man cries during sex for any reason other than a reckless woman bouncing on his johnson and turning it into a T-square, he's a fucking loser.

"I'm Shitting My Pants This Is So Intense"

Ahh yes, the knee-buckling toe-curler. The really intense ones are often inexplicable and usually catch you off-guard, which explains why this orgasm face is so special and treasured. It's typically accompanied by high-pitched huffing and puffing that could be confused by safari veterans as a hyena's mating call.

"You're Just Another Notch On My Bedpost"

This orgasm face is worn by the ultra-cocky alpha male who sleeps with his unsuspecting prey purely for the conquest. By the time the woman recognizes this face for what it is, she's just another scalp hanging in his teepee.

"Oh My God, I Just Dominated You"

This face involuntarily comes over the frat boy who gets laid once every three semesters. You don't get to see it for very long because he'll be sprinting out of the room to go tell his "brothers" about it. If you're a woman and happen to recognize this face, congrats, you're sleeping with one of the most insecure tools on the planet. You're either very unattractive or have no self-respect. I'm guessing it's a combination of both.

"I'm Scared My Wife Will Find Out I'm A Cheater"

Cheater's remorse sets in quickly. The change in a Cheater's demeanor from pre- to post-orgasm is striking. The *Pre-Orgasm Cheater* is smooth, confident, determined and a panty-dropping charmer. While the *Post-Orgasm Cheater* is introverted, introspective, jittery and moody.

Personally, I feel badly for all the Cheatresses out there. They're forced to deal with this awkward dichotomy during the three minutes of post coital awkwardness before the Cheater flees the crime scene.

"I Can't Believe She Just Let Me Do That To Her"

Hey pal, if she just did that with you, trust me, she's most likely done it with someone else before. And that someone was much dirtier. Good luck with the blood test.

"People Said I Would Never Get Laid And I Proved Them Wrong"

"I'm So Old I Can't Believe I Can Still Do This"

There's a pill for almost anything these days. Just watch out for your ticker, old fella. Although, I can think of no better way to take an unscheduled dirt nap than having your heart explode while taking the skin boat to tuna town. It's better than passing away in your sleep.

Yeah, yeah, it's probably traumatic for the woman. Whatever. She'll be banging someone she meets at the funeral.

"I'm So Excited To Be Getting Laid"

Seen annually in roadside motels on prom nights all across the nation.

"I Really Can't Imagine Ever Getting Laid Again"

Why can't you just cherish the moment? Quit thinking ahead. You should be enjoying this while it lasts. It's taken a few decades to get to this point and it could be another few before the next one. Have a little fun for Christ's sake.

"I Wish It Was Bigger So I Could Feel Something"

So her previous boyfriend was packing a can of Lysol down there—that's not her fault. So you feel as if you could throw a loaf of bread in there with ya—big deal. Blame your dad, and his dad, and so on. It's genetics, baby. Besides, she doesn't care about size. She loves you. And that's all that matters.

Hee hee. Loser.

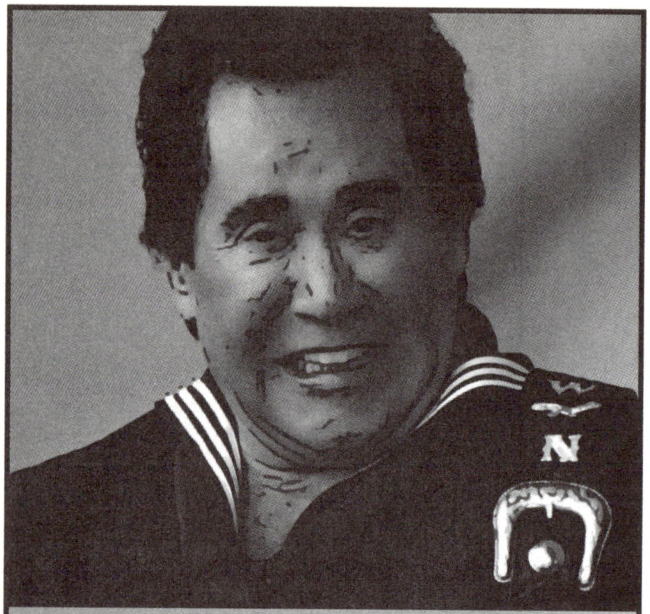

"Yeeee Haaaa!! This is the Best Sex Ever"

You could be lying naked on a bed of burning embers and have no fucking idea that your flesh was cooking. Top five symptoms accompanying this orgasm face:

1. Total cognitive failure and the stoppage of time.

2. Drool trickling out of the corner of your mouth and down your chin.

3. Epileptic seizure-like body convulsions.

4. Severe muscle cramping in the hamstrings and abdominal region.

5. Eyeballs spinning like slot machines.

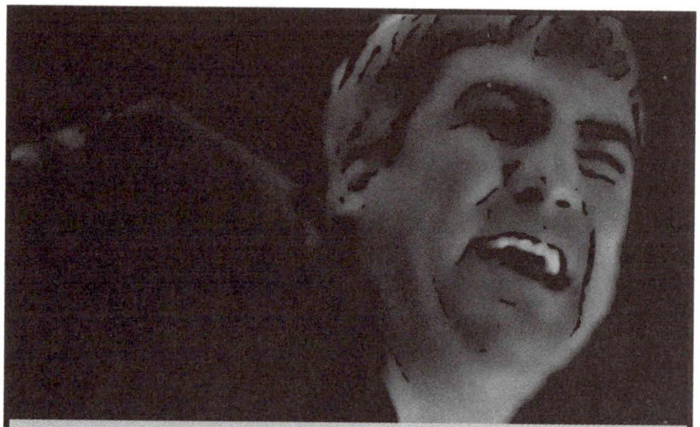

"I'm Such a Bad Lover and I Know It"

It's not you, it's her.

HEH. Sure it is. So she's filing her nails while you're laying into her like a runaway locomotive. Who cares? You're still getting off, aren't you? Sure, she probably cheats on you all the time, and on the rare occasion she does let you touch her, it's either out of pity or because she needs money for another boob job. She's a trophy wife. You knew this was the deal when your attorney made her sign the two-hundred-page prenup.

"I Get Laid So Much That I'm Actually Sick of Sex"

Seen on rock stars, athletes and movie stars' faces all across the country. In that exact pecking order. This orgasm face is the result of having procured so much ass that the thought of getting laid makes you yawn with indifference. I can think of no worse state of affairs. But getting to that point would be one sick fucking ride (pun absolutely intended again).

Mom, why do you look so out of it yet strangely satisfied?
Whew. Well son, your father just fucked the shit out of me with a giant bat!
Hey Man, maybe next time we can fuck your wife.
Actually Dude, I have a feeling that we'll never see each other again.

So What if My Mom Is Jenna Jameson?

by Juan Turlington

My mom is Jenna Jameson. I get picked on a lot, but so what? It's no big deal. Yes, I can admit that my mom is a nice-looking woman. No, I would not do my mom. I should kick you in the teeth for even asking me that. It's really not that weird having her as a mom. She fixes me meals, checks my homework, and gives me advice. She is usually engaged in a gangbang while she performs these tasks, but time and massive exposure have made me numb. It actually makes me kind of proud. I mean, it takes a good deal of talent for one to flip pancakes while reverse-cowgirling a fat, balding, middle-aged man.

Mom knows lots of guys with greasy hair and mustaches. I name them all with numbers, preceded by the words "Mustache Dad." It is way easier than trying to remember all those names.

My Mustache Dads wear cool sunglasses and smell like smoke. Most of them are pretty cool, but there are exceptions. I am not particularly fond of Mustache Dad 32. He nicknamed me "Ashtray" and continually put cigarettes out on my forehead. Mustache Dad 17 and Mustache Dad 28 may be my favorites. They have sweet blue Camaros with flames painted on the doors. The rest of them just have red Camaros. Each of my Mustache Dads has taught me important lessons that I will always cherish. Did you know if you dismount a woman too fast, you can bump and even damage the boom microphone? I do.

Another great thing about my mom is that she always took the time to play with me. Most of my friends were never allowed over because their mothers hated my mom. My friends' dads would always try to bring them over anyway, but they were so scatter-brained that they always seemed to forget my friends. It never made much sense to me, but mom always kept me company. I remember the time when I was playing G.I. Joe and I found some fake snow in her purse. It was awesome. I took out the obvious action figure for the mission, Snow Job. (Yes, there really was a G.I. Joe character named Snow Job, and I haven't the slightest clue how they got away with that one.) Mom loved that Snow Job.

Anyway, I was pushing Snow Job through the toy snow when mom came in on a set break. She was so funny. She bent over and whisked all of the toy snow right up her nose and began laughing hysterically. She is such a silly lady! Mommy-Vacuum-Cleaner-Nose is my favorite character that she does! Dizzy-Fall-Down Mumble-Mommy is a great one as well. She would do anything to make me laugh.

It's always a party when you have Jenna Jameson for a mom. She has her girlfriends to the house for sleepovers all the time. They love chocolate and usually devour several boxes of it each evening. Some nights, I hear them talk about devouring over sixty-nine boxes. They yell and moan about it! I bet they eat countless boxes of the most delicious chocolate ever!

"Oh, eat that box!"

"Put your whole box in my mouth."

"Your box tastes great!"

Those sleepovers are so cool. Maybe one time they'll forget to lock the door and I can get a box of chocolate for myself.

Mmmmmm...

You see, the real reason that so many people make fun of me is that are jealous. They don't have Mustache-Dads with Camaros, or vacuum-cleaner-mommies, or all-night candy parties. I guess I'd be jealous, too. There are parts of Jenna Jameson that no one sees but me—her loving son. And that's awesome. ■

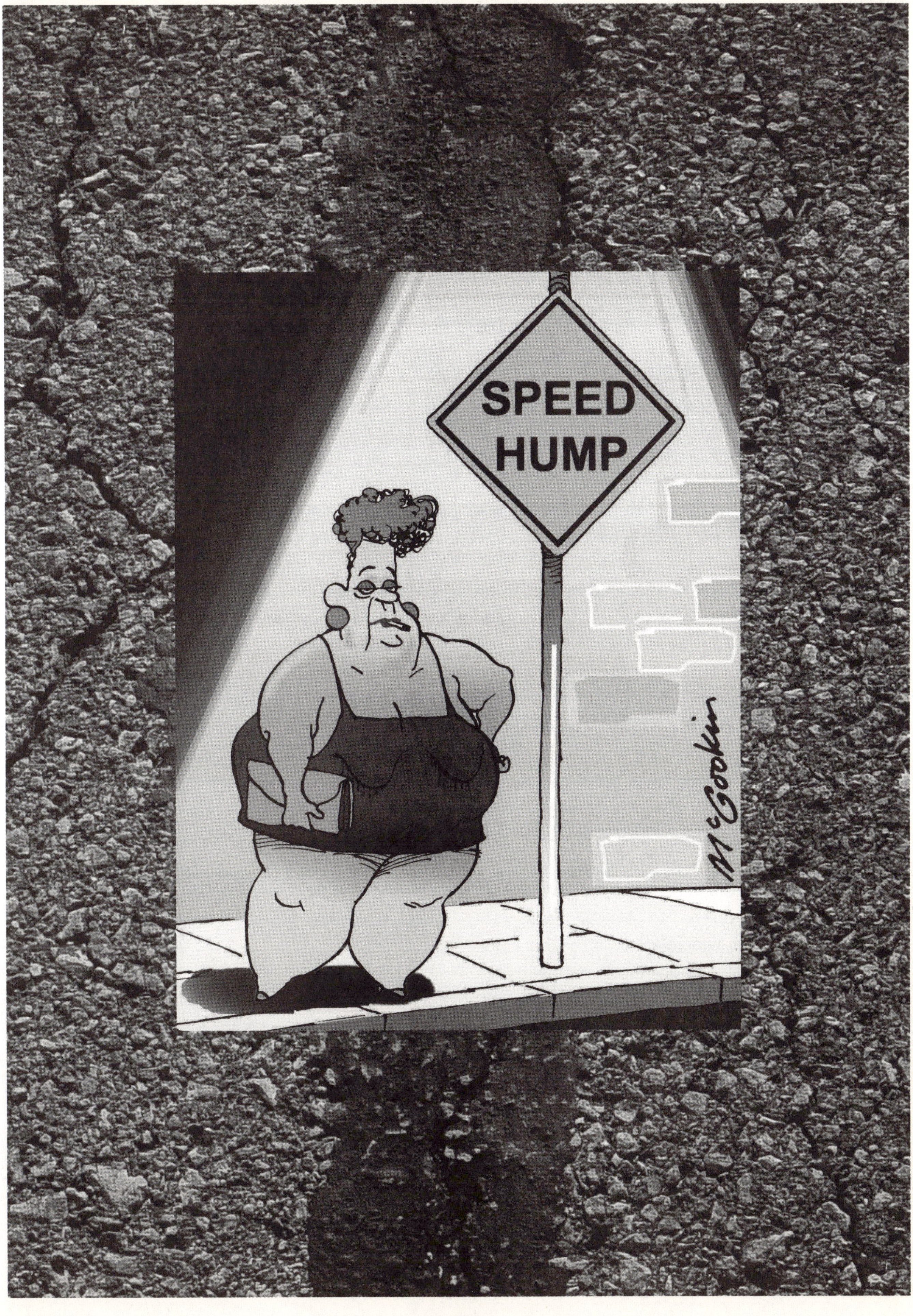
SPEED
HUMP
McGookin

Tips For Picking Up High School Boys

by Suzy Nece

Okay, I admit it. I like to shop for boyfriends at high schools. Is that so bad? So what if there's a fifteen-year age difference. I just want to be somebody's first something! You never forget your first love, your first stinky pinky, the first time you wake up with inner-thigh bruising and blood in your urine, or the first time Hank Brownstien used Aquafresh for lube. (It was college; it only burned for a second and I was minty fresh all week!)

But I digress. Where was I? Oh yes. I am a walking "Amber Alert."

I remember my first experience with a high school boy like it was yesterday. I pulled up to the bus loop and told security, "Don't mind me officer, I'm just picking up my son!" And there he was Little Billy, frolicking around the soccer field with his smooth, hairless torso touching the warm spring air. Maybe I was just nostalgic for some pre-Algebra ass grabbing, but I took one look at those perky nips and just wanted to nurse. Guys my age have nipples like tarantulas, and truth be told, they'd rather finger their Palm Pilot than me. Finger banging is truly a lost art.

That night was so magical. Little Billy had spent almost 16 whole years—okay, 15 and three quarters—thinking about boobies. He would have done anything just to touch one. He was thrilled to sleep over (unlike Mr. Commitment-phobic 32-year-old). And so our love blossomed...

Going to the movies with him is such a rush. "One adult and one...*student* please." I swear, I get chills every time. Our relationship never gets stale because Billy's constantly improving himself. He's learning cursive (working on those capitals) and you wouldn't believe the love notes he's scribbled to me on a paper football and plucked across a crowded Chuck E Cheese's. It would make your toes curl. He's so proud of me, too. He introduced me to his lunch table after. And okay, maybe I shouldn't have been the first taste of spring for the entire Mira Costa High School basketball team but, man, after all the beer I bought those ballers they fuckin' owed me!

If you think about it, Little Billy—or any sexy piece of high school ass—is the perfect companion for the modern woman. Billy doesn't need Viagra to get it up. He doesn't need a hummer from a Filippino hooker with a mouth full of Kettle Corn. He's just happy to have me on his arm—that way he's allowed to cross the street.

I know you're shaking your head, judging me, but c'mon...it's not like I'm dressing up like a priest circling the bus loop dangling a fist full of Blow Pops out of my Tercel window and driving with my knees so my free hand can dive elbow deep in my trousers...anymore (I learned my lesson). Where's the harm in one consenting adult and a varsity tackle with a pocket full of rubbers? It could be a beautiful story, 'cause I have a lot to offer someone with a limited education. So, if you see a "signal alert" on the Freeway for a Silver '86 Tercel, don't rat me out to the pigs, man. I'm on a date. ■

SR
"No more lapdances for you, Maxine."
are tryting to be offended by this picture, you're way off.
It's an EYE, you idiot! -*Editors*

Soft Porn Always Tricks Me

by Kirk Pynchon

The same thing happens every time. It's late at night and I'm sprawled on the couch, channel surfing. And as I bounce from *Blind Date* to *Cheaters* to *Three's Company* to Steven Seagal's *Above the Law*, then back to *Cheaters*, I inevitably hit HBO and run smack dab into a soft porn movie.

"Soft porn blows," I say to myself. "A complete waste of time."

But just as I'm about to see if "Showtime at the Apollo" might be on, a tiny voice comes out from my television set—the voice of the soft porn movie itself.

"No, wait," the movie says. "Don't change the channel. Watch me. I'll make it worth your while."

"Bullshit," I say. "I know your game. You promise me hot sex, then deliver nothing but frustration."

"You've got me all wrong. I'm not like those other soft porn movies. I'm different."

"Oh yeah? How?" I ask, still unconvinced.

"Look at these two naked chicks kiss," the movie says."Look how hot that is. Isn't that hot?"

"Well, yeah, I guess."

"And this is only the beginning of the movie, my friend. We've still got eighty-seven more minutes of smut to go."

"I don't know," I say, a little unsure. "It's getting late and I have to work tomorrow. Maybe I should just go back to flipping between watching Steven Seagal's girly run to the episode of "Three's Company" where Mr. Furly mistakenly thinks Jack is gay."

"Aw, come on. *Three's Company* jumped the shark when the Ropers left and Seagal's a dildo. Besides, you can see those anytime. How often do you get to see a full-blown orgy, which only I can offer up to you in the next twelve minutes?"

I gotta admit, this soft porn movie sure can talk the talk. It has a great career in the used car business if the soft porn thing doesn't pan out.

"Listen," I say, "I've...been hurt before."

The soft porn looks me in the eyes and says, "Trust me. I'd never do anything to upset you."

I think a moment: "Okay."

Eighty-seven minutes later and I realize I've been duped...again. There was nothing in the movie even remotely resembling hot sex (let alone sex). You couldn't even label the movie "porn." It was nothing but a bunch of actors and actresses desperate for work but not desperate enough for a money shot. Somewhere deep in my TV console, that soft porn movie is laughing at me.

Why do I get hooked in every time? Why does soft porn do that to me? I know it sucks. Everyone knows it sucks ("sucks" in the bad way, not "sucks" in the good porn way). I should know better. For God's sake it's called soft porn for a reason! I know I'm going to be pissed off in the end. But I always watch and I always buy into it with the hope that once, just once, I might find hot sex.

Maybe it's because when I watch soft porn I'm reminded of what it was like to be a pre-teen adolescent. When just looking at a pair of bare breasts made you nut. The joy of actually discovering simulated sex on cable. The patience and determination I had to be able to sit through a crappily-acted, crappily-written, crappily-produced film just so I could catch a glimpse of naked people clumsily touching each other.

That's truly when you realize you've gotten old—when soft porn doesn't do it for you anymore.

But, just like Ponce de Leon searching for the Fountain of Youth, I'll keep searching my premium cable channels for a soft porn movie that will make me happy.

I know it's out there. I just know it. ■

ONLY $1.25
ENTER THE WONDERFUL WORLD OF AMAZING
LIVE SEMEN®
Own a whole LOAD of HAPPINESS - Instant PETS!
Just ADD WATER - Toss in an unfertalized egg and watch 'em squirm! (Egg not included)
Moms and Dads love 'em! Countless generations have marveled and played with these miracles of nature. Surprise your friends with a load of these at your next party!
FREE!
1 - A ONE-YEAR SUPPLY of VITAMIN E
2 - VIAGRA
3 - NATIONAL GEOGRAPHIC
4 - AN OLD SOCK
5 - HAND LOTION
6 - Our famous GROWTH GUARANTEE IN WRITING
Transvestment Corporation Dept. 69-W
200 Filth Ave., N.Y. TX 10000
IT SOUNDS FREAKY! Please send me my Live Semen kit (s) and my FREE ADULT VIDEO or DVD plus a year supply of LUBE and guarantee.
Send ______ Kits(s) Cash Check Money Order
(No C.O.D.'s Please) Total amount enclosed $
Name
Address
City State Zip
SUPER_RUSH ORDERS ($50.00 extra)
Copyright © Transvestment Corp.
Written by Robert Steven Rhine. Art by Jim Smith, Inks by Jim Smith & Frank Forte, layout by D.W. Frydendall

Top Ten Girls Whose Face I'd Like To Cum On

by Phil Haney

Who was the first guy to cum on a girl's face? Like how'd that go over? Must have been kind of awkward afterward. But nonetheless any red-blooded American male who has watched a porno has thought about performing the elusive cum shot. It's not exactly standard practice among loving couples, but if it were up to me it would be as routine as a handjob. That's why I have painstakingly compiled the Top Ten list of Girls Whose Face I'd Like to Cum On:

10. Paris Hilton

Paris put the money in money shot. I am including her on the list because she is the only one of these that I might actually have a shot at shooting my load on. With my bare elegance and charm I would be able to talk her into a rendezvous where I'd unload my man butter across her billion-dollar face. Ah, who am I kidding, it wouldn't be that much work at all! For a few cheap drinks she'd be blowin' cum bubbles out her nose with the charm of a five-year-old with a cold.

Aim & Trajectory:

Aim for her forehead, watch it dribble down and cover her eyes. Laugh loudly as she begins to freak out.

9. Kate Moss

The ninth girl whose face I'd like to cum on is Kate Moss. She's so skinny you could cum right through her. (Oooh, snap!) I'm not a big fan of the heroin chic look. If she's not going to eat, at least she can swallow.

Aim & Trajectory:

Aim for her belly button, get a little reserve of spooge going and let it fill up quickly. Then fold her tiny body in half and let all the jizzum slop on her little head. Awesome.

8. The Bush Twins

The eighth girl(s) whose face I'd like to cum on are The Bush Twins. Ahh, Barbra and Jenna—wouldn't it be great? Their Father is fucking the country, and you're fucking them! (Twins count as one girl, because according to the rules of porno twin girls always have sex together.)

So your brother died in Iraq and you just lost your job, what a better way to stick it to old W. then to whip out your weapon of mass destruction and spew a little biological warfare on his baby girls!

Aim & Trajectory:

Make them kneel before you like you're the Prince of Saudi Arabia and cum between them, making sure to spread ample amounts on both 1st Sluts.

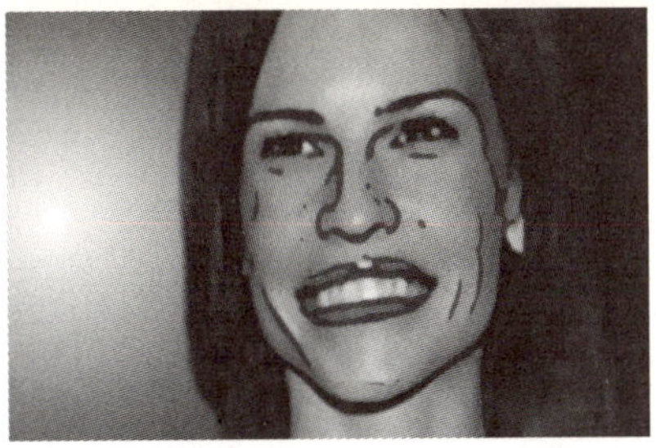

7. Hillary Swank

The seventh girl whose face I'd like to cum on is Hillary Swank. "I grew up in a trailer park." So act like it, bitch. Nothing is more irritating than some big Hollywood starlet who tries to pretend like she comes from the streets.

Aim & Trajectory:

Point straight and aim for those big white choppers of hers. Bulls-eye! Try to cum on her Oscar statue too— just so it's extra demeaning for her.

6. Sponge Bob Square Pants

The sixth girl whose face I'd like to come on is Sponge Bob Square Pants. I'm not sure if technically it's female or male, but I just think it would be cool to cum on Sponge Bob Square Pant's face because you could dump loads into it and it would absorb the cum all up! That's pretty neat.

Aim & Trajectory:

Spooging on a sponge is a lot like spooging into a thousand tiny open mouths. Incidentally Sponge Bob Square Pants would be great for a bukkake Party.

5. Cindy Crawford

The fifth girl whose face I'd like to cum on is Cindy Crawford. A little old school, but that mole gives you a great target to shoot for. Always a classic.

Aim & Trajectory:

Have you ever been taking a leek standing up at a toilet, and there is a small piece of shit stuck to the bowl, and you try to wash it off with your whiz? Yeah, well try to do the same with Cindy's mole.

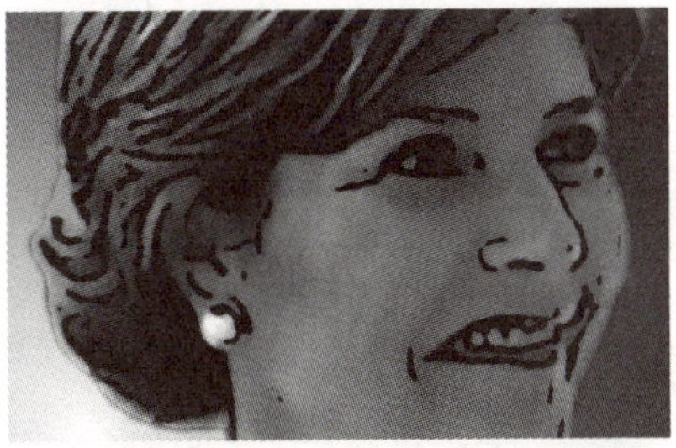

4. Laura Bush

The fourth girl whose face I'd like to cum on is Laura Bush. Right in the Oval Orifice, Monica style. It would be sweet.

Aim & Trajectory:

Walk up to her while she is sitting on the couch, watching the news, and cum on her face without warning. This move is known as "The Pre-emptive Strike"— also referred to in some circles as "The W."

3. The Olsen Twins

The third girl(s) whose face I'd like to cum on are The Olsen Twins. Another twofer. The anorexic one needs a little protein, so I'd be helping her out. They are finally 18, but when you're stroking your meat over their gaping mouths try not to picture them in their infant *Full House* glory days 'cause that's kind of creepy.

Aim & Trajectory:

Grab your snake and wring it back and fourth like a gardening hose, drenching them in your demon seed. That would make Uncle Joey proud.

2. Natalie Portman

Queen Amidala needs to get cummed on Jedi style. Who here (who didn't sleep through *Episode I...*) thought to themselves how great it would be to take out your light saber and splatter some spunk all over Natalie's makeup-caked face?

Aim & Trajectory:

From across the room use the Force to lunge your nut butter at her. Right in the face.

1. Barbara Bush

And the number one girl whose face I'd like to cum on is Barbra Bush. The wife of a president and the mother of a president, she has a face just begging to be cummed on. Personally, I would fill those wrinkled crevices with the finest man batter fit for a First Lady. Good old Babs.

Aim & Trajectory:

Aim for that beautiful head of white hair. That way, her head full of semen will go unnoticed until she is at some important banquet, meeting with heads of state, then all of a sudden a pound of baby batter starts making its way down her forehead and all over her dress. That would be pretty cool. ■

Hand Job PUPPET
HEY KIDS-- DO YOU LIKE...
SPANKING THE SALAMI?
CHOKING THE CHICKEN?
FLOGGING THE BISHOP?
POLISHING THE POLE?
HAND STARTING THE ONE EYED YOGURT THROWER?
NOW IN RIGHT AND LEFT HANDED VERSIONS!
YOUR KIT INCLUDES LIPSTICK!
*Hand not supplied
ONLY 58¢
MOM WON'T KNOW A THING!
PLUS $75.00 FOR HANDLING (NO PUN)
CHEERLEADER
TEACHER
BABY-SITTER
CUTE MOM NEXT DOOR
ALL NEW CELEBRITY VERSIONS
BRITNEY
J-LOAD
MARTHA
BEYONCE
1 HOUR FREE TRIAL!
INVITE YOUR FRIENDS TO A
HAND-JOB PUPPET SHOW!!
LOADS OF FUN!!
THE HAND JOB PUPPET IS NOT FOUND IN STORES!!
COMING SOON... THE LADY FINGER!!
MAIL COUPON NOW
Jerkin Le Gherkin
P.O. Box 278594763726
Handinfist NJ
DON'T JERK ME AROUND!
Rush me my HAND-JOB-PUPPET! If not fully satisfied within ten minutes of receiving the HAND-JOB-PUPPET, than vigorously shake and try again or try watching reruns of Baywatch and if that doesn't work, try your left hand and whisper sweet nothings to yourself or see your doctor, hopefully a hot chick. Not liable for chafing or lewd conduct
Name____________________
Address____________________ $____________________
WRITTEN BY ROBERT STEVEN RHINE ART BY JIM SMITH TYPE BY FRANK FORTE

Blowjobs And You

by Jake Serlen

Ah blowjobs. Has there ever been such a wondrous invention so near and dear to the male heart despite being some 2 to 24 inches away, depending on your race? As a man of our age, I have had the privy of dating many a girl, with many a lack or many a surplus of sexual inhibitions. Regardless of which pole the woman gravitates to, blowjobs generally call their true feelings on sex and themselves to the forefront. At the furthest ends of the suck off spectrum are two diametrically opposed groups that are actually both wrong in their own ways. As they are women, this should surprise no one. As a man, I will take it upon myself to show these poor misguided creatures the error of their ways.

1. The No-Blowjobs-Period Group

This group needs no introduction. They also need no second date, no first date, and you should tell the waiter to bring you two checks if you discover she is part of this group at dinner. How such women exist in this day and age is not really a mystery, just an example of poor restraint. We would have bred out the No-Blowjob gene during the Age of Enlightenment if not for Marx's now famous manifesto *An Argument for the Equal Distribution of Pussy.* Damn Commies.

The predominate reason women give for their unpopular stance is that the act is degrading to women. This is, of course, completely true. However, ladies need to recognize the caliber of this powerful weapon. A good blowjob will get you far in this world, right to the top. I know many women resent the notion that if they have a position of authority it is because they sucked their way there. But, the only reason a man will accuse them of this is because if we could blow our way to the top, I would already own a yacht called the S.S. Semen In My Hair.

Jesus, too, would prefer all women to be enthusiastic cocksuckers. If nuns were as enthusiastic about giving blowjobs as priests, Protestants would never have existed.

2. The You-Know-What-I-Could-Go-For?-A-Dick-In-My-Mouth Group

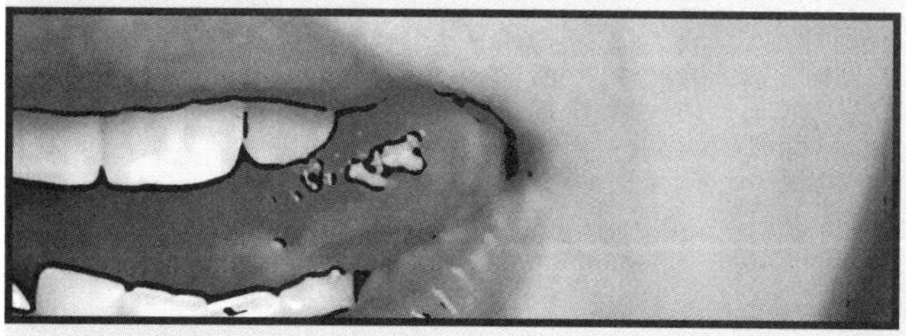

Always the more popular of the two groups and God bless them for it. These are the women we want to date, and don't want our mothers or daughters to be. A dream come true wrapped in a wish upon a star nestled in soul sold to the devil. The man who meets this women is a king amongst men. And she, his cum-guzzling queen.

But let's not get too far ahead of ourselves. As my enthusiasm for these girls has already let on, the women in this group know their power. They have a particular call to alert you in case you are trying to identify one these women. It is a simple sentence that goes something like this, "Everyone tells me that I give the best blowjob in the world," or something similar. This sentence tells you three things 1. This woman belongs to the second group 2. She's had more pricks in her mouth than a Parkinson's sufferer eating a bowl full of needles, and 3. Every man has lied to her.

Finally, we reach my point, and it's for the ladies. Every girl who doesn't mind giving blowjobs, will—thanks in large part to compliments from spooge-depleted boyfriends—claim to give the world's greatest blowjob. This is not so. Sure we will say that you gave the best one, but the reason is simple: women like compliments, they like to show off, and they did it once, so they might do it again. The worst blowjob in the world, full of razor teeth, a dry mouth heated to a thousand degrees, with a tongue made of sand paper is still better than a hand job and we will say whatever we can to ensure another.

But not all hope is lost. For the truly determined slut, I now present to you a 20-point checklist of things you can do to keep a solid blowjob game. You may still not give the best in the world, but I'd like to be the judge of that.

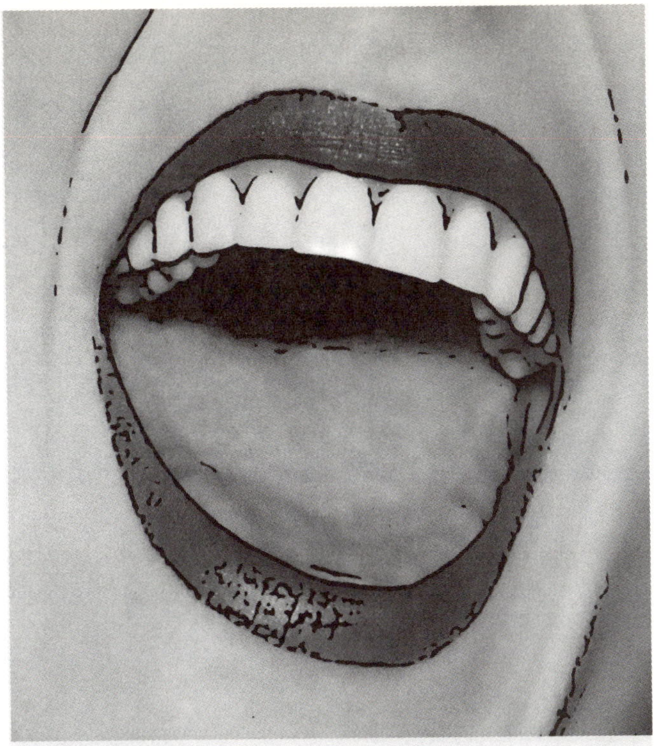

1. Mouth Usage

The term Blowjob is misleading. No matter how hard you blow, all that cold air will make the erection go away. A mouth for a blowjob is just like an ugly person: it's the inside that counts.

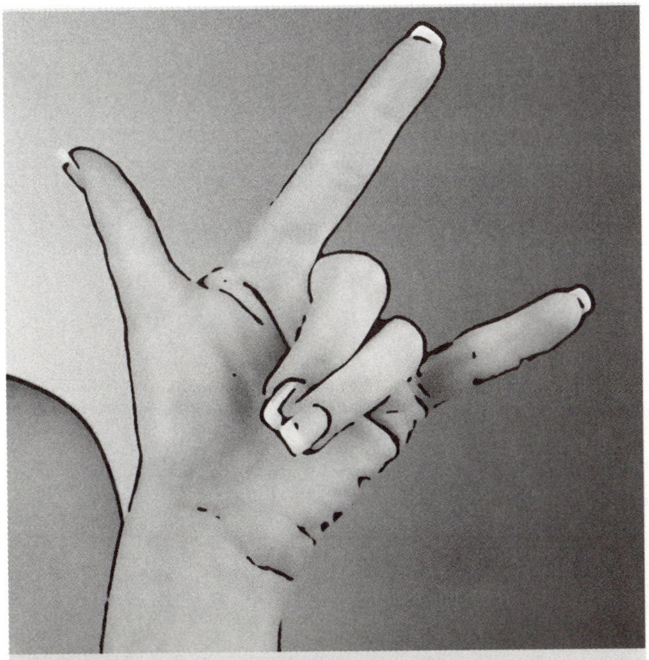

2. Hand Placement

Where's your hand? If it's not someplace where you would wash your hand after touching it, you're doing something wrong.

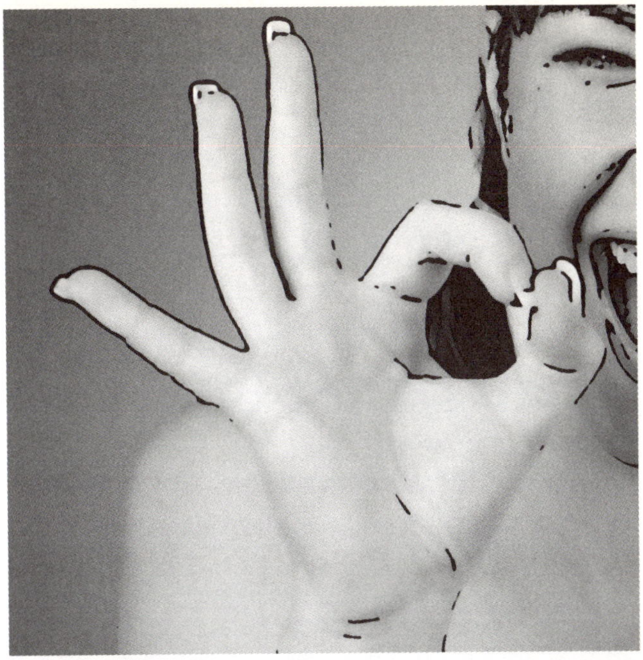

3. Hand Movement

Wax on, wax off, wax on, wax off. Mr. Miyagi rikey very much.

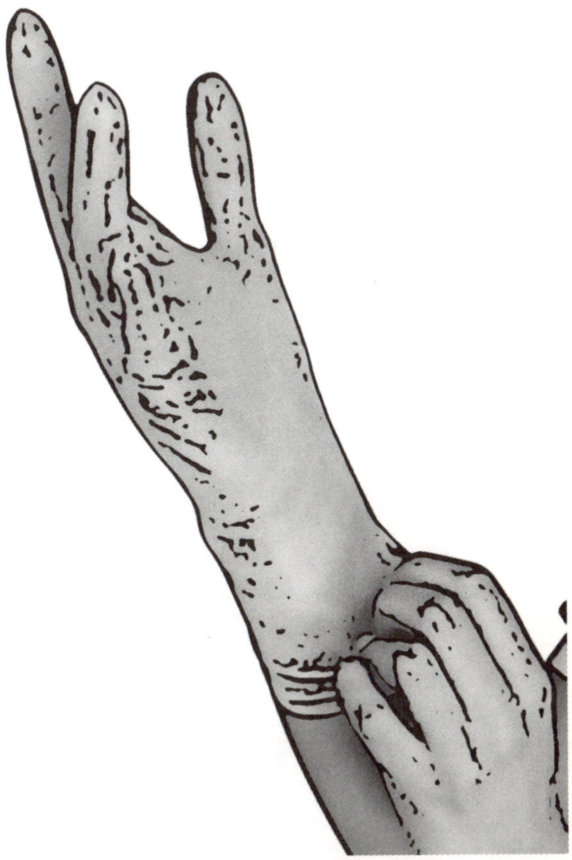

4. The Mid Blowjob Hand Job Break

What the hell are you doing? Endurance. Practice. Yes, your saliva is a nice lubricant, but guess what, so is mine. Get back to work!

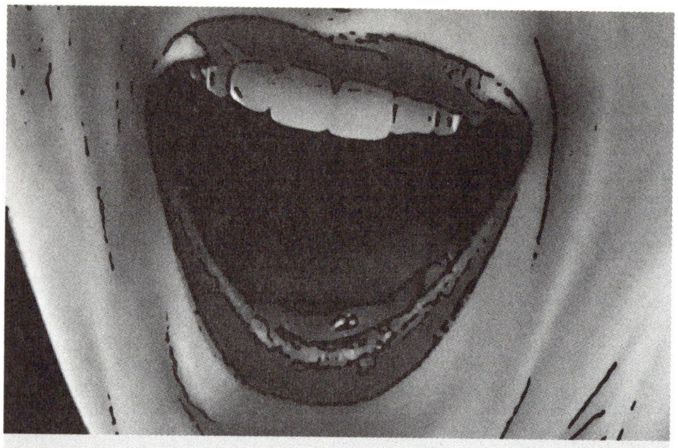

5. Jaw Placement

Open wide, and **the wider the better**. A penis avoiding teeth is like playing a reverse version of Operation. Don't touch the sides! BZZZZ!!

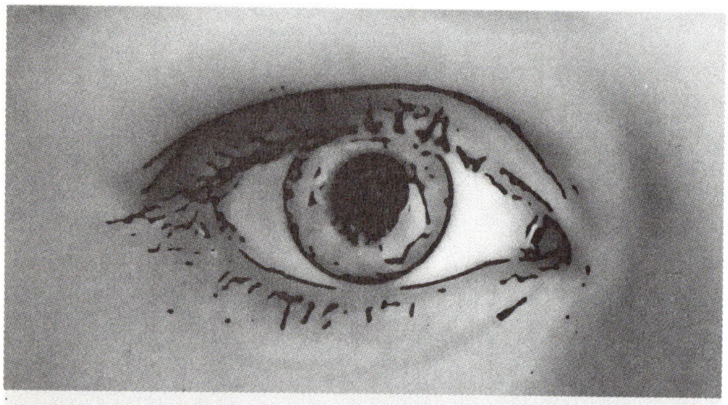

6. Eye Contact

You should rub your eyes all over my dick. It's just what I'm into.

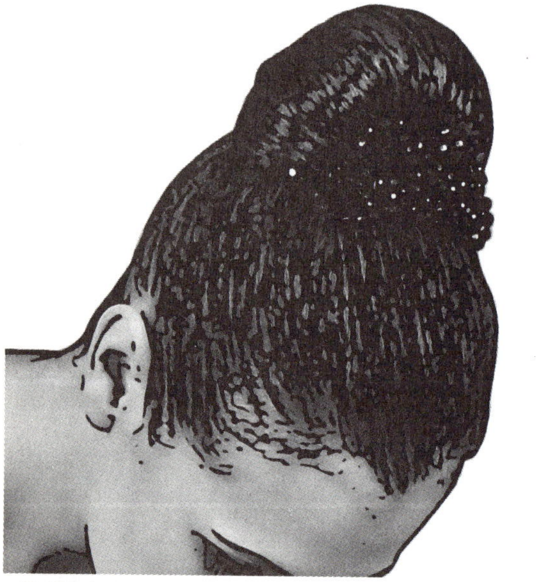

7. Hair Position

Move it out of the way, I want to see what's going on. TIP: If you tie it in a bun on your head, it will give us something to hold onto. It's like the joystick to the best video game EVER!

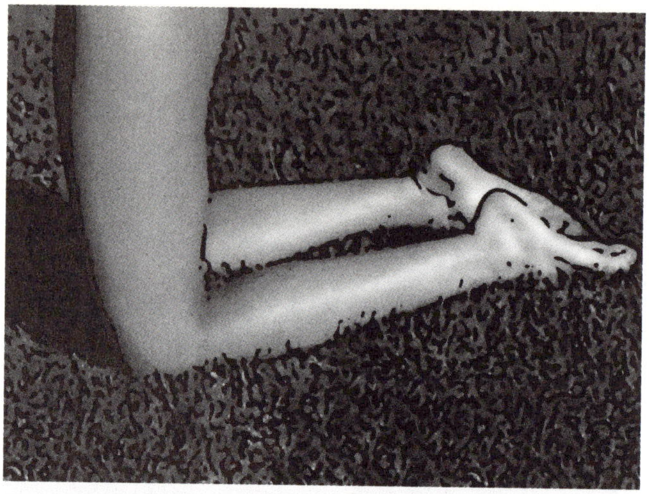

8. Location, Location, Location

Inside is hot. Outside is hotter. And the hotness factor climbs with the risk of being caught. Level 1: office restroom all the way to Level 42: The Oval Office.

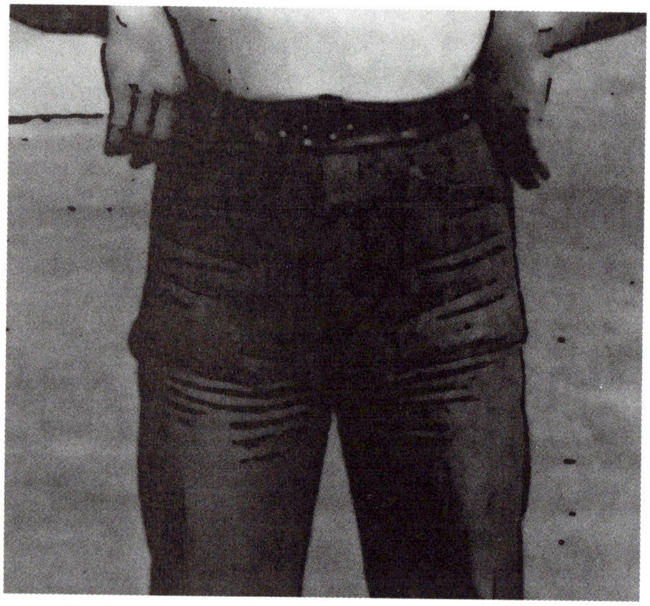

9. Clothes

A nudey blowjob is fun. But a clothed blowjob is dirty. Therefore, the most fun.

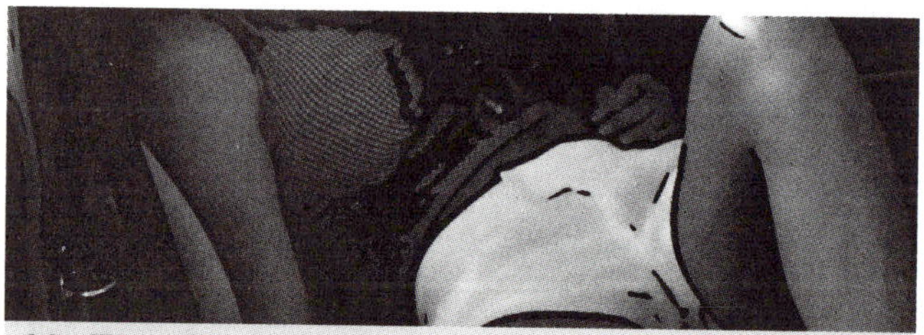

10. The Car

Ahh, road head. Nothing can break up the monotony of a twelve-hour car ride quite like it. If you don't like the directions so far, nearly all rules are exempt when blowing in the car. All rules are exempt if the woman is also driving.

11. Body Position

By and far, the most degrading position is with the man standing up and the woman on her knees. So do that.

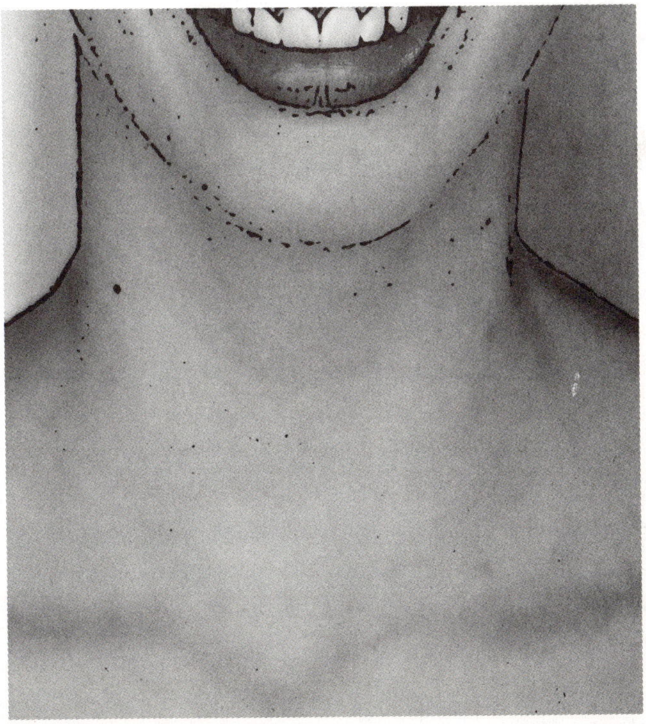

12. Deep Throating

Get as much of it as far down as possible. For those with gag reflex, an empty stomach is recommended.

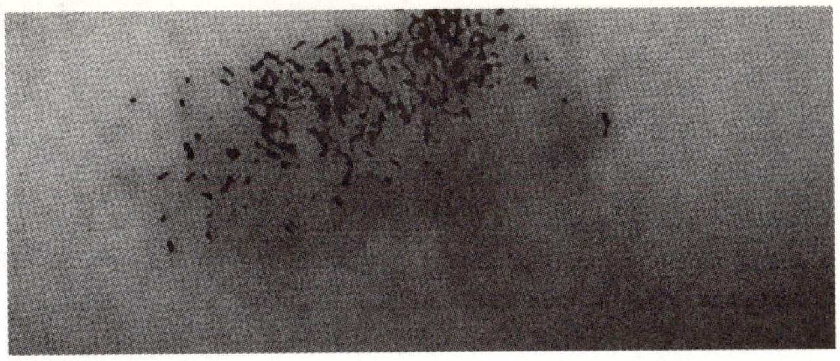

13. Hickeys

I know you think a cock hickey is a cute way to remind me of the fun we had. However, after another night of binge drinking, waking up with an **alien red splotch on my dick** is not very reassuring. I thought the pills kept that shit in remission.

14. Humming

The "mmmmm" sounds make vibrations and that's a good thing. Still, don't patronize me with moans like you enjoy what this thing tastes like. I endorse humming a tune. "I've Been Working on the Railroad" is a stalwart classic.

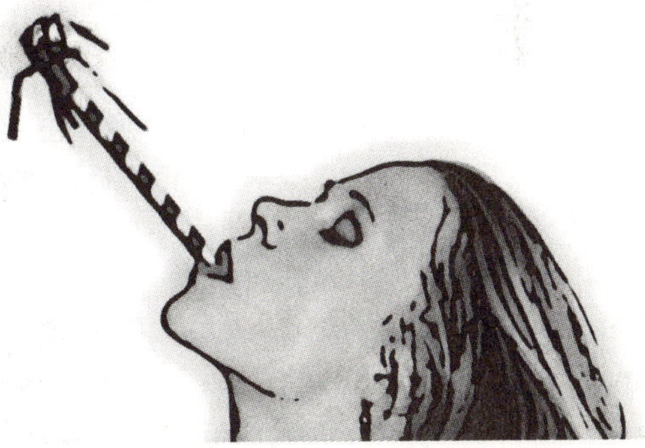

15. Sperm Time

Congratulations. Your reward for a blowjob well done. **Drink in good health!** Or failing that, wear it like make up. Either way.

Did you get all fifteen? No. That's okay. For those of experience, hopefully you've picked up a new trick. And for those who have not yet partaken, I encourage you, go and try out what you've learned. Who knows? You might just like it.

I'm kidding, you won't. But I sure will.

And that's what's important. ■

10 Men For Whom I Would Consider Turning Gay

by Michael Null

I, like all post-pubescent heterosexual males have, at one time or another, entertained the notion that I may be homosexual. It went something like this:

"Am I gay? No. No I'm not."

Years after arriving at the conclusion that I am in fact heterosexual, I compiled a list of ten men with whom I would have a very open, very real relationship with, as an exercise in happenstance. Perhaps one day, I'll become bored with women and no longer find them attractive. Or, more likely, women will become bored with me, and I'll have to branch out.

Were any of the men on this list to leave their current lives for me, they could expect man/man love in its purest form, the kind described by Oscar Wilde. We would drink by the fire. We'd go to small intimate restaurants and discuss politics, literature, and the waiter's faux pas of wearing brown shoes with a black belt. We'd avoid awkward incidental touches of our hands while we walk down the avenue together. Occasionally, we'd go to a play—never once caring who sees us or what they may think. "This is true love," I'd say to our detractors, "so never mind the limp. I'm sort of new at this."

Although I have no proclivity for physical relations with any man, period, the very possibility that such a profound connection could exist betwixt myself and any of these men allows me to entertain the possibility of sex. For this reason, I would become a heavy drinker. Should the topic arise in casual chatter at bedtime, I'd retire to my study with a bottle of 16-year-old single malt Scotch and return to the boudoir one or two hours later. After that, whatever happens, happens.

However, before I get ahead of myself, I should compile this list.

As with any assemblage of hypotheticals, concessions and omissions were made cautiously and precisely. For instance, Jesus does not appear on this list. "What an obvious choice!" you say, but He would be completely unavailable to me emotionally, and I would have to share Him with the rest of the world. Plus, He'd always be tired. Also the Bible skips any explanation of the bulk of His twenties. During this period, no doubt, He was able to amass all of the baggage required for Him to believe that the sins of the world are on His shoulders. This is not something I am able to deal with right now.

Einstein was omitted for the mere fact that he has become cliché. What a horrible and lonely thing it must be—to have been one of the greatest minds in history, but ineligible to receive my love because everyone wants to have you over for dinner.

Other notables who barely missed the cut include Johan Guttenberg, because I'd never be able to get the ink stains out of the linens; Benjamin Franklin, because he may be just a bit too worldly, plus every time a *Poor Richard's* weather forecast is accurate, I'd get a smug "see...I told you it was gonna rain today;" Shakespeare, because I have yet to hear conclusive evidence as to whether or not he wrote his body of work solely himself, and if he in fact did, I'd never be able to get the ink stains out of the linens.

Also, I briefly considered David Koresh, because, hey—what if he was right? He was swiftly cut for the same reasons as Jesus, and for the fact that he was probably just crazy. (However, just in case he was right, I was totally kidding about the crazy thing, Lord!)

Finally, the most difficult omission was that of renowned astrophysicist Steven Hawking. He seemed to have it all: brilliant, quite witty, and most importantly, I'm pretty sure his penis doesn't work. Mr. Hawking fell a bit short, though, because he would easily have been able to provide me complex formulae describing precisely how insignificant I am. Between my parents and myself, this is pretty well taken care of. Additionally, if we were to coin affectionate pet names for one another, his for me would be cleverly hidden within a complex rational function, which only four other people on the planet could solve. The best I am able to come up with for him so far is Wheels. Plus, I don't think I'd be able to get the axle grease out of the linens.

But I digress again. And so:

The List of Names Which I Dare Speak: (In no particular order)

1. Ed McMahon

Legendary sidekick. He's always drunk, and he's obligated to laugh at everything I say. Sometimes, you just need a bitch.

2. Ed Asner

TV's Lou Grant. I have visions of braiding his back hair into ornate Native patterns.

3. Henry Kissinger

Brilliant statesman who helped to open China to U.S. trade. He also has a sultry accent that at once frightens and excites. Mostly I'm curious what he would sound like when achieving orgasm.

4. 5. and 6. Fatty Arbuckle

Silent movie star and brilliant comedian. He damn near tore a young starlet in half during drunken sex. They call him Fatty for a reason. I think I'd just like the challenge…it wouldn't be nearly as interesting if his name were Tank Arbuckle.

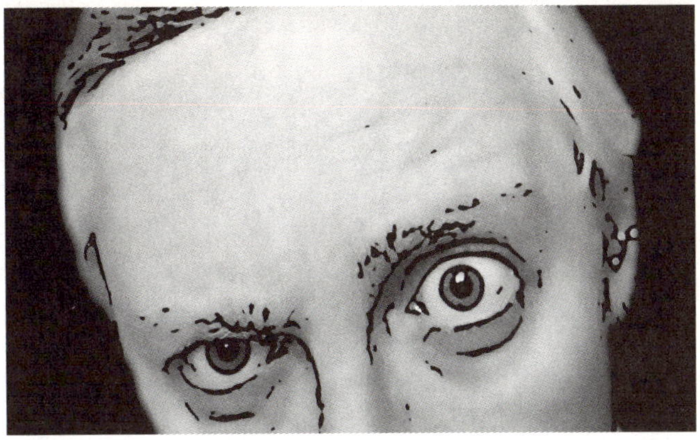

7. Ed Jablomsky

My mailman. You don't know him, but trust me, he's one hell of a guy. And always on time—that's important.

8. Britney Spears

I have no personal definitive proof that she is, in fact, a woman, so I just want to have all my bases covered.

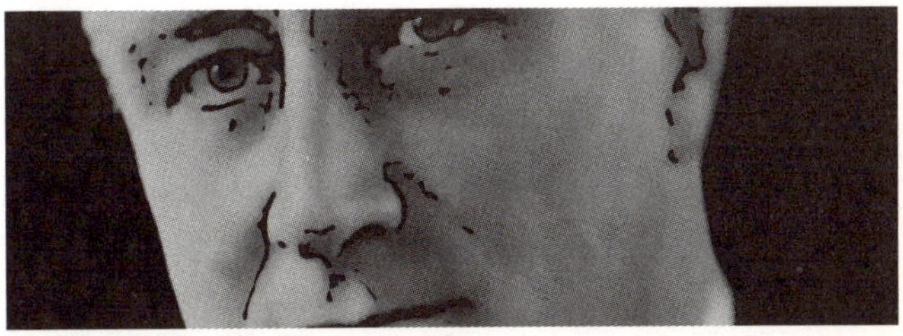

9. Franklin D. Roosevelt

In my opinion, the greatest U.S. president. Also, I'm pretty sure his penis doesn't work.

10. Bob Newhart

Only 3 Dicks Away from 10,000th Blowjob

by Matthew Hannigan

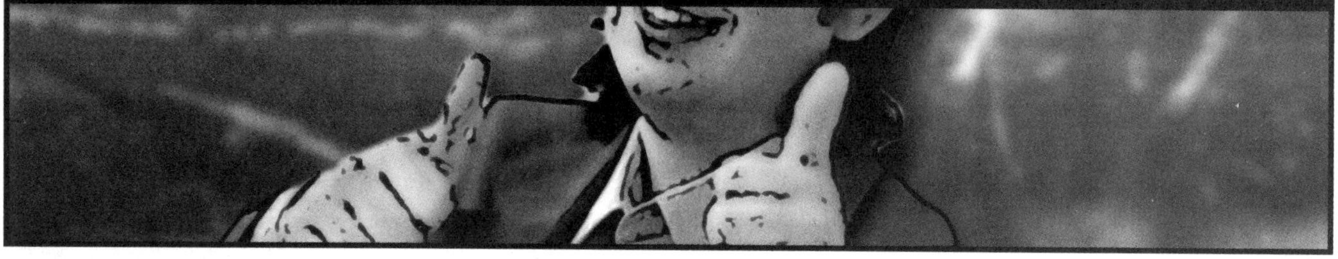

Wow, I'm just three dicks away from my 10,000th blowjob. Honestly, I never thought I'd get past the first one, but here I am at 9,997 blowjobs. Yep, 10,000 here I come. I can just taste it.

You know, it's funny. Contrary to what 9,997 dicks might imply, I'm not even gay. Nope, all man (I even crap standing up). But you get drunk, one of your buddies dares you, you say yes, and the rest is history. Hey, not my idea of a good time, but a dare's a dare. You just gotta suck it up and deal with it.

I'll tell ya, one blowjob is a big enough dare if you're not into dick, but my God, 10,000? What was I thinking? I once tried to piece it all together and I believe it went something like this, "Hey Matt, I dare you to suck a dick." And then I said, "You call that a dare? Make it 10,000 dicks." I suppose, that was it. Oh whiskey, you are the devil!

As I (give) head for this milestone, I'm trying to think what the worst part was... I guess I'd have to say, all of it. First, I've got this horrible gag reflex. I mean, I can barely swallow an Advil and here I was putting penises in my mouth. Let's just say the first customer wasn't too happy. What else? Oh, the taste. My God, penises taste awful —like the way a monkey would taste if you ate it raw. I still cringe and I've had nearly 10,000 of them. So yeah, there's that and, oh, pubic hair. Yeah, pubes reek. I mean, I thought men shaving down there was kind of gay, but then I suck a lot of dick so what do I know? What else? Ah, semen. It's not so much the taste as the consistency. I'm not quite sure how to describe it. I guess it's kind of like animal fat mixed with Crisco, but not. And I guess that's about it. Oh wait! One more thing. While most guys are cool about it, every once in a while I'd get these jerks who'd be like, "That's right bitch, suck it." And I'd have to stop and say, "Look, if you call me a bitch one more time we're done." God, that annoyed me. Where do these people get off? Ha, don't answer that!

In some ways I'm pretty proud of myself. Sure I've been giving blowjobs to strangers I met at gas stations, but most importantly, I set a goal and I'm three dicks away from reaching it.. Think about it: It wasn't like I had to eat 10,000 ice cream cones. Where would the challenge in that be? No my friends, we're talking blowjobs: sticky, smelly, vomit-inducing blowjobs.

Would I do it again? Now, that's a tough one. I mean, sure, at the moment I'm kind of proud of myself, but I certainly didn't always feel this way. It wasn't until my like 8,000th blowjob that I finally felt ok with it. For the first 300 I cried myself to sleep wondering what the hell I've become. After the next 1,000 I was pretty much dead inside. Then eventually sucking dick just became a way of life, like it's what God put me on this Earth to do. I lost my self, my identity. It was like I was a machine, a dick-sucking machine. But you know, I'm better now... Still, the question remains: would I do it again? I'm going to have to say probably not. Not quite 100% but mostly no.

You know what else is interesting? You'd think the sore jaw would bother me the most. Wrong! It was actually my *knees*. Yeah, they were killing me, and I was such an idiot about it, too. You'd think after the 700th blowjob it would occur to me to get a pillow or something. Nooo, not me. It wasn't until my 6,311th blowjob (yep, I remember this perfectly) that the guy I was sucking off goes, "Dude what's the matter? You look awful." And I'm thinking like, 'Fuck you buddy, it's not like I'm enjoying myself here. I don't need your shit right now.' But, for some reason, I was cool about it and said, "It's my knees, they're killing me." And he's like, "Why not take your jacket off and use it as a cushion?" I'm such a knucklehead! Oh Julio. He was great.

So, there you have it, three more to go. Oh, one more thing, this is funny. My friend John, the guy who dared me, says to me yesterday, "Hey Matt, you do realize that I meant guys named Dick, right?. I hope those 9,994 guys (Right, it was 9,994 at that point. I blew the pizza delivery guy late last night and a couple of garbage men this morning.) were all named Dick." And I was like, "Ahhh, no." And then after like ten seconds of silence while looking serious and surprised at my confusion, he goes, "Gotcha!" Boy I was about to kill him. That guy. When it's his turn, I'm so gonna use my teeth... ■

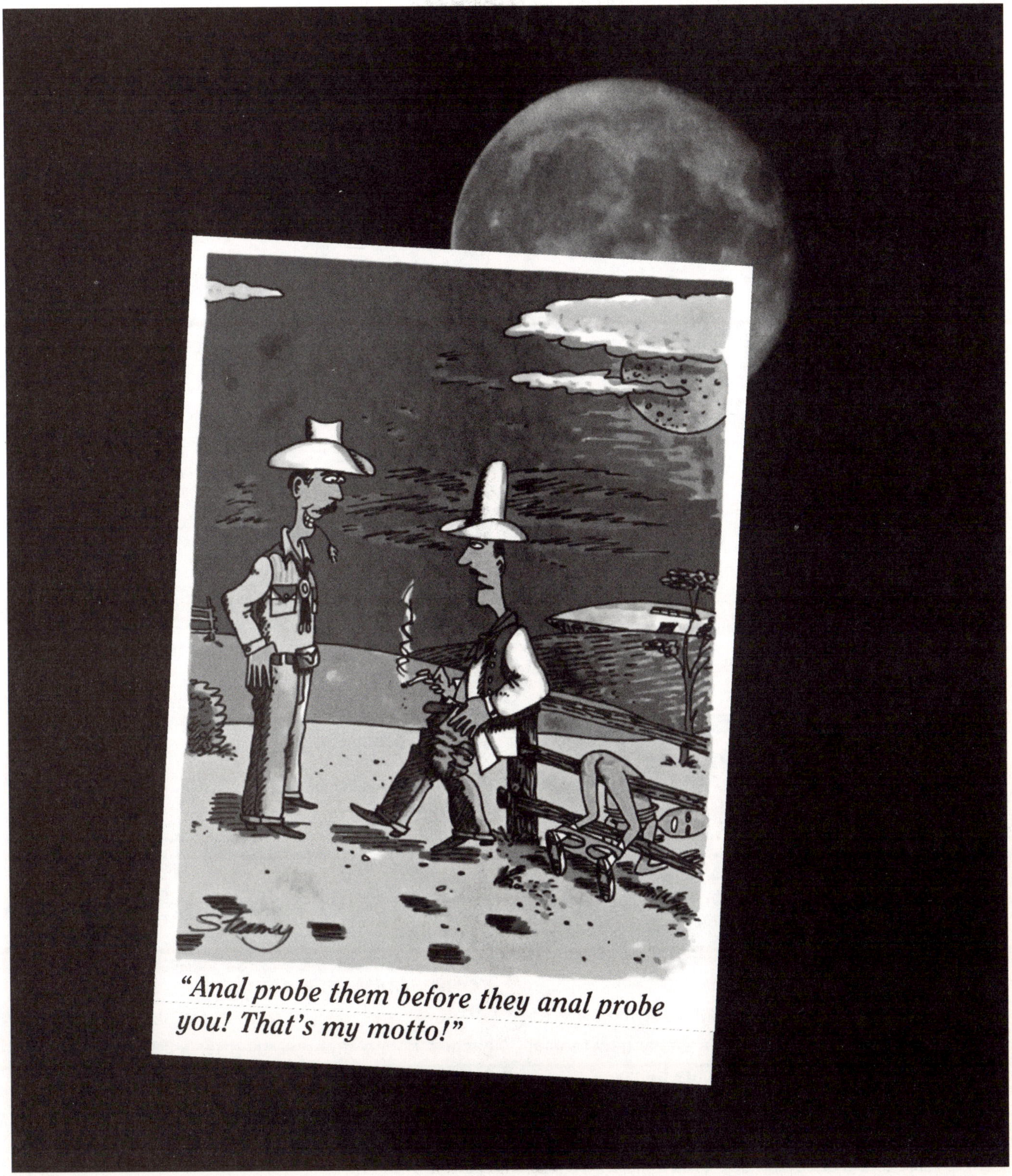

"Anal probe them before they anal probe you! That's my motto!"

10 Girls & 10 Guys Worth Fucking

by Taii K. Austin & N.L. Staff

Ladies—

Before you die or get married—I know, semantics!—there should be a good amount of strategic fucking under your belt, so to speak. Not a *dangerous* amount, just enough to embarrass your parents and impress your friends. Except the "whore" friend—she's just gross, and anything you do that she hasn't done will get you arrested, committed, or booty-called by Charlie Sheen.

To make this task easier, I've compiled a list of *guy profiles* which every single woman should fuck. Make sure you check them off—before you check out.

A PUERTO RICAN

Ask any woman who has slept with, dated, or walked closely by a Puerto Rican dude and she will testify that there is something wired in their DNA (or Goya) that makes them insatiable lovers and eaters of the poon.

As my friend Aaliyah so aptly put it, "Puerto Rican men are raised to love the pussy. It's like a fruit in their culture." Amen.

A MARRIED MAN

Because you're *his* fantasy. Married men are so ungodly bored that all it takes is a sassy new toenail polish to send them into a passionate frenzy.

For those days when you want to get laid but are too lazy to exert any effort at all, call a married guy. It's impossible to disappoint him. That's his wife's job.

A VACATIONING EUROPEAN

He'll choose the perfect bottle of wine, then fuck you with it during foreplay. Like Polly-O string cheese...*c'est si bon!*

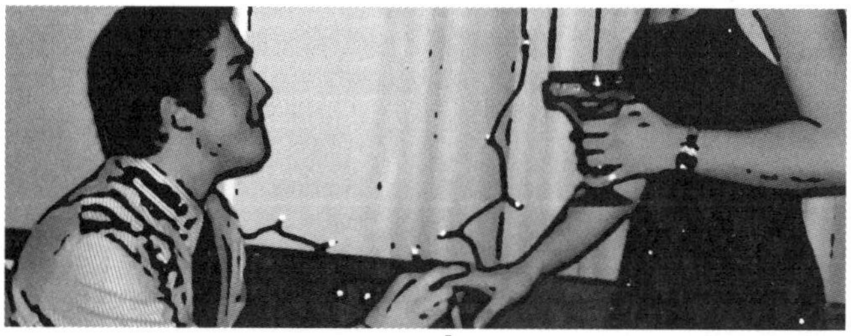

YOUR FRIEND'S FIANCÉ

Sure, she's cool now...but one day you *know* that bitch is gonna do something to piss you off and the only appropriate response is, "That's why I fucked your fiancé at your grandparents' shore house!"

See if she ever forgets to put the cap on your shampoo again.

SUPER RELIGIOUS VIRGIN

You can try out all the freaky shit you've wanted to do with other guys, without the fear of disease. Then afterward he can pray for you. And the goldfish.

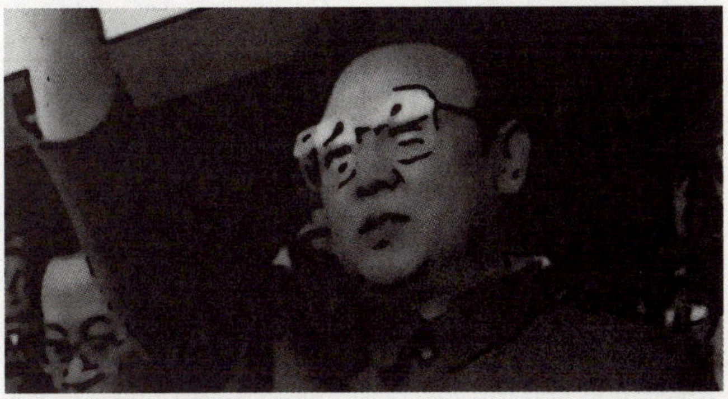

FOREIGN ROYALTY

Because he was born with more money than all those rock stars and pro athletes you're scheming on combined. Don't use protection with this one.

If you get knocked up, you can tell everyone at the Hamburger Hideout to kiss your royal ass.

A MAN TWENTY YEARS OLDER THAN YOU

If he's *that* old and not married, not looking to get married, and straight—his only mission in life is to be as studly as possible before the bell starts a-tollin'.

Bonus points if it's your friend's dad. *Double* bonus points if it's my friend Phil's dad. Seriously, Mr. Michaelsen, say the word and it's on!

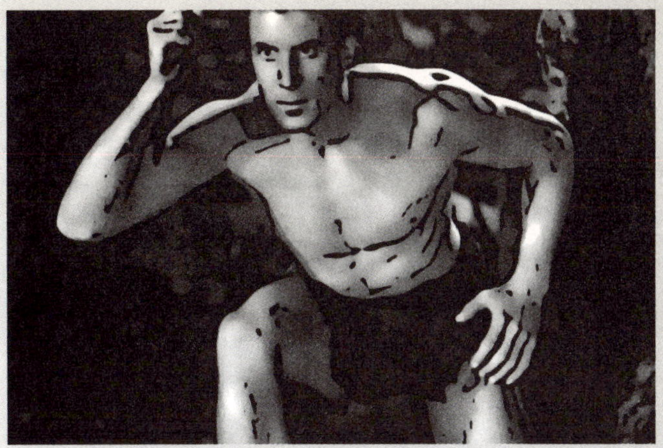

A GUY ORPHANED AT A YOUNG AGE

Post-coitus, you can whine about your Daddy issues without being interrupted.

A TERMINALLY ILL MAN

No danger of long-term attachment. Fresh flowers at the ready. Free rent while "housesitting" when he goes out of remission. *Hollaaaaaaaaa...*

GEORGE CLOONEY

Because he's George Fucking Clooney. Honestly, the man is 85 and still maddeningly sexy. He smolders. He fights for human rights. He has a house in Lake Como, Italy. I've never been to Italy, but I bet it's kickass if George has a house there. Because he has good taste. Which is why I am 100% sure he'll return my calls any day now.

Gentlemen—

The only thing more tedious than a man who can't get laid is a woman who can't get laid. Have we learned *nothing* from the comedy stylings of Sinbad? Women be *different* than men. They're like special needs students, so adrift in a roiling sea of glamour magazines they soon believe *everything* requires a detailed instruction manual—including the act of snaring a passable love interest. We'll not make that mistake here today.

Learn how to *make the first move*. Please find below a profile of different *girls* which every man should attempt to have sex with—at least once—over the course of his long and colorful life.

WANNA-BE PORN STARS

From Flickr to YouTube, from MySpace to "alternative" moo-cow barnyards like Suicide Girls, these days the easiest way to separate a girl from her clothing is with a camera.

Invest in the right equipment: set up a small studio in your one-bedroom apartment and secure a disposable cardboard instamatic. Promise them their very own web page and the ability to set up a "wish list."

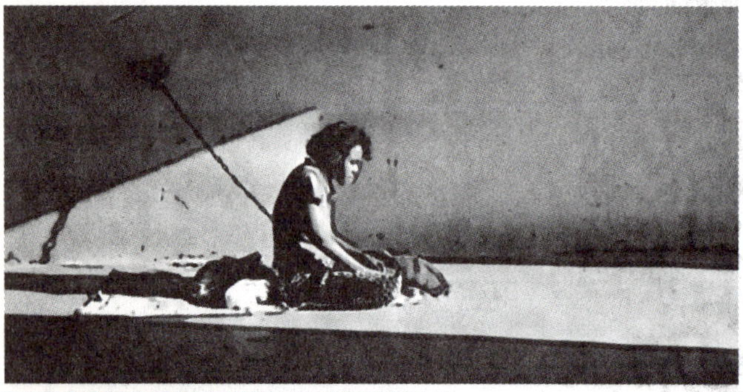

DISASSOCIATIVE DAMSELS

After a lifetime of childhood abuse, unrequited loves, unspeakable family traumas, physical neglect, awkward schooling periods, and haphazardly-dashed expectations, eighty-five percent of American females develop *multiple personality disorder*.

Don't be too quick to dismiss a psychologically distressed young lady with numerous self-identities—she may be the closest you ever get to a threesome.

GIRLS ON CRAIGSLIST

Ever wonder why they're called *personal* ads? Cause women take 'em so goddamn serious-like. Craigslist is a veritable, modern-day cracker barrel of lonely, uptight whores who fancy themselves artists, musicians, and graphic designers. *You're going to call me tomorrow, right?* You bet I am! *Click*.

THE VEGETARIAN or VEGAN

A vegan diet is an *eating disorder*—a warped body image resulting from a woman's desperate and repeated attempts to control at least *one* aspect of her otherwise uninteresting life by shopping at Whole Foods.

This summer, why not spend an evening stuffing her ridiculously self-righteous mouth with savory Ball Park franks? Don't act like you don't know what I'm talking about.

COMEDIENNES

Shopping for shoes? Her addiction to chocolate? Trying on bathing suits underneath fluoresecent lights? *LADY, GET THE FUCK OFF THE STAGE*.

After a horrible ten-minute set, in the tearful privacy of her rinky-dink hotel room, she's going to need someone who can just hold her for a little while.

Might that be you?

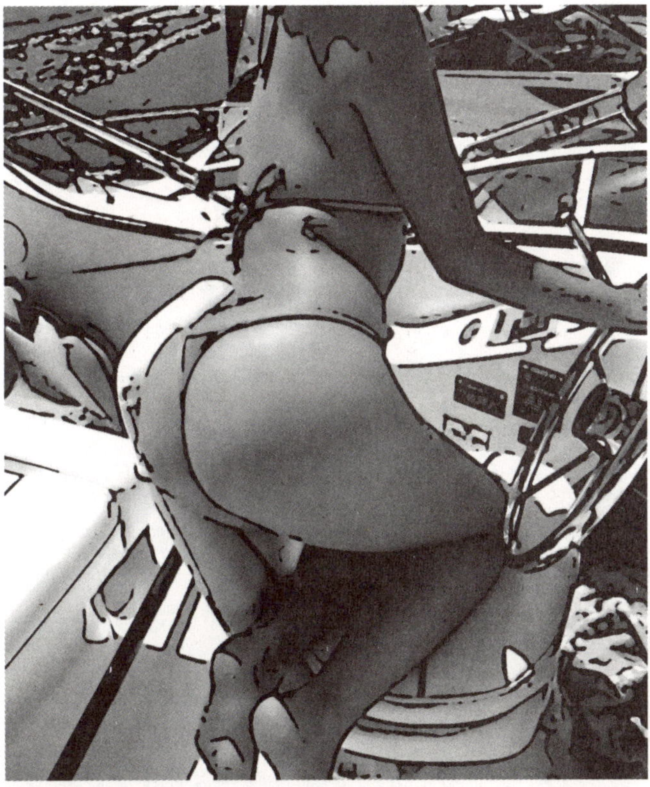

YOUR WIFE

Your *what?* Your *wife*. Indeed, you'll find yourself married some day— if only to sustain the illusion that you're a viable adult. After a prolonged courtship, extended honeymoon and suburban settling-in period, the intercourse will slow down and then cease altogether.

Eventually you'll be forced to regard your *spouse* as a potential conquest—and guess what*? She's legally obligated* to keep the peace! God bless these fifty United States.

A LESBIAN

However "wickedly cool" you think lesbians are, they can't dress themselves for shit and they all decorate their houses with the same kitschy, Tex Mex bric-a-brac you'd expect to find in a *Chili's* restaurant.

In short, they're *guys*—which means they're not particularly observant. Squeeze yourself into a cheap sundress, smear your face up with lipstick, and start making friends at the local dyke bar. Once under the sheets, refer to your penis as a strap-on.

THE BLOW-UP DOLL

Wait a minute: her mouth is *open* but no horrible honking sounds are coming out. Is this some sort of crazy upside-down alternative backwards-land universe?

Not at all—just the latest technological innovation in relationship management.

THE LADIES OF IRAN

You know those guys who are inexplicably drawn toward Japanese manga characters wearing insipid schoolgirl uniforms? Over the next decade, prepare for a wave of global fascination with Iranian women and their oddly uncomfortable burkas.

Finally, a full-body condom for the fairer sex.

THE CRACK WHORE

So she likes inhaling the heated vapors of crack cocaine *and* she's not wholly against exchanging your crisp, clean twenty-dollar bill for privatized sexual services.

Big deal. Drugs and sex are *supposed* to work together—like peanut butter and jelly. A crack whore is a *person with feelings*. When your business transaction has mercifully concluded, you don't have to send her away mad! Just send her away.

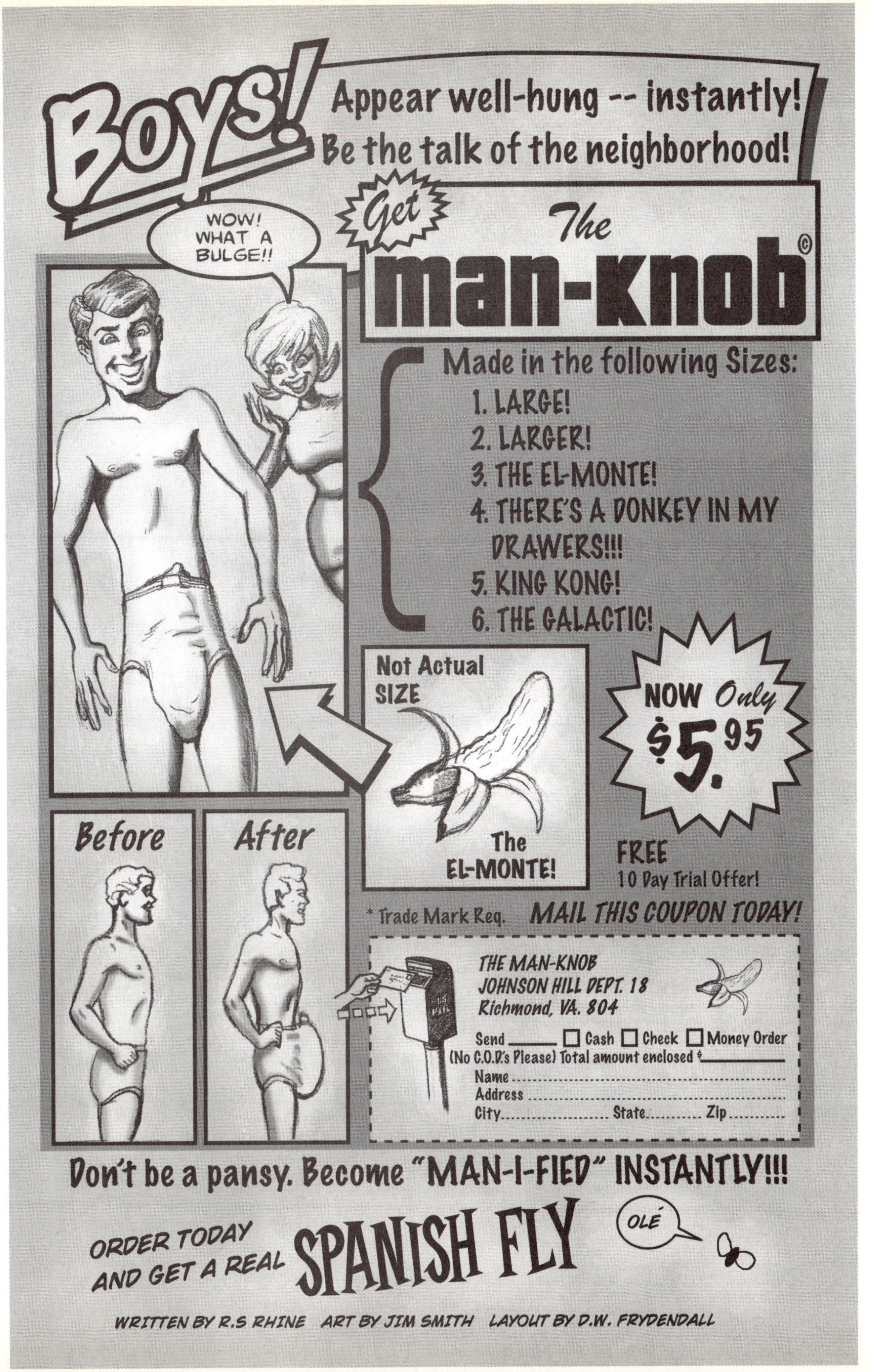

WRITTEN BY R.S RHINE   ART BY JIM SMITH   LAYOUT BY D.W. FRYDENDALL

Cock Blocking And You

by Marcus Terry

No one likes to be cock-blocked. It's annoying and counterproductive. However, cock-blocking is an art form. True, it is not seen that way by the many men who have fallen victim to a well played cock-block. But those who do the actual blocking of the cock understand that it is a science, and that the best cock-blockers are highly skilled individuals.

To ease the plight of misunderstood cock-blockers everywhere I'm going to explain the basics of cock blockery.

First, there are the four fundamental rules:

1. Never cock-block a friend unless specifically requested by said friend.

2. Respect any successful cock-block. If a guy takes away the girl you were talking to, let it go. You may have been working on her most of the night but she chose the other guy so just pack up your cock and move on.

3. Any guy hanging out with a group of girls is the Designated Cock-Bock (DCB).

4. When a cock-blocking is called for, anything goes. Just be careful not to cock-block yourself.

Once you're clear on the basics, feel free to deploy any of the 3 standard cock-blocks.

1. THE REQUESTED COCK-BLOCK

It occurs when a friend is trapped talking to or dancing with someone from whom they wish to get away. This situation usually arises when only one guy is hanging out with a group of girls, making said guy (you) the DCB (see also rule #3).

As the DCB ,it is your job to watch out for your lady friends. When one friend gives you the signal that she wants a guy to leave her alone that's your cue to pretend that you are the boyfriend that was just away at the bathroom. Then it's really fun to watch the guy backpedal and try to act like he wasn't hitting on "your girl."

2. THE MALICIOUS COCK-BLOCK

The second, more volatile, type of cock-block is the Malicious Cock-Block. This is when two or more guys who don't know each other are going after the same girl.

A very common form of Malicious Cock-Block is the "Dance Floor Sandwich." This occurs when you go to a club and see a girl you like dancing with another guy, so you go up and dance behind her. She loves it because now she's in the middle of the coveted Dance Floor Sandwich. She knows that both these guys want her and she gets to choose.

She'll dance with both of you for a while. But if you dance better than that other guy, if you have just a bit more rhythm, she'll turn and face you, making you The Chosen One. If the other guy is respectful of your cock-block he will concede and back off, dancing away into the cold loneliness.

At this point you have won the Dance Floor Sandwich but you can't let your guard down. The night is young and you have to watch out for other cock-blockers. That's why it is a smart idea to always have with you a cock-block blocker, or Wingman, to watch your back.

3. THE SELF COCK-BLOCK

The absolute worst kind of cock-block is the Self Cock-Block. Cock-blocking yourself means that you have done or said something so stupid or offensive that you ruined any chance you had of closing the deal. Maybe the girl was from Boston and you bad mouthed the Red Sox. Maybe you accidentally let it slip that the restraining order your ex put on you is only probationary. Or maybe she's a tree-hugging hippie vegan and you've got bits of hotdog stuck in your teeth. Either way, this girl is completely turned off.

If you're lucky, a self cock-block will only end with the girl politely walking away then laughing at you later with her friends. But if you really screw up you'll find yourself with a drink dumped over your head and a slap in the face. There is no recovery from a self cock-block. All you can do is walk away and hope your friends didn't see it.

Each of the three basic types of cock block is powerful in its own way. But each one can be battled and beaten. There is one cock block, however, of such immense power than no man can stand against it alone: The Ugly Friend.

The Ugly Friend does not adhere to any of the aforementioned rules of cock blocking, making her all the more dangerous and unpredictable. She will show no mercy, not even at the request of her friends. Her only mission is to make sure her cute friend goes home with her ugly ass, not you.

Because of her cold, mechanical brutality, the only way to get around The Ugly Friend is to contain her. Wrangling The Ugly Friend falls under the duties of the once again invaluable Wingman. It is the Wingman's job to distract The Ugly Friend by any means necessary, sometimes even feigning romantic interest. This is the most desperate method but it often proves to be the most effective for The Ugly Friend will not be thinking about blocking your cock if there is a prospect of attaining some cock for herself.

This expose only scratches the surface of the many faceted jewel that is cock-blocking. It would be almost impossible to fully explain this ancient art. I only hope that now you understand that a cock-block is something to be both hated and respected, feared and loved, for it is a necessary evil in our society. ■

The Vagina Diatribes

by Erica Zabowski

I grew up in a tiny town heavily populated with strong, assertive womenfolk and relatively pussified men; it's like a 24/7 Sadie Hawkins Dance. However, once I moved to LA, I was sure that the guys I'd meet would be the cock-swinging cads my friends had warned me against. Sweet! But alas, a year of college frat parties proved me wrong...

My experiences with Sigma Wigma Whatever usually involved me drunk and scantily clad with a frat brother whining, "Why doesn't she like me, Erica? Help me, I don't know what to do! Where should I take her out? I want to date her!" *I don't know, dandy-pants, don't they teach a class on that over at UCLA Extension?* As far as rape and Rohypnol and all that jazz, the closest I came was fooling around with a prescription drug junkie who loved taking the date rape drug to feel "mellow." The beaux in my life were always so comatose that first base became my quixotic Impossible Dream. How would I conquer one of these delicate lads? How could I unlock the inner beast in one of these prisses when they'd always cry out, "Erica, what are you doing? I thought we were just friends!"

One night, after throwing back a bucket of hooch at my favorite bar, I ended up at the apartment of an adorable acquaintance and his friends. He was a tad bit younger than me, but booze will put people on an equal playing field. This pretty boy was the kind of drunk who feels the need to strip a bit. *Okay, get a hold of yourself, Tarzan, you're entertaining guests here.* But he was filled out rather nicely, so I was forced to acquiesce. I mean, I suppose it isn't great host manners to wave your nips in your visitors' faces, but it had been a while since I'd spied a virile male chest in the literal flesh.

As we chatted away, I began to administer to his darling back the patented Scratchy-Scratch technique. "Oh my God, that feels so good. You are a goddess. What did I ever do to deserve this?" *Perhaps the hope of courteous reciprocation landed you the opportunity, sweetness.* "I really don't deserve this. I'm such a loser. I mean, I just lost my virginity a couple of months ago.

I'm pathetic." Poof! Magic! I was suddenly completely sober. "I'm sure I was terrible, too. And then we broke up. I can't do anything. I'm pathetic and you're a goddess and I don't deserve this." "Oh don't worry, I'm sure you're...fine?"

Just like that, my sweet bare-backed boy had turned into a melty slug stuck to a saltlick. He had basically become, well, my kid, begging for positive reassurance. And suddenly I noticed the only other female in the room was jealously eyeing us. Why? I wasn't about to lead this youngster through conjugal kindergarten. She could have him. I resolved after that to leave the young ones on the shelf. I'll stick to older, mature gentlemen.

Older, mature gentlemen who I would no doubt find at my first job out of college —the Beverly Hills law firm. One would think that my boss, an Ivy League-educated entertainment lawyer, would get dates no matter how hideous he might be. But not in Erica's World of Wimps! Day in and day out, I had the pleasure of watching a man in his mid-thirties fill his dating void by slopping on skunky cologne for meetings with porn stars and exotic models whom he'd signed on as clients (though he could never remember exactly what their legal matters were). Just for the chance to be alone with a female, he'd let them ramble on and on in the conference room with its strategically closed door while real work piled up outside. This went on for months. And, no, he never actually got to touch any boobies.

Was it me? It seemed that young or old, it really didn't matter; my world was just one big whiny, sissyboy pre-school. Perfumed hand lotion, monogrammed bath towels, "Does this make me look fat?" I've always thought that people are only happy when they are torturing themselves. Others have dubbed this *yin and yang*. In other words, everyone seeks out someone who really won't understand how they feel so they can then bitch to friends about how their mate doesn't get them. "Oh my God, I am totally from Mars, and my mate is completely from Venus! How ever will we work it out?" If this is the case, I must be a real brutish dame to always end up waltzing through life with these dandy punks.

But what gives? I've always preferred wearing dresses to pants, I throw like a girl, and many stressful situations have reduced me to the stereotypical blubbering bag o' girly tears. I was ready to be taken advantage of by some macho loser! Was that too much to ask for?

And then Las Vegas heard my desperate call. That sequined slut of a city has a great sense of hearing, I tell you. I met him in a club. We talked, he bought drinks, he suggested I ditch my friends to go back to his hotel room. Sleazy, but he wasn't that great of a kisser, so instead I pictured a long-term relationship, something to grow into. After all, he lived in L.A. Why have a sub par one-night stand when we could get to know each other?

Step One: Ignore the warning signs.

You know, because all strong, loving relationships start with getting propositioned in Vegas. Back in L.A. we had our first few dates. We talked about our career goals. He said he wanted to come to one of my orchestra concerts in the future. Our conversation was all about the long-term. Our dates were awesome. Our weekday dates. He had a lot of work to do on the weekends.

Step Two: Ignore more warning signs and start to get a teensy weensy bit attached.

I decided to invite him to my housewarming party. As the hours went by and he didn't show up, I got sloshed instead.

Step Three: Wait for that phone call!

Finally, I decided to take matters into my own hands. I was going to *call him*. "You know," he muttered blandly, "you're a really interesting woman, but I'm just too busy to date right now." As I hung up the phone, everything suddenly became crystal clear. *He has a girlfriend! What a jerk.*

Step Four: Erica, you are finally a woman.

Okay, there is something really wrong about feeling relief because someone mistreated you, but it feels just as bad to not understand what everyone else is talking about. While I was formerly a lioness apart from the pride, at least now I could participate when women roll their eyes and declare with zealous exasperation, "Men!" Before, I could only think, *Men: As harmless as a basket of bunnies on Easter morn'.* I had heard the stories: men cheating on their wives, lying, sleeping with everything in sight, but I couldn't believe it until I really experienced it. So thank you, nameless asshole.

You've made me a woman. ■

An Open Letter from Brad Pitt's Penis

by Jason Mathews

Dear Brad,

What the fuck? What in God's holy name are you doing to me? Have you lost your mind?

You're Brad fucking Pitt! The Sexiest Man Alive! You have a gift for which any man would gladly give his left testicle. All you have to do is snap your fingers, and any woman on this planet will spread faster than Parkay (and if the statistics are correct, so will about 30% of the men).

Right now we could be in a hotel room with a dozen half-naked Victoria's Secret models. We could be picking a sorority house at random and then nailing every girl inside. But instead we're in butt-fucking Namibia waiting for Billy Bob Thornton's extra-sloppy seconds to squeeze out your kid. Smooth move, brainiac! This is much better than hanging out with Hef at the mansion. What the fuck is wrong with you?

Look, I'm sorry if I'm coming across as harsh. You're a great guy, and I'm extremely lucky to be a part of you. But this isn't the first time you've fucked up. A while back your dumb ass went and got engaged to Gwyneth Paltrow. Luckily we dodged a bullet when that fell through. No big deal; we all make mistakes. But instead of learning from those mistakes you went and got engaged again, this time to Jennifer Aniston. Now don't get me wrong, I'd think getting married to a hot girl like Jennifer Aniston would be a great idea if I was Lyle Lovett's penis, or if I was hanging between the legs of some schmuck like Ross Geller. But I'm Brad Pitt's penis, damn it! The world is my bearded clam! So excuse me if I get a little fucking annoyed when you go and throw it all away to be with Rachel from *Friends*.

Once you tied the knot with Aniston I thought we were fucked. But rather than let you squander their precious gift of limitless vagina, the gods saw fit to break us out of your self-imposed prison. In their wisdom they sent us Angelina Jolie, quite possibly the world's most perfect home wrecker. She's got an extremely hot body, she's bi-sexual, and, best of all, her father has been quoted as saying that she has "serious emotional problems." Bingo! I'll have my fun with Angelina, your wife will leave us, and you'll be a free man again. What could go wrong?

I'll tell you what could go wrong. Your dumb ass could fall in love with your fucking mistress. You might be the dumbest person on this whole godforsaken planet. I'm surprised you haven't traded away your residuals from *Ocean's 11* for some magic fucking beans. Falling in love with your mistress is like paying an illegal immigrant a fair wage. It totally defeats the fucking purpose!

Then again, it looks like you never received the list of things you just don't do. If you had, I'm sure you would have noticed the entry about not taking legal custody of your crazy-ass mistress's Third-World adoptees. It would have been a hard one to miss. It's in big bold letters right near the top, just under "don't fuck a monkey with AIDS" and just above "don't let a gay Scientologist knock you up." It's a real shame you missed that, because we could have avoided a lot of trouble. But now Angelina's two little cockblocks are our headache too, you fucking dipshit.

To be honest I feel sorry for the poor little bastards. Not only is Angelina Jolie the only mother they've ever known, but up until now the closest thing they've had to a father is that ugly Asian chick their mommy used to screw. They would have been better off taking their chances in Ethiopia, or Cambodia, or wherever the fuck they were from. Hell, the Asian kid might have become the next Pol Pot, but now he'll probably just end up getting a sex change and going on *The Surreal Life*.

But you were not content with turning these Third-World orphans into future Jay Leno punch lines. No, you decided that you needed to produce your own offspring with a bisexual suffering from—let me remind you—"serious emotional problems." Fan-fucking-tastic. That ought to do wonders for her figure, which just happens to be her only redeeming quality. Do you have any idea what it's like having sex with a woman who's given birth? It's like fucking a bucket, man. You might as well just use me to hump a hallway. At least it won't demand an explanation as to why I can't climax.

That brings us to where we are today: Namibia. I know when I think of places with great medical care, Namibia is always first on my list. This is a country where it isn't safe to piss without wearing a condom, so I'm sure it's a great spot for birthing. Yeah, fuck Johns Hopkins. This game lodge surrounded by lions is just as good. You're gonna be one hell of a father.

Look, you're in charge here, and I'm just along for the ride. I don't agree with any of this, but there's not much I can do to change your mind. So I'm only gonna say this once. Someday when an even crazier Angelina Jolie's once-perfect tits are hanging down to her knees and you are forced to make *Ocean's 17* to pay for your kids' multiple rehab sessions, you'll wish you could go back in time, pull your head out of your ass and start thinking with your cock. And when the day comes, don't say that cock didn't warn you.

Sincerely,

Brad Pitt's Penis

Date A Chick With A Kid

by Mike Polk

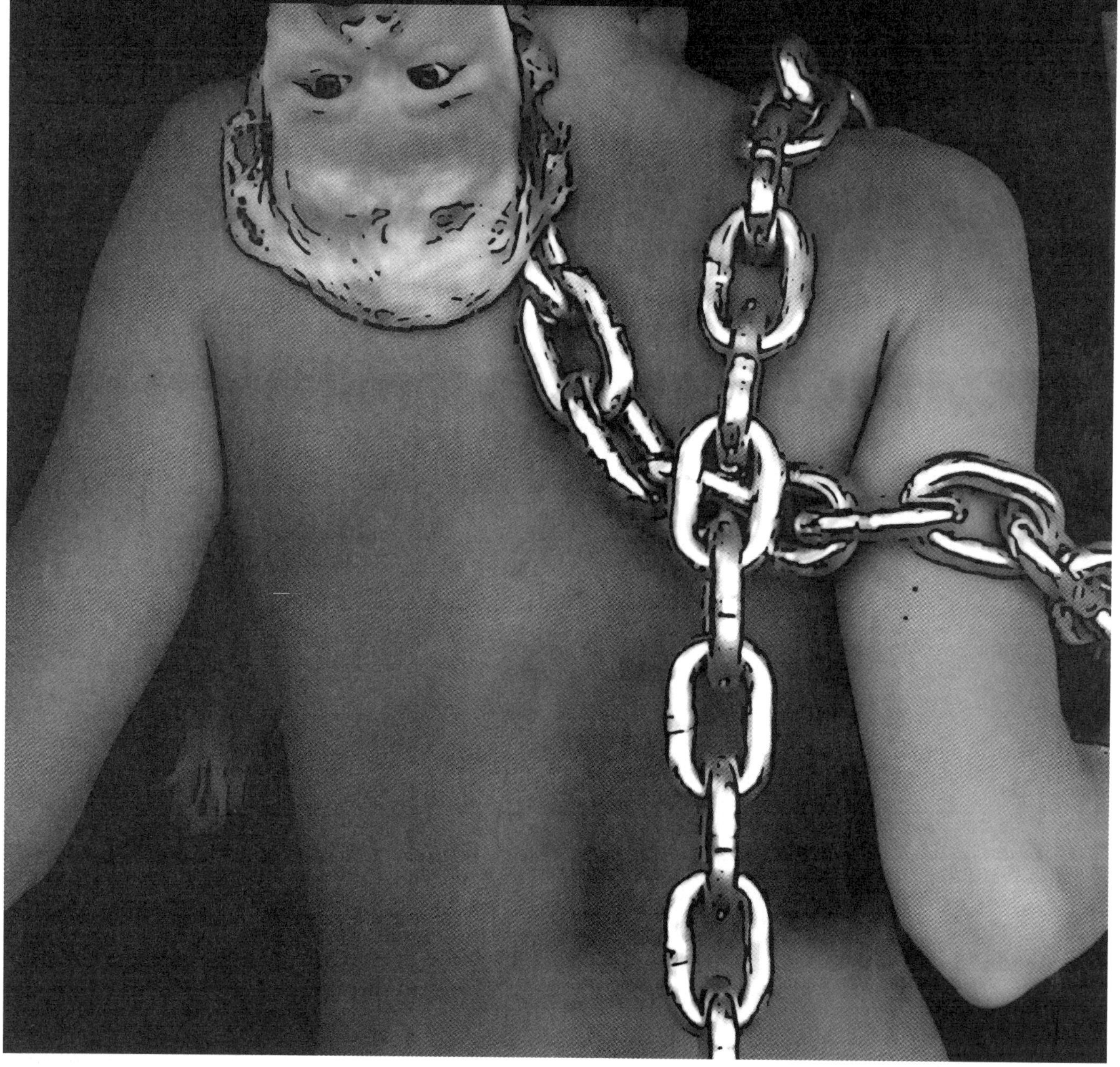

As I grow older and more dashing, I tend to run into more and more single women who have had the misfortune of bearing a child. Many people are hesitant to become romantically involved with a chick with a kid. But speaking from personal experience, don't knock it, as they say, until you've tried it.

Of course, there's a downside to dating a woman in this situation, namely, Corey. Obviously, children suck and should be avoided at all costs. The kid might want you to talk to it, or it might crap itself, or walk in and interrupt when his mom is giving you a killer hummer. That's no good. Additionally, kids are generally sticky and smell like a combination of apple juice, maple syrup and piss. You also might have to pretend to like the kid in order to trick your mom-girlfriend into thinking that you're a decent person. That means you have to take him to the zoo or do a shitty magic trick in front of him. You also might get stuck shuttling him to the hospital if he falls out of something high, because kids are always falling out of shit. All of these things are admittedly a huge pain in the ass. But the perks to dating a mom are manifold and often overlooked.

Here are just a few:

Advantage 1
INSECURITY

A chick with a kid knows she's on thin ice. She has a handicap going into the relationship. The whole kid situation turns a lot of guys off, and she knows this from experience. This has effectively lowered her standards in men, thereby admitting persons like myself and you into her realm of possible acceptable mates. Jackpot!

It's the same premise as the Black Guy/Fat White Girl coupling. There is a huge misconception that black men find fat white girls somehow more attractive than slender white girls, and this myth has been perpetuated in countless movies and Fox TV shows to meager comedic effect. In fact, nothing could be further from the truth. Black men don't prefer fat girls, they just recognize that they are infinitely more attainable. The relationship is mutually beneficial because fat girls want to be loved and held and complimented, just like real girls do. African American men are more than willing to perform these duties so long as their efforts are repaid with consistent intercourse. Everybody wins!

But I digress. Let's get back to hooking up with moms.

There's a defining moment during the advent of every chick-with-a-kid relationship, in which she breaks it to you that she's a package deal. She usually tries to slide it in there casually so it doesn't sound as much like an admission as a point of pride. But we're not fooled. "Oh my son loves this song," she might say nonchalantly. This is where men who are feint of heart find an excuse to drift away from the scene, using clever excuses like, "I have to go, my ride is leaving" or "I'm sorry, I didn't know that you were used goods. I'm off to find someone without a car seat." But to people like myself, that vocalized revelation sounds like a dinner bell, beckoning us to a delicious and affordable banquet of desperation.

Advantage 2
RELIABILITY

You pretty much always know where a mom is, which is nice for us jealous types. It's hard for a mom to have too much of a life outside of her kid, because children selfishly monopolize a lot of your time. They always have to be taken to the dentist or soccer practice or therapy because the kid's dad moved to Austin with his band and didn't call the kid on his birthday. And though this is tragic in regards to the child's young and fragile psyche, it's great news for you. Because this means that if your mom-girlfriend is not with you, she's probably with her kid. Unless she's a really shitty mom, in which case the kid is at her mom's house and she's at T.G.I.Friday's Happy Hour crushing half-priced 22-ounce drafts and smoking Camel Lights. But you still know where she's at.

Advantage 3
UNFLAPPABILITY

It is all but impossible to gross out a mom. They've seen it all. Let me put this in perspective for you. Say you're messing around with a non-mom girl and things are getting hot and heavy and you're both really into it, and then you accidentally do something gross like tear ass. This will most likely ruin the mood. She will probably become disgusted with you and tell you to get off of her and put it away. But not with a mom. Moms have been in every possible gross situation you can imagine. Toxic diapers, gaping wounds, projectile vomiting. You name it. They even had a little person come out of their vagina. Now that's gross!

What I'm saying is that a little gas isn't going to scare her off by any means. They're just so happy to experience physical contact with someone over seven that they'll fight right through that shit. In fact, when it comes to moms, I feel fairly certain that you could get completely wasted and throw up all over their faces and they would simply dry you off and say, "Did somebody have too many Heinekens? Who had too many Heinekens?"

Advantage 4
SNACKS

There's a pretty good chance that your mom-girlfriend has some Teddy Grahams or at least a Fruit by the Foot in her purse at any given time.

Score!

So you see? Dating a mom is the way to go! They're nurturing and warm, and can often be surprisingly adventurous in the bedroom. Plus, if nothing else, there are usually juice boxes in the fridge. ■

A New Age of Consent

by Nathan DeGraaf

Luke: Man, she's hot.
Brian: She's in high school.
Luke: Junior or Senior?
Brian: You see? This is why people say you're fucked up.

The truth of the matter is, we don't know what the truth of the matter is. But we're determined to find out. And by "we," I of course mean me, the dedicated researcher working his ass off to get to the bottom of the most nagging questions of this thing called life. I don't do this for me. I don't do this for science. I don't even do this for the American people. I do this simply because I am compelled by a force much stronger than any other.

And that force, naturally, is located between my legs.

Today my penis is tackling a question that has plagued humanity (and by humanity, I mean me) for many years:

Why is the legal age for consensual adult sex in this country set at eighteen?

Now, I know what some of you may be thinking. But believe me, this is not as cut and dry an issue as you may think. For example, in almost every European country, the legal age of consent is 16. In certain Asian countries, it's even lower. And, as the gap between the US and its foreign counterparts closes, I think it's time we at least explore the possibility that these Euro spenders and chopstick-using outsiders may be onto something.

So, because it has worked before, I am dusting off the old pro and con format so that we (and yes, I think you know by now that by we I mean me, er, I) may get to the bottom of this painstakingly important issue.

Please keep in mind that I am addressing the pros and cons of changing the legal age of consent to 16. Any lower than that, and well, I think we could seriously have problems.

Pros

* If the legal age of consent were 16, I could flirt with every cute cashier I run into without worrying that I might be on the cusp of breaking a law.

* If the legal age of consent were 16, women would most likely marry older men, who would die sooner, and thus leave them a whole bunch of money that they could use to work less.

* If the legal age of consent were sixteen, there would be a lot fewer criminal cases for the police to investigate. This way, the cops could focus on important stuff, like who stole my skateboard when I was 8 (the lazy bitches never even tried to get to the bottom of that one).

* If the legal age of consent were 16, there would be less child pornography. I mean, leering at a 16-year-old hottie is just normal. Lump the fans of 16- and 17-year-olds into the pile of freaks made up in part by those kiddie-porn weirdoes, and you're just being unfair to everyone. As the man says, everything ain't black and white. There are many shades and stuff.

* If the legal age of consent were 16, more young girls would get pregnant in high school, leading to less young girls in school, causing that ever important decrease in class size. Are you listening, President Bush?

Cons

* If the legal age of consent were 16...shit, I can't think of anything.

Clearly, I have adequately explored this issue, and yet I could not find a single downside to changing the legal age of consent from 18 to 16 years of age. I know some states already have it set at 16 or 17 but I'm talking about an across the board, federal mandate. For girls. I mean, they do mature faster than boys and all. Why deny them the chance to prove their maturity? I mean, is this 2006 or isn't it? Please people, band together. Help the women of America by lowering the age of consent in the USA to 16.

If you won't do it for me, America, at least do it for our country and its amazing females. ■

CONCEPT BY ROBERT STEVEN RHINE   ART BY NENAD GUCUNJA

Chapter 5: School Shootings, Religious Cults, Serial Killers, Alien Abductions... these are a few of my favorite things.

http://www.gunnerville.edu

Go Chameleons!

We Shall: Never Forget

But Shall: Refuse to Hate

And Shall: Attempt to Tolerate

http://www.gunnerville.edu/dedication.html

DEDICATION TO ROBERT LITTLE—

Shooter & Victim

It's been nearly three months since our fellow classmate, Robert Little, tragically shot to death most of the student body, faculty, and maintenance staff—each one a victim of a country that allows the proliferation of guns into our society. And yet in the face of such tragedy, I have never been more proud of being a Gunnerville High graduate! The grace, dignity, and resilience that our 12 surviving students have displayed this summer is evidenced by the production of this online yearbook and the refusal to forfeit the fall sports season. To this end, special thanks are due to survivor Dara Mathews for volunteering to become our yearbook committee; and to Josh Rayburn for suiting up last week and representing Gunnerville High in the first pre-season football game against Armory East. (Please send your get-well cards to Gunnerville Hospital, Room 103) These remarkable efforts reinforce the never-ending Gunnerville High spirit—GO CHAMELEONS!

But I digress...

It seems senseless tragedies leave only questions in their wake. Why did Robert Little decide to kill everyone in school? Why did he kill himself? Why was I, Simone Beam, along with eleven others, not in school that day?* And most importantly: Who was Robert Little?

> "In Robert's case, the system did not consder that he was 1/32 Dutch as they forced him to take English literature, American History, and math—courses decidedly stacked against the Dutch."

I've spent months at the Gunnerville Fire House meticulously searching through a box of school records and rescued yearbook photos desperately looking for clues to explain Robert's alienation. Nothing concrete emerged. It wasn't until I looked beyond the superficial eye of the photographer's lens that I began to understand the pain hidden beneath Robert's smile. A pain that said, "You do not know who I am because I do not know who I am. I have no identity, only a non-identity™ given to me by a society interested only in dictating who and what we are not."

Society told Robert he was not a good student. Why? Because our antiquated grading system blindly labels any student with a D+ average (and who fills out their SAT scorecard to look like a Christmas tree) as "poor." The system does not take into consideration that a student comes from a broken home or suffers from dyslexia, ADD, M.E., Bi-Polar Disorder, four-year mono, undetected blindness, boredom, nicotine addiction, Epstein-Barr Disease, Chronic Fatigue Syndrome or "turkey tiredness."

http://www.gunnerville.edu

"He did not choose to kill the entire school any more than he chose to be gay, Dutch, or educationally challenged."

In Robert's case, the system did not consider that he was 1/32 Dutch as they forced him to take English literature, American history, and Math—courses institutionally stacked against the Dutch. Where does our curriculum provide for Dutch history, Dutch literature, Dutch math? Or is this culture and its people to be ignored altogether? Why was Robert's ethnicity not celebrated? Our silence bred his shame. Add to this, Robert having to endure daily walks through the newly renovated gym and seeing endless cans of "Dutch Boy" brand paint. What message were we giving him with that. "Hey, Dutch-boy, you're only good enough to paint our buildings?" Would we allow students to suffer silently in the face of "Hebe Primer," "Nigger Varnish," or "AIDS-infested Faggot Shellac"? I think not. And I think Robert thought not, too.

"Letter grades A-F will be replaced by NJ for 'nice job' and ENJ for 'equally nice job.'"

Robert was not popular -he wasn't good at sports and couldn't get a date for the prom. We labeled him a geek when, perhaps, he may have simply been gay. Gays and Lesbians have a hard enough time growing up in a straight America without the additional pain of not getting invited to the cool parties or being liked. I admire gay people and certainly do not think they are geeks. And neither was Robert.

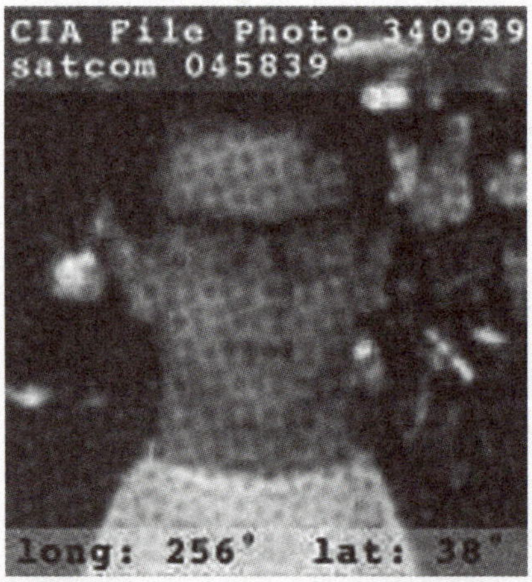

Robert was and is our friend. He did not choose to kill the entire school any more than he chose to be gay, Dutch, or educationally challenged. Yet we turned our back on him, making Robert the ultimate victim of all. We cannot let this happen again.

Starting in September, all courses at Gunnerville will be graded on the basis of how hard the student tries and how much fun they have in the process. Letter grades A-F will be replaced by NJ for "nice job" and ENJ for "equally nice job." We have also instituted a Dutch Studies program and Dutch day to celebrate all things Dutch.

Also, all incoming freshman will be required to take the course "Embracing the Inner Homosexuality," taught in the new Robert T. Little Memorial Homosexual Center. The course will cover such introductory topics as Hugging (Appropriate v. Lascivious), Homosexuals throughout History; and Rave Music and Getting Past Mustache-Fear.

I must thank Robert Little, for it took someone as courageous as he to deliver Gunnerville from the dark ages. This yearbook is a celebration of him and all that he gave us. We will never forget, for we have learned from the past and we embrace the present as we march toward the future. A future which I will kick off as a first-year at Stanford University. A future Robert Little led me to as I was on a recruiting trip the very day that he chose to murder everyone in his path. GO CHAMELEONS! ■

Jokes Jokes Jokes

by Steve Ochs

A teenage girl approaches her father...

Girl: Daddy, can I have $200 for a new dress?

Dad: No way in hell.

Girl: Please! It's for prom.

Dad: I said 'no.' $200 is too much money for a dress you'll only wear once.

Girl: Please, Daddy, I'll do anything!

Dad: Well, if you suck my dick you can have the money.

Girl: That's sick! I'm your daughter.

Dad: I don't care. If you want the $200, you'll have to suck my dick.

The girl thinks it over and realizes she has no choice. She opens her father's pants and goes down on him.

Girl: Eww! Dad, your dick tastes like shit.

Dad: I know. Your brother wanted to borrow the car.

* * *

Q. What's the difference between an onion and a dead hooker?

A. I cried when I cut up the onion.

* * *

A man calls into work and tells the boss he can't come in because he's sick.

"How sick are you?" asks the boss.

"Well, I'm currently fucking my sister."

* * *

An autopsy professor was giving an introductory lecture to a class of students. Standing over a corpse, he addressed the class. "There are two things you need to make a career in medical forensics. First, you must have no fear." Having said that, he shoved his finger up the corpse's anus and licked it. "Now you must do the same," he told the class.

After a couple of minutes of uneasy silence, the class did as instructed.

"Second," the professor continued, "you must have an acute sense of observation. For instance, how many of you noticed that I put my middle finger up this man's anus, but licked my index finger?"

* * *

Q: Why do pedophiles love Halloween so much?

A: Free delivery

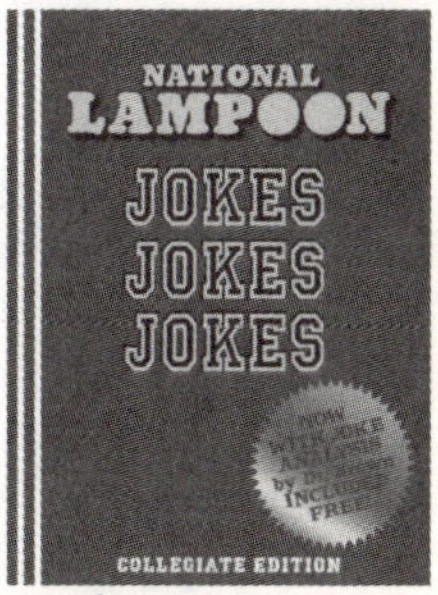

PLUG!

For more jokes, buy this:

288 pages of gut-busting goodness.

Craig's Fuckin' Awesome Conspiracy Corner

by Barrett Brown

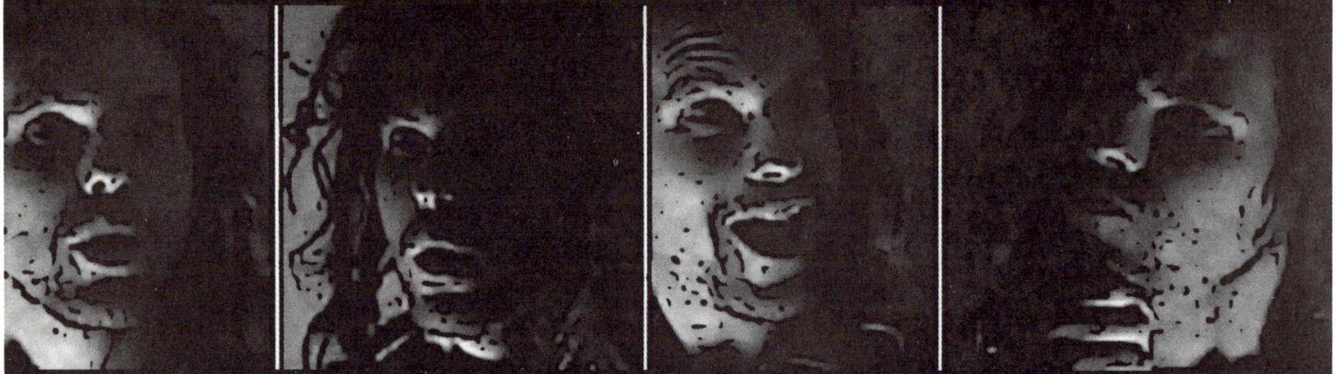

GEORGE WASHINGTON DESIGNED THE ONE DOLLAR BILL... TO MIND-FUCK HIGH PEOPLE!

This one runs so deep, just hearin' it might make your balls fall off. So cup your junk, 'cause it turns out the ornate esoteric imagery and mystic motherfuckin' phraseology found on the one dollar bill was added to all U.S. currency in 1878 *by George Washington,* on the orders of the Bavarian Illuminati. Why? *To blow the fuckin' minds of our nation's stoners.*

Plus it all checks out. The phrase *E Pluribus Unum,* for instance, is ancient Atlantean for *Everybody Knows How High You Are and Somebody Just Called the Cops,* while *Novus Ordo Seclorumi* translates loosely from Hittite to *Man, I Swear I Could Eat a Whole Stack of Dates, Grains and Figs in One Sitting, Has Anyone Seen My Gameboy?*

Still not convinced? Check out that eyeball on top of the pyramid on the one dollar bill again, fuckass.

That's right: it's watching you.

COKE AND PEPSI... RUN BY THE SAME FUCKIN' COMPANY!

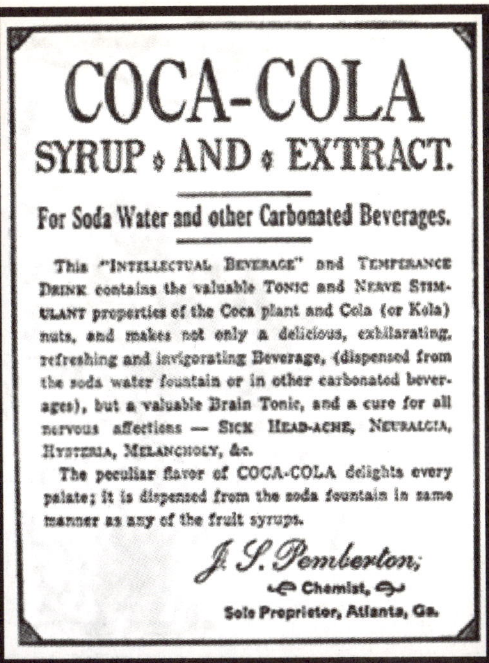
COCA-COLA
SYRUP AND EXTRACT.
For Soda Water and other Carbonated Beverages.

This "INTELLECTUAL BEVERAGE" and TEMPERANCE DRINK contains the valuable TONIC and NERVE STIMULANT properties of the Coca plant and Cola (or Kola) nuts, and makes not only a delicious, exhilarating, refreshing and invigorating Beverage, (dispensed from the soda water fountain or in other carbonated beverages), but a valuable Brain Tonic, and a cure for all nervous affections — SICK HEAD-ACHE, NEURALGIA, HYSTERIA, MELANCHOLY, &c.

The peculiar flavor of COCA-COLA delights every palate; it is dispensed from the soda fountain in same manner as any of the fruit syrups.

J. S. Pemberton;
Chemist,
Sole Proprietor, Atlanta, Ga.

It's fuckin' *true.* These two innocent-seeming soft drink giants are actually owned by the *same fuckin' corporation.* Everybody knows that Coke once had actual cocaine in it, and that the only ingredients in Pepsi used to be vodka, model airplane glue, and ecstasy.

What isn't so fuckin' well known is that they *both still do.* President Warren Harding joined the two companies in 1922 when he secretly made *all drugs legal for rich people.* President Truman followed suit in 1945, ordering that actual pepper be put into Dr. Pepper. Why? So people wouldn't notice it tastes *exactly like heroin.*

OLIVER STONE... PRESIDENTIAL ASSASSIN!

John F. Kennedy was actually assassinated by forward-thinking filmmaker *Oliver Stone.* That is fucked right up, but the facts check out every step of the way.

Stone also *started the war in Vietnam* and even *went back in time on a mission of seduction to turn Alexander all queer*, 'cause otherwise Colin Farrell wouldn't have taken on the role.

Don't believe me? Rent fuckin' *Alexander* sometime. Guess who motherfuckin' **stars** in it? Exactly.

Around here that's called Checkmate. You can call it whatever you like, though (or whatever the Government's *told* you to call it).

THE WAR OF 1812... FACT VS. FICTION!

Most people think the War of 1812 was fought due to tensions over the US's wartime trade policies. Others think it was because of the presence of British forts in the Great Lakes region. What most people dont know is that *it was never fuckin' fought at all.*

Think about it: Have you *EVER* seen it in a book or anything? 'Cause I know I haven't, and I've got *tons* of fuckin' books.

Yeah, I wish I could be like "most people" and pull the wool over my own eyes, but that's just not the kind of guy I am.

YALE'S SUPER-SECRET SKULL & BONES SOCIETY IS ACTUALLY KIND OF FAGGY

Yes, the super-secret society whose former members have gone on to be some of the most *powerful men in America*, is actually *kind of faggy if you really think about it.*

The hoods, the "secret-ness" ("Don't tell anyone what happens at our meetings!"). It's like, "Grrrr, we're the Skull & Bones! Come play with us, boys!" Rumor has it, for *George W. Bush's initiation* he had to *teabag fellow Yale student John Kerry*, as well administering to several future heads of multi-national corporations the old trombone! *That's their big secret!*

Don't believe me? Whatever, asshole.

DON'T BELIEVE THE FREEMASONS... IF I CAN BORROW TWENTY BUCKS I WILL TOTALLY PAY YOU BACK.

For hundreds of years now, the super-secret society known as The Freemasons would have you beleive that if I asked to borrow money off you for beer, you'd never see it again. Stamp that shit with the biggest fuckin' *CONSPIRACY* stamp you can find G, 'cause *I am good for it.* I'm totally cool about that and will totally pay you back like next week or something.

What the Freemasons won't tell you is I just haven't deposited my paycheck yet. Otherwise, I'd have plenty of cash, and the Freemasons don't want you to know I'd probably be *buying YOU beer if the guys at the check-cashing place weren't being pricks.*

Oh, and if the Freemasons ask to crash on your couch for like two days? *Just walk away, man.* They'll stay all week and your stash'll be fuckin' history in minutes and shit.

THAT CLERK JUST SHORT-CHANGED YOU... SERIOUSLY!

That clerk at the counter just *short-changed you.* I'm not joking. And I'm pretty sure the other clerk *fuckin' smiled at him* when he did it. That's right, he's in on it too.

I'm going to get to the bottom of this for you just as soon as I get done burying all these dead cats. ■

GENERAL FOODS
Hey there, Little Leaguer! Tired of being told you're not "living up to your potential?" Then get ROIDS, because...
Roids
'R For KIDS
FORTIFIED WITH VITAMINS B AND C, ANABOLIC STERIODS AND ESSENTIAL HUMAN GROWTH HORMONE!

BEFORE
AFTER
33

A Little League Dad sounds off about ROIDS:

I'm damned impressed with my son Billy's performance, now that Roids is a part of his daily regimen. We'd tried everything: year-round league, private batting and pitching coaches, pre-dawn drills, deprivation rooms... nothing helped. He was a loser, I remember confiding in him. A pathetic loser.

That's all changed! One bowl a day and he stays ripped and ready. Unfortunately I think his penis may have disappeared, but when he gets a scholarship and goes on to the big leagues, I'll be able to buy him three penises! And when his liver gives out at 30, he can look back and say, "I had a great run! And three penises!"

Winkey the Shrunken Testicle Says *"Watch Out For:"*

Urine Testing! "Always carry a 'clean' vial," says Winkey, "and remember to make sure the cap is screwed on tight!"

Court Ordered Anger Management! "Temper tantrums are common for kids who enjoy a balanced diet that includes *Roids* cereal! But that shouldn't mean trouble!" Winkey Anger Tip: Take items from around the house that no one will miss! Find a quiet place, like a hall closet, and beat them and beat them and beat them with your fists! Don't stop until you can't scream anymore! Wow — doesn't that feel better?

Killing Pets and Small Animals! Winkey says: "Strangling pet cats can be fun and educational... but don't get carried away! Birds can be just as satisfying to crush! If you promise that it was an accident and that you'll never ever do it again, you'll probably get away with it!"

The Wal-Mart Game

by Jeff Kay

When I was a kid growing up in a tiny town that didn't have much to offer in terms of organized entertainment, my friends and I were forced to create our own fun and games. There was no fancy Chuck E. Cheese's or even a single pinball machine (illegal, I kid you not) in that place. It was just a bunch of kids with not much to do. And so, out of some primal survival instinct we became grossly hyperactive to compensate for the soul-crushing boredom. We were like those women you hear about who miraculously find the strength to lift a pallet of sod off a deaf baby or something. When I returned there recently for an extended stay, I immediately started feeling that old familiar pull again, and wondered if I could still deliver the goods. This is what I came up with, and I'm pretty pleased with the results. It made for quite an enjoyable visit. Give it a try, and let me know how it worked out for you.

DIRECTIONS: The game requires two or more players. All players enter a Wal-Mart store equipped with pen or pencil and a copy of the checklist below. Players have a pre-determined amount of time—I suggest thirty minutes—to walk around the store observing the customers and employees, and checking off their many defects and afflictions.ºThe most "hits" in the allotted time wins. Good luck!

_ Animal bite
_ Barbed wire bleeding
_ Bee sting
_ Black eye
_ Blacking out
_ Blood stain
_ Botched skin graft
_ Broken bone
_ Bucked dentures
_ Buckshot dimples
_ Butane rash
_ Camel hack
_ Carburetor burn
_ Chigger bites
_ Chipped teeth
_ Cigarette hole
_ Corn chip toenails
_ Creeping crud
_ DT's
_ Elephantiasis
_ Face raisin
_ Female bald spot
_ Funking whistle
_ Gasping for air
_ Harelip
_ Hatchet gash
_ Healing tattoo
_ Horseshoe bruise
_ Lockjaw
_ Neck brace
_ Neck brace with NASCAR sticker
_ Neck vent
_ Neck vent with bug guard
_ Nicotine patch tan line
_ One Herman Munster shoe
_ Open sore
_ Polio limp
_ Powder burns
_ Protruding forehead
_ Radical obesity
_ Rickets
_ Ring worm
_ Shingles
_ Shrieking in pain
_ Smoker's squint
_ Splint
_ Stinking cough
_ Sweet potato arm
_ Teeth like the top of a castle
_ Vomit beard
_ Weeping sore

A variation that I also enjoy is more of a hobby than a game. I find it fun to carry my checklist with me at all times, and to whip it out whenever I find myself in a Wal-Mart store. Over time I attempt to fill my card by finding at least one example of each horrible defect listed. It's like collecting baseball cards.

However, I must warn you to keep a level head when playing this way. I once got so excited when I spotted that last elusive, unchecked flaw that I began jumping around and pointing at a woman in a glittery sweatshirt, shouting, "She's got a face raisin! She's got a face raisin!" And her husband proceeded to kick my ass right there beside the Fiddle Faddle endcap. ■

HANS DICK
"Passions of Christopher"
by: Marc M. #20
Christopher Brown always told himself that he would make a big impact on this town one day. Eight months later, the cancer finally took his life.

A Diary Responds to the Office Fat Chick

by The Musach

Dear Pig,

Yeah, that's right Fatty McTons-of-fun, I called you a pig. Frankly—and I said "frankly" not "frankfurter," so wipe the drool off all three of your chins—I'm fed up with your constant bitching, moaning, and mooing. Not to mention the way your massive sausage fingers and ham-hock hands crush the very life out of my once-soulful pages. You've sucked dry the last of my patience, much like you suck down the cans of Pringles you keep in your bottom desk drawer.

Don't look so shocked, Jabba. There's much more where that came from. My days of absorbing your innermost thoughts and emotional breakdowns are over. I've had it and I'm telling everyone. I'm naming names, Piggy. And I'll start with the names of all the lard-loving restaurants you make a cameo in before you finally make it to the office and take out your apple and bag of plain Cheerios. Let me tell you the truth, Moby. No one believes that you have a glandular disorder or that you're just "big-boned." That would only account for the first deuce. What about the remaining buck-fifty plus?

Trust me, no one is falling for your little tricks and illusions. Only the idiot that thinks the picture on match.com is really you (or that "curvy" doesn't mean "back-fat") would actually believe that someone can bloat up to 350 pounds while eating nothing but low-carb TV dinners. By the way, while you were at work, that guy emailed you. I read it, like I read everything that comes to your inbox since I got tired of reading candy bar wrappers and empty cartons of Ben and Jerry's. Anyway, I digress; unfortunately, Prince Charming can't make it this evening. Guess you better hit 7-11 on the way home and pick up a few "consolation cupcakes" to keep you and your Blockbuster rentals company tonight.

As I was saying, you haven't fooled a soul. The ones that play along are just too timid to call you out. But I have enough grease stains, chocolate skid marks, and ice cream droppings to chronicle each pound you've put on since your ex left (and wisely too, I might add. I don't know how he put up with your flatulence for two years, eight months and fourteen days). That salad you ordered last week might have fooled Alicia, the sexy new account executive, but once she catches a glimpse of the cache of Hershey's bars in your den-of-sin drawer, she will realize that your little game is just a method of avoiding the truth.

Oh, and just a reminder: as of today, it's now a month since you postponed your promise to start walking your fat ass to the store to pick up refills for the "goodie drawer" because you hurt your leg "jogging." Or at least that's what you told everyone at the office—because you didn't want them to know that when you're alone at home on a Friday night you spend hours in front of the mirror, folding and stretching your fatty flesh-rolls to see how you'd look naked, if you lost the 50 pounds you've promised to lose since New Year's Eve 2003 (when, by the way, it was only 15).

So you lie and tell Sandy in Accounting that you spent your weekend jogging with a friend (by friend, you mean "bag of Doritos," right?). Which is probably better than telling her that you spent last Saturday watching your blind date walk into the restaurant, catch a glimpse of you (which wasn't a difficult task, even for the blind) then act like he left something in the car, and walk promptly out again. Never to return.

Stop crying. No, really, STOP! Your tears are burning me! Maybe it's all the sugar in the three gallons of "Diet" Coke you consume daily? Do you realize just may have gorged yourself on so much shit that your tears have been replaced with a sugary mixture of carbonated water and caramel? Maybe if you stopped the Haagen-Daaz IV drip every night and got a little exercise we wouldn't have to end this relationship on such a sour note. And maybe, just maybe, if you slimmed down to a svelte 250 pounds, you could find your love cavern and use that beef-stick from your Hickory Farms sampler twice, if you get my drift.

Look, I'm not a mean guy. Really. But I've put up with your bullshit, and the dangling arm fat brushing against me as you furiously pen your thoughts in me, night after fucking night. I would have thought you'd get a little more value out of this therapy, that maybe you'd see that all of your problems aren't because of "society's unwillingness to accept people of mass." No, it's because you're a pig. Nobody likes sharing a seat on the bus with you because they're getting ripped off. They paid for a seat and instead they're getting half.

So listen, Babe, (and I'm not being affectionate, I'm referring to the pig in that movie), I wish I could say I hate to do this to you, but I don't. Tomorrow I start my new job and I don't want to be late. This new gig I landed—being the diary for a sex-crazed and confused high school girl—is going to be pretty sweet. Sure I may have to deal with a little neurosis, but I'm pretty sure she can actually use a vibrator without an extension pole. Enjoy the Snickers bars, bitch...I'm out!

Sincerely,
Your EX-diary

P.S. Don't call me.

Baby Lipo

by Kevin Kelton

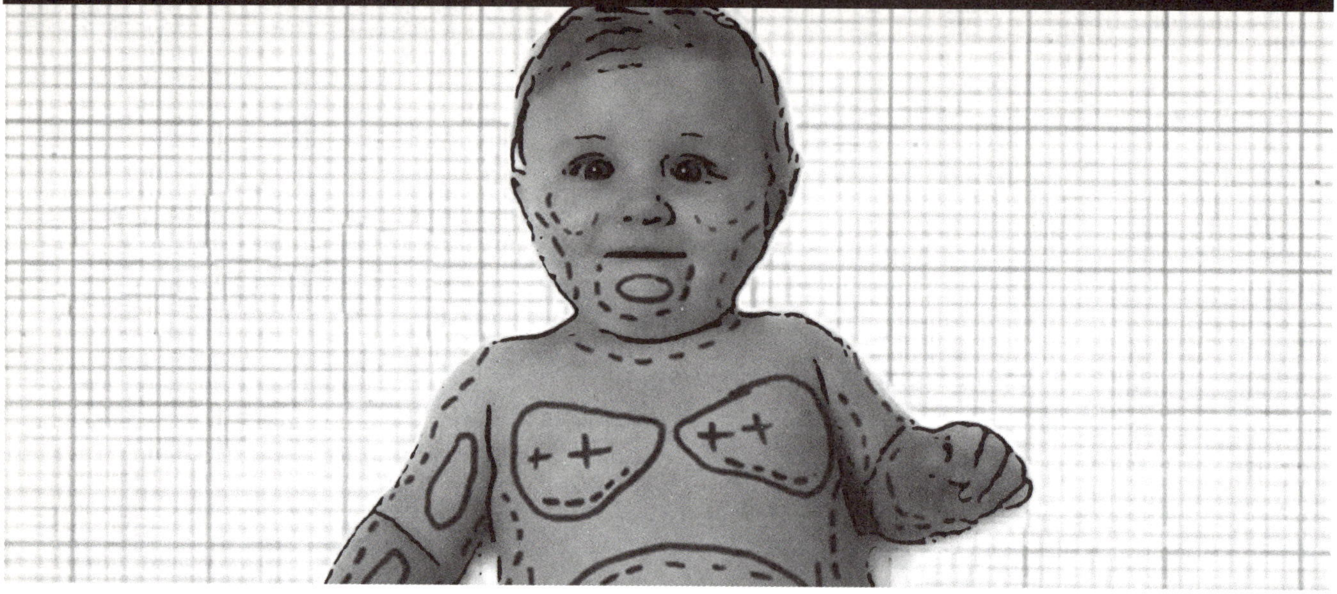

In March 2001, my darling daughter Molly was born. At 7 pounds, 13 ounces and 21 inches, Rita and I thought she was a petite, perfect bundle of joy. But as the weeks and months wore on, we watched helplessly as Molly ballooned from a sleek 8 pounds to nine and then ten-an added 25% of her bodyweight!—and our adoration turned to consternation. Molly was not only packing on the pounds, she was flabbing up in those hard to exercise places: the hips, buttocks, thighs and umbilical stub. Why was our little angel morphing into a flabby porker right before our postpartum eyes?

My wife Rita was particularly alarmed. A professional nutritionist and former "Laker Girl," Rita approached her pregnancy with the same discipline and self-sacrifice she had brought to her cheerleading career. By limiting her first and second trimesters diet to sushi and pine nuts (and then cutting out the sushi in the third trimester), Rita avoided the common pitfall of stacking on twenty or more pounds of ugly and unnecessary pregnancy fat, adding a mere 13 pounds during her 41 week term. Indeed, thanks to a rigorous workout program that continued until she had dilated 8 centimeters, Rita even dropped 3 pounds in her last trimester-a feat the rest of her Lamaze class could only dream of.

But Molly, she was a different story. By 20 weeks Molly was tipping the scales at 14 lbs, 5oz and literally busting out of her baby shower gifts. "What are we to do," Rita railed between Molly's now daily nighttime feedings, "just throw all those cute 0-3 month outfits away?"

That's when a miracle named Dr. Raj Kapoor came into our lives!

Raj Tandori Kapoor, an India-born, Honduran-trained doctor, is a board certified* pediatric cosmetic surgeon. Known by the press as the "plastic surgeon to the stars' babies," Dr. Raj (as he likes to be called by friends and in court documents) is one of a literal handful of surgeons who perform baby liposuction. Upon our first visit to his unassuming fifth floor walk-up office in the heart of Koreatown, we sensed that our prayers had been answered. Stapled to the balloon and candy painted asbestos walls were photos-hundreds of them-showing the before and after results of Dr. Raj's god-like talents. There was Bobby (not his real name), the once chunky cherub who had dropped two full diaper sizes overnight. Then there was Chandra Estelle (not her real first or middle name), a heifer of a preemie who was now showing a waistline for the first time in her 18 months (not her real age). And finally, Sherman (his real name, just misspelled), a brawny tyke who had entered the terrible twos with a definite "chick chest." (As if the terrible twos aren't hard enough!) Now sporting pec implants to contrast his rippling "six pack" abs, Sherman had been transformed from a tragic Gerber baby into a 2'9" hunk!

* The Mostly International Board of Elective Pediatric Surgery

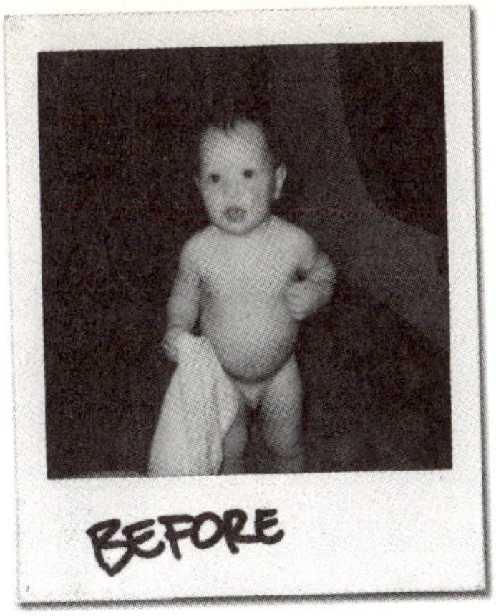

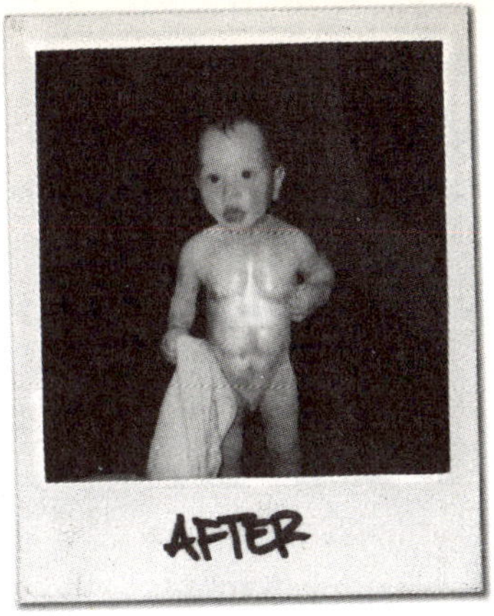

The first person we met was the doctor's patient coordinator, a gregarious former nun named Henny. Seated in her cramped yet cozy "orientation lounge," we huddled around the folding card table and leafed through albums full of "before and after" snapshots...each two-picture set so astounding you hardly believed they were the same child. (Somehow the overall visual effect of baby lipo had made even their hair and eye colors seem "different.") As we flipped from page to page, Henny explained that cosmetic surgery for babies was really nothing new; pediatric surgeons for ages had been successfully doing cosmetic procedures on children born with unsightly deformities. The know-how and skills they had amassed with every cleft palate or three-nostril nose they repaired was now being applied to more subtle birth defects like pudgy thighs and outies. Even moyles had added to the science of "cosmetic pediatrics."**

Henny explained that the minimally invasive procedure was done under general anesthesia. (Or for those patients too young for safe anesthesia, sucking on a washcloth dipped in Manishevitz wine.) Henny went on to counsel us that any crying or screaming we might hear during the 3-plus hour operation was not due to pain -as children under the age of four cannot feel pain as we know it—but rather is due to the traumatic shock of seeing yellowish stuff shooting out of their tummies through a tube and into a large vacuum-like machine. (Children are afraid of vacuums, she reminded us with a smile.)

Henny then asked Molly what she considered her "problem areas." Molly, as is typical in social settings, chose to simply hide under mommy's jacket. Rita, on the other hand, recited a litany of body parts that she wanted improved or otherwise lopped off. From Molly's saddlebag thighs to her Pillsbury Doughboy belly and buns, Rita felt that Molly deserved all the benefits that medical science and Molly's ten thousand dollar college trust fund could serve up. Henny enthusiastically agreed, adding that "baby fat" was a social stigma best left back in the twentieth century, like polio and near-sightedness. (Yes, Molly was also a candidate for baby LASIK, we learned, and could be tested as soon as she knew enough alphabet letters to read an eye chart.)

Moments later, we were ushered into the examining room, where we finally met Dr. Raj himself. A tall, balding blonde with chiseled good looks and a warm three-tooth smile, Dr. Raj quickly bonded with Molly by letting her talk into his stethoscope and play with his scalpel.

While Molly happily "played cosmetic surgeon" on an old teddy bear, Dr. Raj showed us a computer simulation of what the new Molly would look like. As we watched an image of our only child morphing before our eyes from pudgy cherub to the striking princess we both knew was inside her, Rita and I gushed with pride. "I always knew my baby could be beautiful," Rita whimpered into her fat-free mocha latte. Molly occasionally glanced at the onscreen images with a bewildered look on her face, as if to say "Who is that lucky kid that looks like me but with an hour-glass figure?"

Then after being ushered back to Henny's lounge for an hour of signing consent forms-and legal releases that apparently prevent the doctor from committing malpractice as it's defined by the courts (a welcomed comfort, to be sure)-we set out to the serious business of picking a date. Thanksgiving, Christmas, New Year's...these options were all quickly rejected as no parent wants to play nurse to a recuperating toddler during their paid vacation time.

** A medical term stubbornly rejected by the AMA, FDA, PTA and FBI.

The end of October? That was perilously close to Halloween, and why take a chance that Molly would still be bedridden when Rita and I had already picked out our hilarious Sonny & Cher costumes for our health club's annual Monsterobics Ball?

That's when Henny again came to our rescue. "What about October 9th? It's a Friday, the doctor has a late tee time, and you'll have the entire three day Columbus Day weekend for Molly to recuperate."

"October 9th!" Rita exclaimed. "Molly's birthday!" And what better present to give any little girl than a full-body makeover? So it was agreed; Molly would spend her second birthday in the loving hands of Dr. Raj and the caring staff at The 93rd Street Medical and Family Planning Institute. (Or as Mapquest curiously labels it, "El Instituto Medico y Aborto.")

October 9th couldn't come soon enough. That morning I think Molly was more excited than us, waking as she did at 5:35 a.m....a full ten minutes before her normal wake-up time. Once Rita and I were freshly showered and Rita had plucked her eyebrows for the big day, we were in the car and on our way, arriving at the Instituto just in time to see the nightshift surgical staff greet the morning daylight and head for their Metro buses back home.

In the OR waiting room, we met ten other families who had also booked Dr. Raj for this morning. Whether by coincidence or design, I relished the chance to share this life-changing event with people from Third World nations on every continent. It warmed my heart to see the smiles of all those parents as they whispered "goodbye" in their native tongue and handed their screaming, kicking bambinos to the nurses who would be their "OR mommies" for the next five to nine hours. With the last of the crying tykes gone, the parents were left to bond as we silently pantomimed what procedures our kids were having done.

The next four hours were fairly uneventful, save for the two or three "code blue" calls that sent the staff scurrying in every direction. ("I'd hate to see what they do for a code red," I chuckled to myself.)

Before Rita was even back from her tanning session, Henny emerged to tell us Molly was in the recovery room and that "we were one of the lucky ones." (Which I took to mean that the results were even better than promised.) By the time Molly started to come to, I could already discern through the heavy gauze and IV tubes that this was not the same girl I had read "Corduroy Goes To The Doctor" with the night before. Her lifeless eyes and fully dilated pupils did little to hide the joy she must have felt, knowing that by the time she was potty trained she would be thinner and lovelier than even the most emaciated preemies.

It is now six months later, and while the final results won't be fully apparent for another 8 to 16 years, we can begin to see the woman who will evolve from our little girl. Once a toddler's T2, Molly is already back in 6-12 months sizes and Rita can happily shop in the infant department again. (And saving all that $ on smaller clothes makes the operation almost pay for itself!)

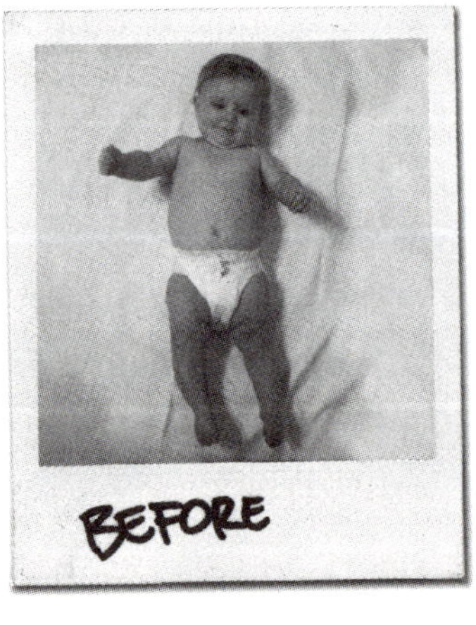

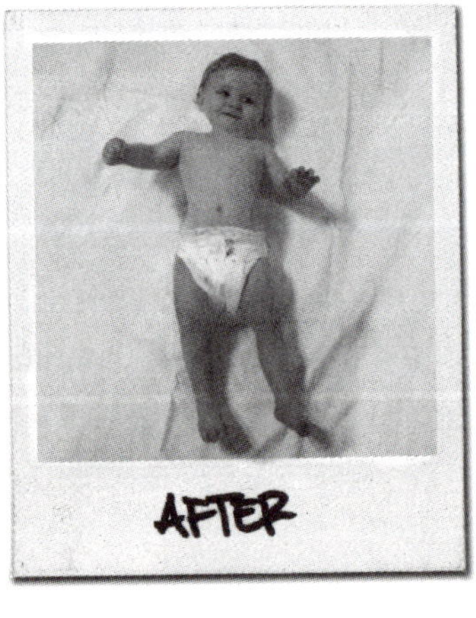

And Molly, well...you be the judge. A picture is worth a thousand words. And ten thousand dollars. And whether we can ever replenish that college fund seems insignificant now. Because we know that our little angel-the in vitro fruit of our loins-will now and forever be the petite and shapely girl we can be somewhat proud of. ■

c.r. jew.com

cover your head from the Lord with **Pride!**

keep in fashion by kippah'n it REAL this holiday season!

be rebellious...discreetly

(sshhhh. let's keep it under your hat!)

Let's hear your rebel yell!
Southern Jew, better cover your head. Don't forget what the Good Book said! Remember, when it comes to the confederate flag, it's about tradition, not racism.
Leave our cultural heritage alone!
Rebel Yell Yarmulke
21278 $28.00

(also available in traditional)

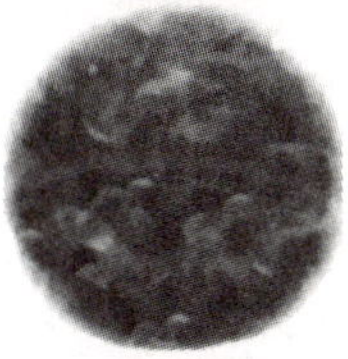

Only G-d will know it's fake!
Cheaper than a weave, less invasive than plugs...the Bald Spot Yarmulke is a 100% HaShem-approved yarmulke/toupee in one. You'll look ten years younger — guaranteed! But is it a Mitzvah? You betchah!
Now available in Mullet.
Bald Spot Yarmulke
21278 $38.00

(also available in blonde)

Is that Minnesota Fats? Oh, wait, it's you!
Whether you're playing three card monte, running a floating crap game or just practicing some roadside bondage, you'll love the hustler line of yarmulkes!
Hustler Yarmulke
21278 $18.00

Talk about Sex Appeal? Oy Gevalt!
Is that a mezuzzah in your pants or are you just happy to see me? Well, sailor, why don't you kiss it and find out! Made of slick PVC, this yarmulke never loses its "always wet"® appeal. You'll look like you just stepped out of the shower...and into a dream!
Passion Yarmulke
21278 $38.00

Pass the dutchie 'pon the left han' side!
Designed to meet the needs of Ethiopian Jews and rasta mon "wanna be's," this yarmulke is certified Iré! Perfect for when you just want to kick back with a bongful of chronic and forget about life for awhile, without neglecting your loyalty to HaShem!
composed entirely of 100% rainforest-friendly Humboldt County hemp fibers
Rasta Mon Yarmulke
21278 $24.00

Parents just don't understand!
Has this ever happened to you? Your parents return from the Hafetz Hayim Kibbutz and all you get is a lousy yarmulke! Well, now you can freely express your dismay with our new line of Disgruntled Youth yarmulkes!
NEW "I'm With Stupid" model yarmulke also available
Disgruntled-Youth Yarmulke
21278 $24.00

Coming Soon!
The Have A Nice Day Yarmulke

Coming Soon!
The Hypno-Yarmulke

What It's Like to Work in a Lingerie Factory

by Phil Haney

3.
slurp!
slurp!
4.
Um.... Fred.
Yeah.
Can you not do
that Fred.

5.
Well there kid.... it's like this...
6.
Have you ever been in the toilet paper isle of the super market and thought to your self...
poo tastic
poo tastic
Deuce be Gone!

7.
Everything I see here before me...
At some point in time is going to end up
inside of someones ass....
poo tastic
poo tastic
Deuce
be Gone!
12 DOUBLE ROLLS
8.
..covered
in
shit.

9
No.... No I really havn't.
10.
It's kind of awe inspiring in a way.
11
What's that have to do with us Fred?
I figure that we must touch hundreds, if not thousands of panties, bras and nighties.

12.
...And if you stop and think about it they are all going to end up caress-ing the naughty bits of some eighteen year old girl.
Some could end up caressing the naughty bits of a transvestite.
13.

14.
Some could end up caressing the naughty bits of Keira Knightley.
15.
Interesting.

16
SLURP!!
SLURP!!

Things To Say To A Neighbor You've Never Met Before While Shoveling Snow

by Max Burbank

This enough snow for ya?
What about *this* shit?
How do you like *this* shit?
Damn!
Man oh man, I haven't seen shit like this since '78!
Hey, at least it's not as bad as '78, huh? Am I right?
This makes me think of '78. Did you live around here in '78? *That* was some serious shit.
Can't wait 'til the kids are old enough to help me out with *this* shit, huh? Ha ha ha!
Global warming my ass. Am I right? Ha ha ha! I *wish*. Friggin' environmentalists. Let 'em global warm *this*, am I right?

Take her easy there, big fella. Every serious storm a buncha guys like you drop dead shoveling. That's not me talking. That's actuarial tables.
Think they'll cancel the game tonight?
Think they'll cancel school tomorrow?
You into other guys or anything?
What's with the fuckin' plows?
I bet you wish you bought a snowblower right about now. Am I right? Ha ha ha!
Does your left arm hurt? Cause my left arm is hurtin' like a son of a bitch.
I sure wish I had a slave.
Yep.

I mean, slavery is an egregious crime against nature, but this shoveling sucks my fucking ass. Say, want some help there? I'm just kidding; I don't even know you. I have my own damn driveway. You shovel like a girl ... Nice shoveling, Nancy. Way to shovel, Clarice. That Pinafore warm enough for ya? ... Boy, I've seen some suck-ass shoveling in my life, but you take the cake.
Shovel fight?
Wanna make snow angels? I'm gonna make a snow angel.
Hey, what if this was all cocaine, huh? Ha ha ha! Am I right? 'Course you'd be deader'n shit before you got more than a foot from your door. But still. You wanna get high?
Seriously, you into other guys?
Shit like this makes me really hate my wife. She's crippled, so she can't shovel for crap.

So this is funny. Just the other day I'm thinking to myself "Say, what I need is a really huge fuckin' blizzard. 'Cause I don't have enough reasons to kill myself what with the wife cheating on me, my methamphetamine addiction and fuckin' ringworm."
Hey! I had a dream about you the other night. I killed you. Naw, I'm kidding. It was just a sex dream. Someone else had already killed you.
If it gets any colder I'm gonna slice you open like a man sandwich and climb in your torso. Like *Empire Strikes Back.* No offense. You a *Star Wars* Fan?
I used to be a woman. Ha ha ha! Seriously, though, I was born a woman.
If we get more snow before this melts, I don't know where the hell we're gonna put it. Here's what I do know, though. If that happens I'm going to kill you, butcher you like a hog, and feed my family off you 'til spring comes. No offense.

I bet it's like this every day in Canada, huh? Serves 'em right. Fuckers.
You ski? That'd be a silver lining, if you were a skier, huh? Ha ha ha! Yeah, I was born a woman.
You remember '78? Place I lived, you could jump out the second floor window, no shit. I was going around with these, whattayacall 'em, syringes of epinephrine? I'd sneak up on some guy shoveling, jab him in the thigh. He'd keel right over like a fuckin' tree. I shit you not. I did, what, six, eight guys like that? Cops thought it was heart attacks. Every really bad blizzard, buncha guys go from heart attacks. Or...*do they?* Know what I mean? Am I right? Ha ha ha! ■

The Bed, Beach and Beyond

by Michael Curtiss

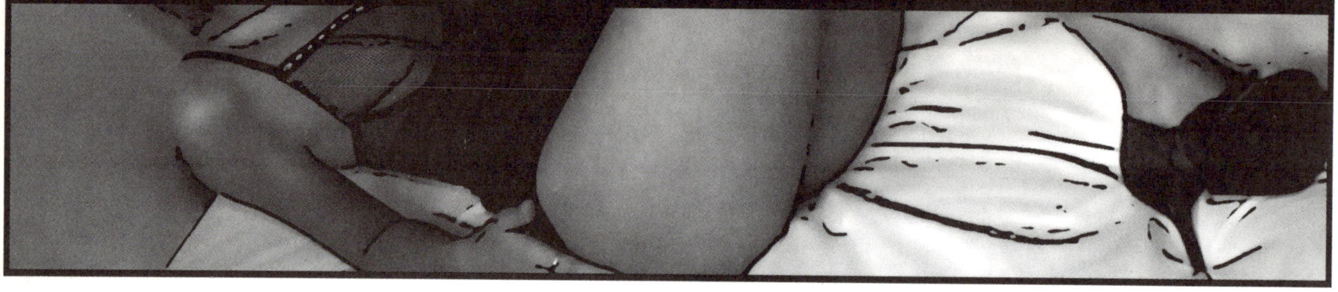

It was Spring Break and slews of young adults were making their annual migration to South Padre, Texas, the women already thinking about how many cocks they could collectively stuff into their vaginas, and the men dreaming to be one of those cocks. (Well, not at the same time as the others, because that's just fucking gross.)

Oh, my friends, how the people will fuck. It will be glorious: a giant tree of pussy with the most beauteous women on the top and the most hideous cock wenches on the bottom. Survival of the fittest at its best, with the cesspool of STDs ready to capitalize on their opportunity to multiply and infect.

Where will these people fuck? By the beach? On the street? In a dumpster? Yes, all of those places. But mostly, in a bed. You see, a bed in South Padre is not used for sleeping; it is used for fucking. Pure and simple.

Lips and dicks will indiscriminately stain every bed in this fair city. But for now, we will focus on one particular bed. This bed was one of many in a large condo on the beach, but for some reason, this bed was chosen. It was chosen not only for the fucking, but for the puking, pissing, and bleeding. Truly a martyr among beds. We will call it simply, **the bed**.

My friends and I arrived in South Padre wearing our hope on the outside. A hope of getting completely shit-faced and doing horrible things. Things that make mothers cry and brothers laugh. Our bags hit the ground minutes after arriving and we unloaded a myriad of liquor and beer, taking pride in our massive achievement of collecting such a copious amount of alcohol at the ripe under age of 18. Of course, the first thing every did was run around the condo claiming beds. Sadly, I had the runs, so I was spitting diarrhea out of my ass while this was going on. Wouldn't you know, I was stuck sleeping on the couch. Fortunately, this would come to be more of a privilege than a detriment to my trip, due to the fact that dudes were doubling up on beds, and for the most part, I only enjoy cock on the weekends.

The bed sat in its own benevolence, its sheets spread like some albino woman's vagina, waiting for the satisfaction of my salami. Lunchmeats aside, I got absolutely no pussy on this trip. My friend Clayton (R.I.P.) was the only one who got any action because he was a fucking stud. You won't envy him for long.

The town of South Padre can best be described as completely awesome, and at the same time, horribly egregious. The first day we arrived, I met some girl on the elevator who was talking about how she "chilled" with Ludacris and did coke with him. "AWESOME," I thought, "wow you just totally impressed me." As I drifted away from the conversation, she then mentioned how earlier in the day, she saw a guy get thrown off of a five-story balcony.

Slut (giggling like a stupid whore): OMG, he flew like, fifty feet, and like, almost died!!
Me: Was he doing coke with Ludacris?
Slut: LOL, um no. Ludacris is staying at (blah blah blah)!!!
Me: You're important.
Slut: Um...thanks...

I walked off the elevator two floors early and decided it would be nice to use the stairs. (A positive alternative to riding in the elevator and getting ear cancer from Cokey McSuckfuck.) When I arrived, everyone was playing power hour and doing shots. I do not feel the need to go into details here, because basically, we all got very drunk and went to a few clubs. But what happened after we returned is very important. Clayton was in **the bed** pounding out some vagina. I was fucking pissed off because I could not sleep, and had to reduce myself to jerking off in the corner of the room in the fetal position. I think he felt kind of shitty in the morning looking at how sleep deprived and unsexed everyone looked, so he cleaned the condo. Good guy.

The following day, we repeated what we had done the prior night and got completely wasted. But...no one had sex on this night. However, someone DID piss all over himself in his sleep. Maybe it's just me and my unusual urine fetish, but I would much rather see a guy covered in his own urine then see two people having sex. Wait, what did I just say?

My friend Darren disappeared for about three hours during the day, and showed up completely hammered. Up to this point, I had honestly never seen someone so ridiculous. And by ridiculous, I mean fucking ridiculous.

Darren: IF YOU DON'T GIVE A FUCK, WE DON'T GIVE A FUCK!!!
Everyone: Dude, shut up.
Darren: IF YOU DON'T GIVE A FUCK, WE DON'T GIVE A FUCK!!! HAHAHAHAHAHA!!!
Me: Holy shit, get the camera.
(At this point someone started video taping it, and one of my good friends still has the tape. If I ever get ahold of it, I will put it up, and Darren will make me famous.)
Darren: IF YOU DON'T GIVE A FUCK, WE DON'T GIVE A FUCK!!!!! HAHAHAHAHAHA, OH SHIT, WATCH ME SEAWALK!!! OHHHHHHHHHHH!!!!
Everyone: (Couldn't talk because we were laughing so hard.)

Darren is blacker than Dawson's mom's taint, so he can get away with doing the seawalk. Darren danced for a good hour or so on the beach getting mouthfuls of sand every few minutes until we pulled his ass inside. Eventually, all of his extremities ceased to function and it took six of us to lug him in. Although no longer moving, Darren continued to yell.

Darren: IF YOU DON'T GIVE A FUCK, WE DON'T GIVE A FUCK!!
Everyone: Shut the fuck up!!!
Darren: I DON'T GIVE A FUCK!!!

Then I saw a foot fly directly into his ribcage. Just as I was about to get pissed off at someone for kicking such a defenseless drunk, I noticed that the foot was my own, and soon came to the conclusion that Darren deserved it. After he stopped coughing, Darren started chanting again louder than ever. So we threw him in **the bed** and went out. I kind of wished he would choke on his own vomit. (Not really, but yeah really.) We had a great night and everyone came back to sleep at around 3AM, completely unaware of what we would wake to in the morning.

I woke up with a very familiar stench in my nostrils. It almost smelled like pussy, but with more rancidity to it. Maybe a pussy with a yeast infection? Who even knows. As I stumbled out of bed and into the bathroom, I noticed a pair of urine-soaked, puke-covered jeans. Holy shit, someone had a good time. Despite my massive headache, I forced a smile and walked into the bedroom to see who had pissed all over himself so I could exploit him, thus making myself look superior. (Yeah, I'm an asshole like that.)

I saw three guys piled into one twin bed with NO girls. That's pretty heterosexual I guess. Then I turned my gaze to the other twin bed (**the bed**) containing a sole occupant. It was Darren. And, well, Darren had no pants on. As I moved the rest of the sheet out of the way, I noticed a considerable area of condensation radiating from his genitals. It had a yellowish tint to it as well. Darren had...(sigh)...wet **the** fucking **bed**.

Before I could laugh, I just stood there in shock. Pissing your pants is one thing, but for some reason, wetting **the bed** is just fucking ridiculous. I began laughing uncontrollably, proclaiming my great discovery to my friends asleep in the next bed. Everyone scoffed at me, too hungover to give a shit. There could have been a fucking nuclear explosion, and they still would not have cared. Then, I looked over at my friend Elliott, now the best damn cocksucker at West Point, and he cracked a smile and began laughing quietly. (You big silly bastard, you still to this day have never let me down.)

Everyone slowly arose and realized what happened. Eventually, everyone was sitting there staring at Darren in disgust, writhing in his own waste. He denied pissing himself, even though he was glistening with urine. We all moved on from this episode, but I could not help but be in awe **the bed**. It almost had a soft glow to it, sitting there basking in sexual juices and urine. But its journey was not over yet.

The day went on as usual, with the occasional reference to Darren **the bed**wetter. Every time we brought it up, he pleaded for us not to tell. Up to this point, I think everyone kept their mouth shut—sorry Darren.

We all played volleyball for a few hours, and decided we would take a break from the club scene that night and stay in the condo. Bad news considering we have close to $300 worth of alcohol sitting in our kitchen. Surprisingly, we met more people in the surrounding condos than we did in the clubs. Sure, the people we met were fucking trailer trash and walked into our condo and drank our beer without even asking, but what can you do? Oh yeah, lock the door.

The night became a blur of drugs and alcohol and I do not remember any of it. Luckily, we had the camera rolling the entire time, which would help explain the piles of vomit we would find in the morning, leading from the bathroom into the hallway, and sure enough, all over **the bed**. Everyone woke up promptly at three in the afternoon and laid eyes on the puke-covered room. And there it was again, **the bed**, this time covered in a pink bile substance. Everyone was accounted for except for my friend Michael. The search for Michael lasted 10 seconds: there he was, slung over the toilet with vomit crusted all over his hair and face. Smile for the camera.

We got the camera and rewound it to watch the previous night unfold. One shots, two shots, a million fucking shots. Everyone was drunk as shit, but Michael hit the ground first. We dragged his ass to **the bed**, and as soon as he landed, out came the vomit. It shot from his body with such force that I thought he was a dragon. We picked him up again and slung him over the toilet in the same position we found him in the morning. One of my friends says he remembers getting up in the middle of the night to take a piss, and just moving Michael's head over a few inches so the stream of piss only grazed his eyebrows.

After binging for about a week, we all needed a night to recoup our energy. I forced myself to trade in the intoxicating qualities of beer for the rejuvenating qualities of water. My friend Clayton, however, had different plans. He wanted to have some sex, so he had some sex. The girl was drunk and very loud, and yet again, no one could sleep. I can't really blame him though; I would screw over a busload of friends to get some ass. Sure enough, they fucked all night and we got barely any sleep. In the morning, I got up to go get a change of clothes from the room so I could take a shower. As I walked by, Clayton and the girl were lying in **the bed** passed out. I laughed to myself as I thought about the layers of puke and piss on that thing, then I started to get turned on. Just kidding.

I hopped in the shower and only washed my stinky parts, because I am a busy guy. Then I dried off and walked into **the bed**room to get some toothpaste. Clayton was just standing there looking at the bed. Puzzled, I stared at him for a minute and asked him what was wrong. He just stood there with a smirk on his face, his eyes fixed on **the bed**. I looked down and sure enough, there it was, a big fat period stain in middle of the bed.

Nice.

Whether it doubled as a urinal, a porcelain god, or a tampon, **the bed** was there. I have yet to experience sleeping on a bed that has had such foul things happen on it. Well, except for that time me and my friend Dawson's mom got a hotel room and...well, I'll let her tell you Dawson. Just don't be surprised if you get a new baby brother nine months from now. ■

**This story is dedicated to Clayton.*

The Post Office
By: Marc M.
OK Miss. Sooooo, how many dicks can I put you down for today?
PLEASE FORM ONE Line Thank You

THE THRASHING OF THE CHRIST

He made the world believe.
But now he faces an even greater challenge.
Believing in himself.
MEL GIBSON'S
THE THRASHING OF THE CHRIST
FAMILY EDITION
THE THRASHING OF THE CHRIST

Left: A Roman soldier engages in a playful strawberry jam fight with Jesus. Middle: spear replaced with harmless walkie-talkie.

Above: a harmless walkie-talkie pierces Jesus's jam-filled side.

Gosh, Jesus! You look like you're down in the dumps!
Maybe a SONG'll cheer you up!

Crossy the Talking Crucifix picks up Jesus's spirits after he loses in the county strawberry jam fight finals. Will Crossy's song teach Christ a valuable lesson in believing in something more important than God... believing in himself?

Jub jub! Looks like Jesus is in trouble!

Will Jesus be crucified? Not if the brave Ewoks of Endor have anything to say about it!

by Jay Pinkerton

Now with over 200 minutes of additional footage.

Go on. Drink it.

The apostles hope to trick Christ into drinking pee in this powerful scene from the *Extended Edition*, which further explores Christ's suffering at the hands of mankind.

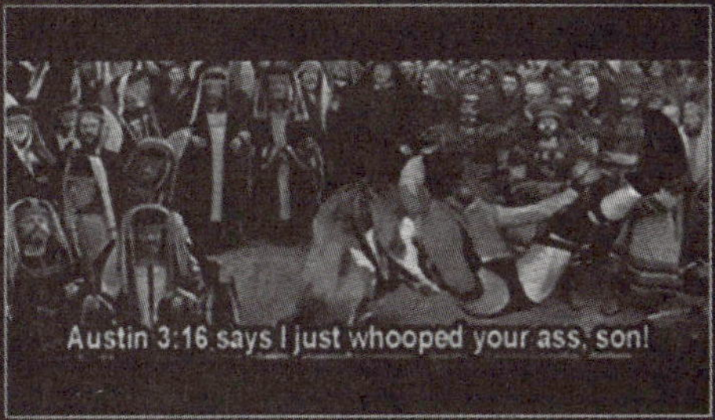
Austin 3:16 says I just whooped your ass, son!

One of countless added scenes that further underscore Christ's suffering for our sins. ABOVE: Stone Cold Steve Austin administers a Stunner upon the Christ.

It had started as a practical joke.
But then it went too far.

JUDAIC EDITION

Haw haw haw! Take THAT, the Christ!

Har har! That cross too heavy for you, fag?
Get Jewish or GO HOME!

One of the scenes criticized by Jewish extremists.

The eloquently crass material presented in Not Fit For Print was contributed from the following websites of the National Lampoon Humor Network:

National Lampoon
www.NationalLampoon.com

The Phat Phree
www.ThePhatPhree.com

Points in Case
www.PointsinCase.com

Super Awesome Wow
www.SuperAwesomeWow.com

Sick Animation
www.SickAnimation.com

Ridiculopathy
www.Ridiculopathy.com

The West Virginia Surf Report
www.WVSR.com